AF333291

EXPLORATIONS IN ETHNOHISTORY

Explorations in Ethnohistory

Indians of Central Mexico
in the Sixteenth Century

Edited by
H. R. Harvey
Hanns J. Prem

University of New Mexico Press / Albuquerque

Library of Congress Cataloging in Publication Data

Main entry under title:

Explorations in ethnohistory.

Includes bibliographies and index.
1. Indians of Mexico—Mexico, Valley of—History—Addresses, essays, lectures.
2. Indians of Mexico—Mexico, Valley of—Social life and customs—Addresses, essays,
lectures. 3. Indians of Mexico—Mexico, Valley of—History—Sources—Addresses, essays, lectures. 4. Nahuas—History—Addresses, essays, lectures. 5. Mexico, Valley of
(Mexico)—History—Addresses, essays, lectures. I. Harvey, H. R., 1931–   . II. Prem,
Hanns J., 1941–   .
F1219.1.M53E96 1983   972'.500497   83-16853
ISBN 0-8263-0712-4

Manufactured in the United States of America.
Library of Congress Catalog Card Number 83-16853.
International Standard Book Number 0-8263-0712-4.
First edition.

Contents

Illustrations

FIGURES

TABLES

MAPS

1

Introduction

H. R. Harvey
Hanns J. Prem

The native cultures and societies of Central Mexico have stimulated a widespread interest since the days of the Spanish conquest. The study of what in recent years has been termed "ethnohistory" is rooted in the writings of that era. In the past two decades especially, significant advances have been made in this old but newly labeled field, as methodological perspectives from many disciplines have been increasingly applied to a more ample and reliable data base.

For the Europeans, contact with New World cultures resulted in an intellectual challenge. For the native cultures, the challenge was physical survival in the face of a new, and often disastrous, set of circumstances, further exacerbated by the loss of cultural self-reliance. European conquerors, colonizers, missionaries, and administrative officials wrote and assembled numerous reports on diverse subjects relating to the Spanish dominions in the New World; above all, they wrote about the central highlands of Mexico. Correspond-

ingly there were efforts on the part of the Indians to analyze their
own past and the colonial present, to preserve and legitimize their
identity by means of the written record. The different literary bases
of European and Indian authors became clear in the early postconquest years. Subsequently these differing perspectives merged; the
unique synthesis is particularly evident in indigenous, pictographic
historical reports from the colonial period. The interweaving of the
two traditions, native and European, along with the survival of a
considerable mass of documents, have combined to create an unusual
stimulus for Mexican ethnohistorical research.

The awareness that ethnohistory is a legitimate, distinct subdiscipline that cuts across the boundaries of anthropology and history
has had important implications, not the least of which has been the
continuing debate as to where or even whether its methodological
and substantive boundaries should be drawn. Among others, two
anthropologists (Sturtevant 1966; Carmack 1972) and a historian
(Cline 1972–75) have commendably reviewed the subject. More
recently Spores (1980) has carefully examined the enormous growth
in the field of ethnohistory in the 1970s. Proper ethnohistoric goals
are now generally accepted to include both synchronic and diachronic emphases. The former takes prehispanic ethnography as its
objective, while the latter is concerned with the transformation of
native society—the process of adjustment and accommodation to
changed conditions imposed by the Spanish presence. Beginning in
the first half of the sixteenth century, humanistically educated Europeans, with their broad range of interests, pursued what we have
come to call ethnohistory as they wrote comprehensive works about
native civilization, regardless of what their original purpose was.
When applied to Central Mexico, then, "ethnohistory" both em-
braces a broad spectrum of analytical approaches and treats widely
diverse themes. Its unifying theme is a concern with what Europeans
encountered in their conquest and the all-pervasive impact of their
presence in the decades and centuries that followed.

CENTRAL MEXICAN ETHNOHISTORICAL RESEARCH

Over four and a half centuries have elapsed since native society
in Central Mexico was first the subject of attempts by Western
observers to chronicle its past and describe its present. Over this

long period objectives and methodologies have changed from time to time. It is not our purpose here to provide a detailed summary of Central Mexican ethnohistorical sources and syntheses; that task is admirably performed by H. B. Nicholson (1975). Rather, it is sufficient to examine and evaluate the general directions in terms of their present relevance.

The rich and varied corpus of sixteenth-century writings contains materials of both European and Indian authorship. Unfortunately the missionary zeal of the Spaniards resulted in the wholesale destruction of preconquest pictorial records, but copies or redrafts of a few were made and the substance of others was preserved in the textual record. From its start the textual record also included ethnographic descriptions and accounts of native history and traditions. The earliest writers were able to draw upon personal observations and first-hand accounts from native informants. Some, such as Sahagún and Durán, utilized native artists to provide the illustrations which complement their texts.

As the generation of primary observers thinned, emphasis shifted to the production of compilational synopses of existing materials, mostly derived from secondary sources, which were then processed into comprehensive historical works. Torquemada's *Monarchía indiana* (1615) is a giant compendium of "facts" about native culture and history, assembled (often uncritically) from a multitude of sources and, as was the custom of the times, without acknowledgment. A well-written synthesis, also compiled largely from available published sources, is Clavigero's *Historía antigua de México* (1780–81). Because of the expulsion of the Jesuit Order from Mexico, the *Historia* was written during Clavigero's exile in Italy, where he had access to only a limited selection of source materials, basically older compendia. Among them was Torquemada, his most important source.

In the seventeenth and eighteenth centuries, writers largely ignored native pictorials as sources. An exception was the native historian Alva Ixtlilxóchitl, who drew upon his own private collection. He may have used, for example, the Codex Xolotl and other pictorial documents from Acolhuacan. A century later Lorenzo Boturini, an Italian, spent seven years in Mexico (1736–43) engaged in an indefatigable pursuit of native source materials. His efforts

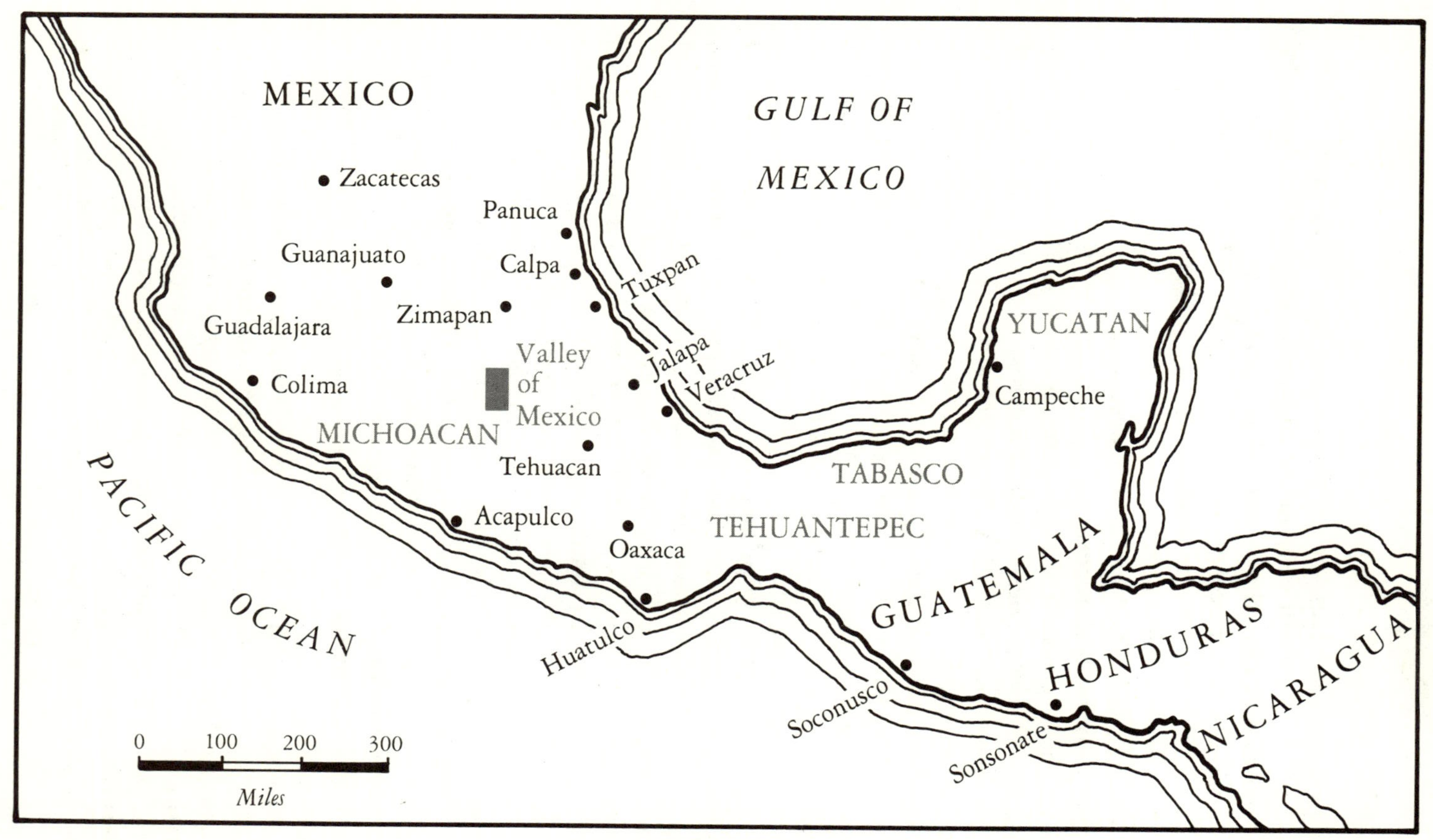

Southern Mexico

resulted in the formation of a huge collection of original manuscripts, but he was thwarted by the crown's suspicion of his motives; the collection was confiscated by viceregal order. His collection did, however, provide fresh source material for nineteenth-century scholars, who became increasingly aware of the shortcomings inherent in grand historical syntheses based upon a two-hundred-year-old pool of secondary sources. As these investigators became cognizant of the potential wealth of information in the long-overlooked native manuscripts, they described, analyzed, and published them, but often without critical evaluation of the data they contained (León y Gama 1832; Aubin 1849, 1893; Kingsborough 1831–48; Humboldt 1810).

About the same time that studies of native manuscripts were initiated, a definite archaeological interest began to emerge. Shortly after the turn of the nineteenth century, the Spanish crown sponsored a mission under the direction of Guillermo Dupaix to conduct an archaeological survey in its overseas realm (1805–9). Dupaix was well prepared for the task because of his educational background, his long personal experience in the region, and his sensitivity to the worth of native achievements in art, science, and engineering that were evident in the sites he explored. Publication of his findings excited great interest throughout Europe and the United States and gave birth to the field of archaeological research in Middle America.

Another important stimulus to ethnohistorical research was set in motion by the closing days of the eighteenth century. In 1785 the crown initiated efforts to concentrate the massive collection of documents that had accumulated on its overseas empire by establishing the Archive of the Indies in Seville. Mexico followed that precedent in 1823, just after gaining its independence, by establishing its own public archive, now called the Archivo General de la Nación.

The general approach of seventeenth- and eighteenth-century writers was to compile secondary sources as a basis for composing their standard histories. By the early nineteenth century, however, emphasis had begun to shift toward the search for new sources, in addition to new methods of analysis. This growing concern with critical analysis and the application of scientific method laid the foundation for modern ethnohistory.

The search for new sources not only involved their location in institutional and private collections, but also their translation, in the case of native language documents. A large corpus of native prose sources recorded in the Latin alphabet had accumulated since shortly after the conquest; the study and translation of these Indian language texts was begun by the middle of the nineteenth century. Many of these early translations remain unpublished, and still other important native prose sources are as yet untranslated.

There also arose within the first half of the nineteenth century a historical analysis with a conscious and distinctly ethnohistorical direction. William H. Prescott's *History of the Conquest of Mexico* (1843) was a landmark contribution in both substance and methodology. Neither his seriously failing eyesight nor the prodigious task of locating and analyzing primary sources deterred him. Although his approach possesses some shortcomings, judging by present standards, it does satisfy modern methodological criteria. Later historians were influenced by the direction of Prescott's pathfinding work; Mexican historians, in particular, have engaged in detailed analyses and have produced comprehensive descriptions which are still of great ethnohistorical interest.

Very important to the development of ethnohistory in the second half of the nineteenth century was the first International Congress of Americanists, held in 1875 in Nancy, France. It established a forum for both the formal and informal exchange of information and ideas, and marked the first substantial entrance into the field of investigators from the United States, Germany, Great Britain, and France. The earlier emphasis on description and publication of Indian pictorial manuscripts was now accompanied by critical analysis and commentary (Léon de Rosny 1869, 1876; Ernest Theodore Hamy 1899a, 1899b; Antonio Peñafiel 1897; Eduard Seler 1904–9). The study of Indian philology resulted in the first reliable translations of large sections of the Nahuatl texts of Sahagún (Seler 1927) and Chimalpahin (Siméon 1889), so fundamental to historical ethnographies of the central highlands. Ethnohistorians from Mexico during this period continued with textual analysis and also began to use the texts as basic source materials in the preparation of their own comprehensive histories (Orozco y Berra 1880; Chavero n.d.).

In the United States the controversial historian H. H. Bancroft introduced an "assembly line" technique for the research and writing of his important *Native Races* (1874–76).

Shortly after the first Congress of Americanists, Bandelier's three detailed studies of Aztec sociopolitical organization appeared (Bandelier 1877, 1878, 1880). He drew upon a wide spectrum of sources to focus on the analysis of very specific topics—warfare, land tenure, and social organization and government—toward the purpose of mustering support for Lewis Henry Morgan's general theory of the evolution of human society. While the Morgan-Bandelier thesis is no longer accepted by most scholars, Bandelier's three studies stand as an important bench mark in the development of a distinctly ethnohistorical strategy for source utilization.

The collection of basic source materials continued as an important scholarly activity in the latter half of the nineteenth century and continuing into the twentieth century. It should be remembered that the massive historical documentation relating to native cultures was widely scattered, and that materials of fundamental importance remained to be discovered or rediscovered. Scholars such as García Icazbalceta and Paso y Troncoso devoted a significant proportion of their energies to the search and publication of primary documents rather than to analysis. Through such efforts many more documents have been published than have been critically analyzed, but their accessibility itself has contributed to the advancement of the field.

The trend toward the use of primary source materials which began in the nineteenth century intensified in the twentieth century, and with it came a growing awareness of the need for "quality control," so often ignored by earlier writers. Three definite temporal concentrations emerged: the protohistoric, the contact period, and the colonial, each dependent upon its own combination of sources for reconstructing native culture and tracing its development and changes under Spanish rule. More attention in the central highlands was initially accorded to the Basin of Mexico and the Nahua area, but by the 1920s and 1930s areas such as Oaxaca and Michoacán also began to attract attention. Maya research was well underway by the beginning of this century, already having emerged as a well-defined cultural-geographical subfield of ethnohistory. While some early researchers, such as Eduard Seler, were able to cross linguistic and cultural boundaries, there has been a marked tendency to concentrate within specific regions and to expand methodologically rather than spatially. In general, intricate analysis has superceded description, and with it has come greater caution in generalization.

For the first half of the present century the growth of ethnohistorical research was very gradual, impeded as much by the circumstances of the time as by anthropological perceptions of priority. Many ethnologists, for example, were concerned with obtaining descriptions of native cultures before they disappeared in the wake of modernization, especially after the Mexican Revolution of the second decade. And the community study as a conceptual model paid little attention to a community's specific history, often generating very misleading interpretations of otherwise more explicable phenomena. However, Gamio (1922) carried out a monumental study of Teotihuacán which successfully combined archaeology and ethnohistory in a multidisciplinary program of research; a few years later Manuel Moreno (1931), a student of Alfonso Caso, helped to change the distorted image of Aztec society propounded by Bandelier.

After World War II the field again began to expand, and as Cline (1972–75) has pointed out, the term "ethnohistory" (coined by Fritz Röck in 1932) came into vogue as explicit recognition of a field of specialization emerged. Clearly the importance lay not in the term but in the implication of its label; in the convergence of methods carefully honed by historians with the substantive and theoretical perspectives of anthropology.

Many scholars have had an indelible impact on the field of ethnohistory in the various directions it has taken in recent decades; among them are Alfonso Caso, Paul Kirchhoff, Robert Barlow, and Wigberto Jiménez Moreno for the central highlands. As an example, Barlow's contributions in the ten short years before his untimely death at the age of thirty-two were spread across a broad horizon. His collaboration with Martínez del Río in the Tlatelolco Project successfully combined ethnohistorical and archaeological research, and underscored the importance not only of an interdisciplinary approach, but also of focusing research on the local level. Barlow was as comfortable with native pictorial and prose sources as he was with the chronicles. A comparison of the accounts of Durán and Tezozomoc led to his (1945) postulation of "Crónica X" as a lost source used by both these early colonial authors, and hence to a justification for the critical examination of source materials. His study of the "Matrícula de Tributos" (1949) provided a different dimension for understanding the structure and dynamics of Aztec imperial expansion. Barlow was interested not only in advancing knowledge to which his own research contributed, but also in encouraging others to follow their own paths. He established, with George Smisor, the journal *Tlalocan,* dedicated primarily to publishing analyses of historical and linguistic source materials. Barlow's efforts, combined with those of others such as Caso, Kirchhoff, and Jiménez Moreno, contributed to what Nicholson (1975) has called the "quantum leap forward" in ethnohistorical research in subsequent decades. More than a quarter of a century has passed since Barlow's time. In this period ethnohistory has gradually been accepted as an important subdiscipline of anthropology and history. Part of this development is attributable to the increasing number of new scholars attracted to the field. However, it is the variety of specializations, orientations, and cross-disciplinary perspectives within ethnohistory that has provided the field with new vitality, with its "hybrid vigor." Ethnohistory has also been influenced by developments in its core disciplines. While ethnohistory has not abandoned its traditional synchronic focus on historical ethnography, in recent decades there has been a modest but discernible shift toward recognizing the importance of the postcontact period and of diachronic studies of process. Evaluating the impact of Spanish conquest and domination on native society and culture is far more complex than has previously been thought. We now recognize that this impact fell unevenly on native institutions, completely shattering some and even enhancing others. This growing awareness has had an important bearing on the use and evaluation of our overwhelmingly postconquest source materials, and has served to broaden the field of ethnohistory by encouraging the documentation and analysis of the past events and processes which have shaped the mosaic of cultures that constitutes today's Mexico. The postcontact period still lacks attention as compared to preconquest times, and there has been a dearth of studies in the middle and late colonial periods; but this gap will certainly be bridged. Gibson's (1964) impressive study of the Valley of Mexico between 1519 and 1810 has done much to stimulate interest in this hitherto largely neglected period and has brought to our attention the great need for more such research.

The quantity, time depth, and nature of basic source materials on Middle America have provided a constant incentive for ethnohistorical research. At the same time, the logistics of working with source materials too often hidden away in private and institutional collections has impeded progress, just as it did two centuries ago. In recent decades there has been an increase in the editing and publishing of these materials, some of it attributable to technological advancements in publishing and to a larger, more affluent clientele for ethnohistorical publications. But in addition, ethnohistorians have increasingly sought complete and reliable reproductions of source materials, both pictorial and textual. Considerable effort has also been expended in cataloging and annotating important collections of source materials, resulting, for example, in the four-volume *Guide to Ethnohistorical Sources,* included in the *Handbook of Middle American Indians* (Cline 1972–75).

One of the most significant recent developments in ethnohistory is the greater variety of problems approached and methodologies employed. As a result, long-accepted generalizations now provide challenging hypotheses to be tested. Recent ethnohistory has clearly become dominated by problem-oriented research and pays less heed to the more traditional goal of producing descriptive compilations. This, in part, explains why contemporary ethnohistorians have not devoted themselves to producing comprehensive areal syntheses such as those of Orozco y Berra and Bancroft; there now appear to be too many topics that still require detailed and resourceful analyses.

There has been a marked tendency to emphasize the local level and to meet its requirements for documentation whenever possible. Source materials long neglected, avoided, or unknown are increasingly being sought and analyzed. With the greater abundance of primary information, we now recognize that the local and regional variation encountered in modern complex societies was no less characteristic of complex societies in the past.

EXPLORATIONS IN ETHNOHISTORY

The essays assembled in this volume are representative of current trends in Middle American ethnohistorical research in their concentration on problems, focus on local-level materials, use of native pictorial and textual documents, and their employment of a wide variety of analytical methods and techniques. They utilize new sources as well as long-familiar ones. They reflect, implicitly or explicitly, the growing consciousness of local and regional differences. And they also necessarily reflect the topical specialities of their authors and the long persistence of many of them in refining their analyses, not only toward a better understanding of specific local situations, but also toward more detailed comparisons with other localities.

A number of the essays included in this volume were presented at the 43rd International Congress of Americanists, which met in Vancouver, British Columbia, in August of 1979. Two symposia provided the stimulus for the present volume: "The Contact Period in Mesoamerica," coordinated by H. R. Harvey, and "The Mexican Project," coordinated by Hanns J. Prem. Temporally the essays cover the preconquest to midcolonial periods; geographically they center on the Valley of Mexico and the Puebla-Tlaxcala region. Both of these areas were predominantly Nahua speaking in late preconquest and early colonial times.

Analysis and interpretation of sources are tasks all ethnohistorians share. The sparsity of early records, the gaps in their coverage, and the confusion in the semantics of native terms also challenge the ethnohistorian. Woodrow Borah's essay discusses other common problems confronted by ethnohistorians in working with the source materials. He notes that there has been a tendency for scholars to assume that Indian authority is more reliable than Spanish, in part because Indians are perceived to have been more knowledgeable in the intricacies of their own society. In some instances reliance on one over the other has led to basic differences in the interpretation of native institutions, with far-reaching implications in the reconstruction of native society. Borah emphasizes that no source, whether Spanish or Indian, should be accepted without a careful consideration of all the circumstances involved in its production.

Three of the six essays concerned with the Valley of Mexico directly or indirectly bear on land tenure (Harvey, Cline, and Offner), a subject basic to an understanding of native social stratification, the taxation system, inheritance patterns, and so forth. Alonso de Zorita's (1891) explicit description of Indian land tenure has frequently been accepted uncritically by scholars who have elected either to overlook or to reconcile discrepancies suggested by other source materials. Yet Zorita himself was careful to point out that there were variations in the pattern, although he did not describe them. Harvey's essay investigates the viewpoints that have prevailed since Bandelier's time, utilizing the data from Tepetlaoztoc preserved in that town's unusually detailed archival record, as well as other archival collections from the sixteenth century to the present. His analysis of this long record suggests a greater complexity of rules and possibly a greater flexibility in their application than has been previously assumed. Since there has been so little observable change from the 1540s to the present in the land-tenure patterns of the nonelite, the basic configuration appears to predate the conquest. Offner's detailed analysis of household organization as recorded in the Codex Vergara leads him to question prevailing views of land tenure, and he, too, senses greater complexity in this important native institution than assumed by most contemporary scholars. His analysis of Tepetlaoztoc's households, when compared with those of other localities in the Valley of Mexico, such as Tenochtitlan and Acolman, also points to local variation in household composition. He finds as well that the patterns prevailing in Tepetlaoztoc occurred elsewhere, such as in Tepoztlan as analyzed by Carrasco (1964). Clearly, even within regions and provinces ancient Mexico was not homogeneous in terms of social, economic, and political structure.

Cline approaches the problem of land tenure and inheritance through individual case analysis. Until recently, very little attention has been accorded to local, personal documents, particularly those in Nahuatl. Part of the significance of her essay lies in analyzing the potential of this important source of material for testing the generalizations found in more traditional sources. Her concern is with the translation and analysis of over sixty wills from Culhuacan, recorded in Nahuatl during the final quarter of the sixteenth century. Despite its small size, the sample contains a wealth of information

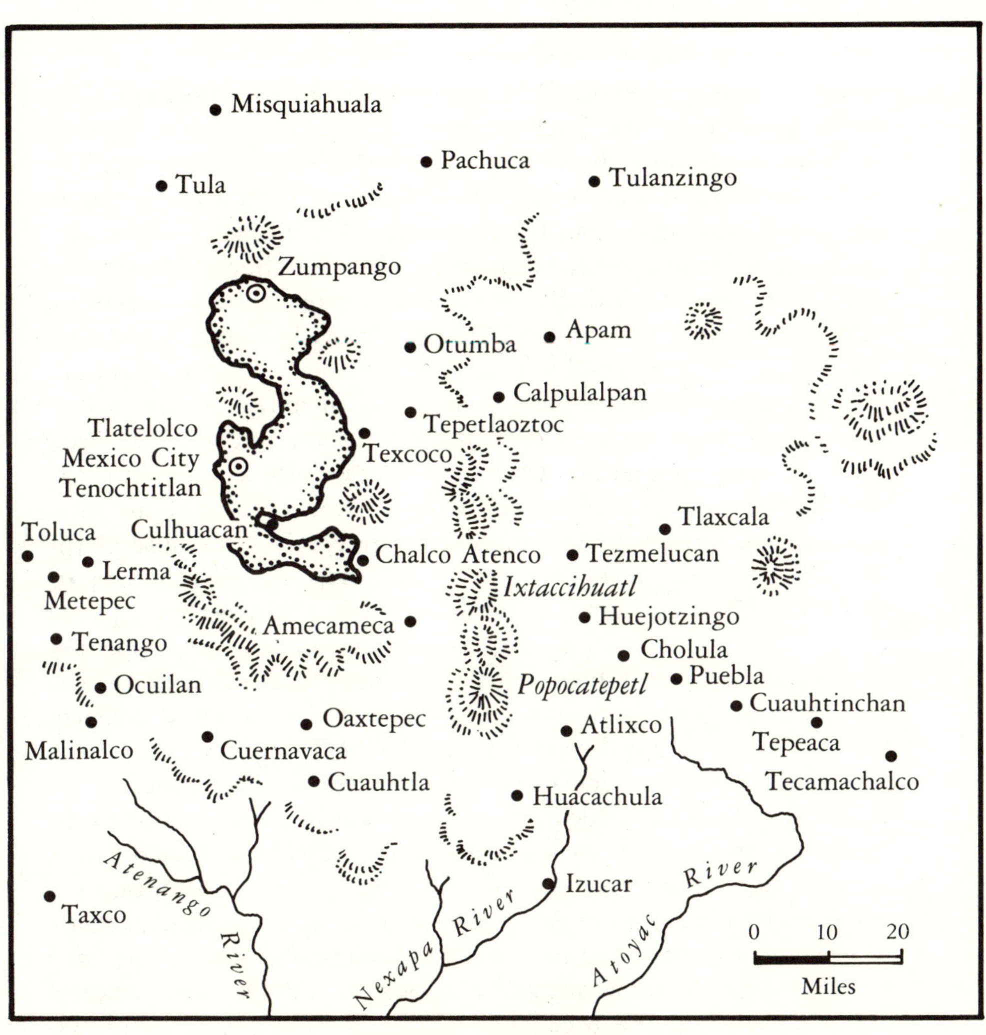

Nahua-speaking area

about a variety of behavioral patterns; it includes both male and female testators, nobility and commoners, and a range of capital goods and real estate. Not all estates involved land, but of those that did, the parcels were for the most part small and widely scattered, and were identified by their location, size, previous owners, and civil category. These prehispanic categories persisted, even though the functions implied by such classification had altered. The wills also suggest that a more complex land classification was in use at the local level than has generally been thought.

Carrasco's analysis of royal marriages in the Valley of Mexico also utilizes the case method. Because such marriages were so important in the structure and dynamics of native society both before and after the conquest, standard chronicles contain an abundance of genealogical information and other details pertinent to this theme. Bringing to bear his expertise in social organization and his familiarity with the source materials, Carrasco very carefully and exhaustively analyzes this complex data set. Many misconceptions about royal marriage patterns have arisen in the past precisely because of the lack of systematic analysis of these materials. Even more importantly, as Carrasco demonstrates, local differences between power centers in mode of succession must be viewed from the perspective of the position each held in the dominant/subordinate political relationships prevailing at a given time in the Valley of Mexico. Kinship organization allowed for considerable flexibility in adjusting to changing political and economic expediencies over time.

Although the native economic system was of great interest to the Spaniards who first observed it and then adapted and modified it to serve their own ends, surprisingly little systematic attention has been paid to the role of labor in preconquest urbanism. Frederic Hicks's essay is the third in a series of studies which he has devoted to analyzing the structure and function of different categories of labor involved in the urban network. Combining the use of traditional source materials with archival data, the essay provides a good example of what rich yields these sources can have when subjected to innovative lines of inquiry. For ancient Tetzcoco (modern Texcoco), with its rather dispersed population, rotational labor provided a mechanism for uniting the kingdom, while responding to the varying demands, seasonal and otherwise, for unskilled labor.

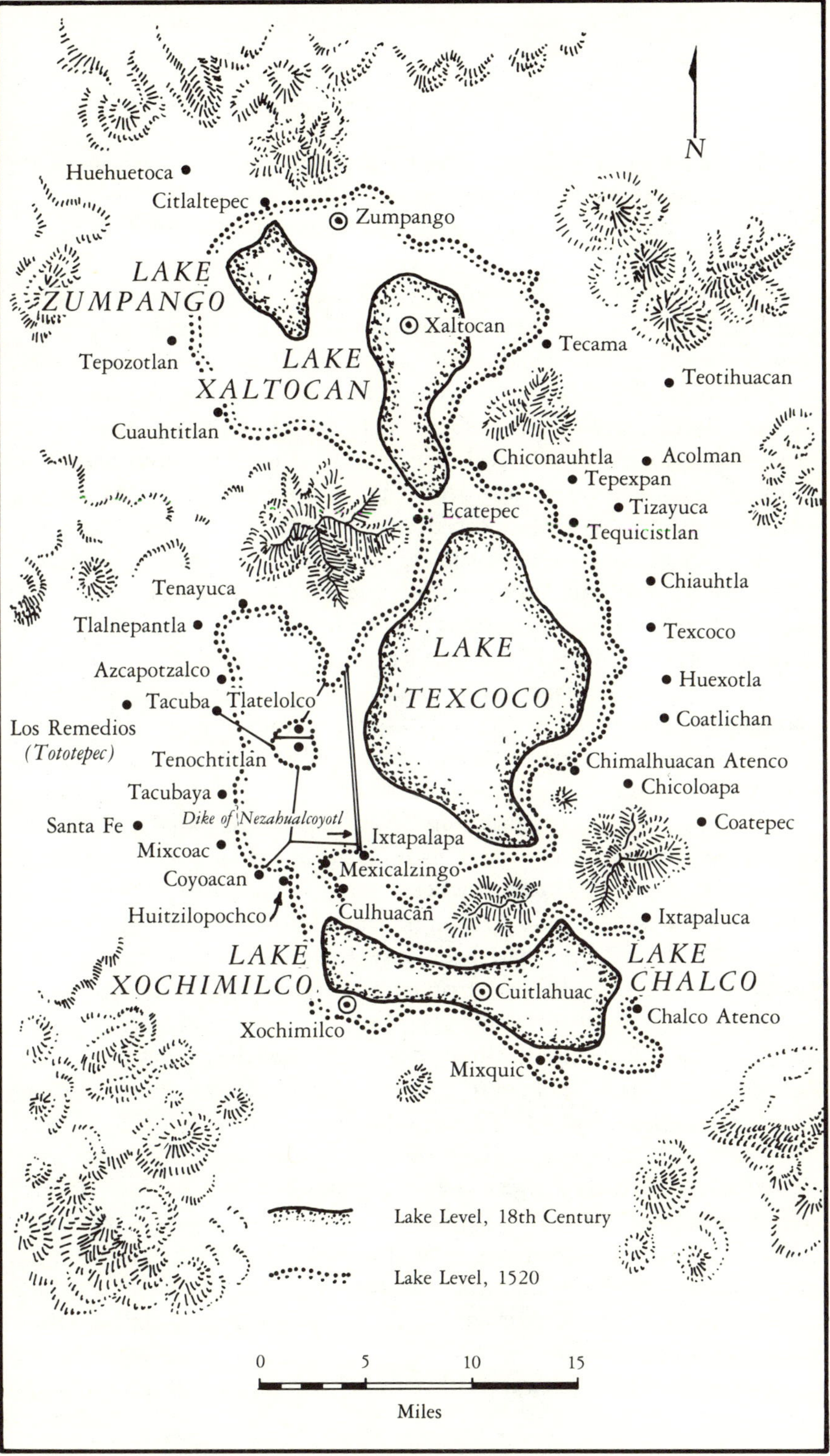

Lake Texcoco region

Most importantly, this study helps provide a new dimension to our growing awareness of the complexity of the system of cross-cutting economic, political, and religious networks, that provided the dynamic fabric of Middle American societies.

Agriculture was the basis of subsistence in prehispanic Mesoamerica. Even by conservative estimates it was sufficiently productive to support a large native population and it was sufficiently varied in its broad array of crops and ecological settings to imply a fair range in techniques practiced by native farmers. And yet its tool technology was relatively simple; hand tools predominated. As Rojas's essay indicates, however, the "simplicity" in tool types was more apparent than real, often exaggerated by the application of generic terms such as *uictli* and *coa* to a range of distinct cultivation implements and the tendency of chroniclers to ignore actual differences in agricultural tool types. Scant attention has previously been accorded this subject; Rojas's thorough examination of pictorial and written sources turns up direct evidence of important differences among tools used in this crucial aspect of indigenous technology.

A number of writers in the early colonial period commented upon the native system of recordkeeping; among the records maintained were cadastral registers and maps. Williams's essay analyzes, for the first time, the native conventions used in the preparation of cadastral records from Tepetlaoztoc, where two important sets of pictorial registers have survived. Although these codices have been known for a long time, they had been largely ignored; they contain few Spanish glosses, and to interpret and analyze the wealth of socioeconomic data required first decoding the native glyphic conventions. Once deciphered, these native landholding texts show that some unexpected data were gathered for cadastral purposes, including the area and soil types of fields.

The essays by Dyckerhoff, Prem, and Trautmann are derived from the Puebla-Tlaxcala Project of the German Research Society, a long-term, multidisciplinary program of integrated regional research. These essays collectively cover the prehispanic through the colonial periods and provide examples of the increasing emphasis which contemporary ethnohistorians place on diachronic models in their research designs.

For certain time periods and regions in Central Mexico, only the barest documentation exists. Ethnohistorians must circumvent these informational gaps or attempt to fill them by other than documentary sources. The analysis of toponyms provides a potential means for accomplishing this. Toponyms can provide data which are useful both in the establishment of area chronologies and in disentangling the complexities caused by multiethnic migration and conquest. In Mexico the study of toponyms has long been very limited in scope, largely devoted to the etymology of place names. By contrast, in Europe the field has been extensively developed as an important instrument in reconstructing the evolution of settlement. Dyckerhoff's essay illustrates that the application of rigorous linguistic methods to the analysis of toponyms yields more accurate etymologies and expands the data base for historical reconstruction. She calls attention to the regional dialect diversity in Nahuatl that existed in the sixteenth century, which will have to be taken into account as sophisticated analyses comparable to her treatment of Huejotzingo toponyms are extended to other regions.

In order to understand the adjustment of Indian society to Spanish rule, it is necessary to look closely at Spanish activities during the period of adaptation. The founding of the city of Puebla and the subsequent colonization of the Atlixco Valley was an experiment designed to establish an alternate system to that of encomienda. Prem's essay examines the settlement process in detail by comparing the Audiencia's objectives with the patterns that actually evolved. The granting of small plots of land in the Atlixco-Puebla area was designed to provide both the wherewithal and incentive for individual Spaniards to farm their own small parcels. It also came to provide a source of wage labor for Indians. By the middle of the sixteenth century, however, allotments of land to individual Spaniards had increased in size and individuals were also combining the small plots into larger estates and purchasing additional lands from Indian owners. While the demand for Indian labor to operate these expanding farmsteads may not have increased in absolute terms, the Indian population severely declined in the sixteenth century, thereby placing a proportionately greater burden on those who survived.

Trautmann is concerned with the Spanish and Indian interaction which resulted in modifications of the Tlaxcalan cultural landscape throughout the colonial period. When analyzed from a geographic perspective, seemingly disparate data on settlement size, location, growth and decay, the genesis of haciendas, barrio organization, ethnic and racial composition, occupation structure, and migration can all be described by a single spatial model, which he terms "center-periphery." The center-periphery pattern is discernible at both local and regional levels. The causes underlying these distributions are arrayed in a second, systems model, which shows the relationships between the elements of Tlaxcalan state and society, the processes in operation, and the resultant effects. As Trautmann points out, spatial models can serve as heuristic devices for simplifying complex data and understanding historical processes, but to date they have not been widely used by ethnohistorians.

Over the last twenty years, the number of investigators who have undertaken research in Mesoamerican ethnohistory and archaeology has mushroomed. An important consequence of this increase is that formerly neglected topics, themes, and geographical areas have been attracting investigation. The larger pool of scholars also brings with it a broader intellectual perspective, as well as a greater array of methods and techniques for interpreting and reconstructing the past. The eleven papers included in this volume constitute a selected sample of directions that ethnohistorical efforts have taken in Mesoamerica in the most recent decades.

The core area of the central Mexican highlands, the Basin of Mexico and neighboring Puebla-Tlaxcala to the east, has been the focus of continuous ethnohistorical activity since the Spanish conquest. It is in fact the oldest area of genuine ethnohistoric inquiry in the New World. Scholars today are pursuing many of the same goals as they did in the sixteenth century, goals directed toward achieving a more thorough understanding of native civilization and its particular components. But that pursuit follows a greater diversity of paths, including considerable rethinking of topics and themes and employing a battery of theoretical and methodological perspectives. As research emphasis has shifted from the macro to the micro level, local and regional variation has become increasingly apparent. The view that is emerging of ancient Mexico is becoming more complex, more intriguing, and even more interesting.

REFERENCES

Aubin, Joseph Marius Alexis
1849   Mémoire sur la peinture didactique et l'écriture figurative des anciens Mexicains. Paris: Paul Dupont.
1893   Histoire de la nation mexicaine depuis le départ d'Aztla jusqu'à l'arrivée des conquérants espagnols (et au de la 1607). Paris: Ernest Leroux.

Bancroft, Hubert Howe
1874–76   The Native Races of the Pacific States of North America. 5 vols. San Francisco: A. L. Bancroft.

Bandelier, Adolph F.
1877   On the Art of War and Mode of Warfare among the Ancient Mexicans. Tenth Annual Report of the Trustees of the Peabody Museum of American Archaeology and Ethnology 2: 95–161.
1878   On the Description and Tenure of Lands, and the Customs with Respect to Inheritance, among the Ancient Mexicans. Eleventh Annual Report of the Trustees of the Peabody Museum of American Archaeology and Ethnology 2: 385–448.
1880   On the Social Organization and Mode of Government of the
–   Ancient Mexicans. Twelfth Annual Report of the Trustees of the Peabody Museum of American Archaeology and Ethnology 2: 557–699.

Barlow, Robert H.
1945   La Crónica X: versiones coloniales de la historia de los Mexica Tenochca. Revista Mexicana de Estudios Antropológicos 7: 65–87.
1949   The Extent of the Empire of the Culhua Mexica. Ibero-Americana 28. Berkeley: University of California Press.

Carmack, Robert M.
1972   Ethnohistory: A Review of Its Development, Definitions, Methods, and Aims. Annual Review of Anthropology 1: 227–46.

Carrasco, Pedro
1964   Tres libros de tributos del Museo Nacional de México y su importancia para los estudios demográficos. Actas y Memorias (del) XXXV Congreso Internacional de Americanistas, México, 1962. Vol. 3, pp. 373–78. México.

Chavero, Alfredo
n.d.   Historia antigua y de la conquista. *In* Mexico a través de los
[ca. 1887] siglos. Riva Palacio, ed. Vol. 1. Mexico: Ballesca y Comp.

Clavigero, Francisco Javier
1780–81 Storica antica del Messico. Cesena: Georgio Bisiani.

Cline, Howard F., ed.
1972–75 Guide to Ethnohistorical Sources. 4 vols. Handbook of Middle American Indians. Robert Wauchope, gen. ed. Austin: University of Texas Press.

Gamio, Manuel, ed.
1922 La población del Valle de Teotihucan. 3 vols. México: Secretaría de Agricultura y Fomento.

Gibson, Charles
1964 The Aztecs under Spanish Rule: A History of the Indians of the Valley of Mexico. Stanford: Stanford University Press.

Hamy, Ernest Theodore
1899a Codex Borbonicus. Paris: Ernest Leroux.
1899b Codex Telleriano-Remensis. Paris: Imp. Burdin.

Humboldt, Alexander von
1801 Vues des cordilleres et monuments des peuples indigènes de l'Amérique. Paris: F. Schoell.

Kingsborough, Lord (Edward King)
1831–48 Antiquities of Mexico, Comprising Facsimiles of Ancient Mexican Paintings and Hieroglyphs. 9 vols. London: Hawell, Colnaghi.

León y Gama, Antonio de
1832 Descripción histórica y cronológica de las dos piedras . . . que se hallaron . . . el año de 1790. México: Alejandro Valdés.

Moreno, Manuel M.
1931 La organización politica y social de los aztecas. México: Universidad Nacional Autónoma de México.

Nicholson, H. B.
1975 Middle American Ethnohistory: An Overview. *In* Handbook of Middle American Indians. Vol. 15. Robert Wauchope, gen. ed. pp. 487–505. Austin: University of Texas Press.

Orozco y Berra, Manuel
1880 Historia antigua y de la conquista de México. México: Tipografía de Gonzalo A. Esteva.

Peñafiel, Antonio
1897 Nomenclatura geográfica de México. Etimologías de los nombres de lugar correspondientes a los principales idiomas que se hablan en la república. México: Secretaría de Fomento.

Prescott, William H.
1843   History of the Conquest of Mexico, with a Preliminary View
           of the Ancient Mexican Civilization, and the Life of the Con-
           queror, Hernando Cortes. London: Richard Bentley.

Röck, Fritz
1932   Versuch einer terminologischen Synthese der menschheitsge-
           schichtlichen Wissenzweige: Rassenforschung, Kulturfor-
           schung (Urgeschichte, Völkerkunde, Volkskunde, Geschichte)
           und Sprachforschung. Mitteilungen der Anthropologischen
           Gesellschaft Wien 62: 295–304.

Rosny, Léon de
1869   Archives paléographiques de l'Orient et de l'Amérique pub-
           liées avec des notices historiques et philologiques. Paris:
           Maisonneuve.
1876   Essai sur le déchiffrement de l'écriture hiératique de l'Amé-
           rique Centrale. Paris: Maisonneuve.

Seler, Eduard
1904–9   Codex Borgia, 3 vols. Berlin.
1927   Einige Kapitel aus dem Geschichtswerke des Fray Bernardino
           de Sahagún aus dem Aztekischen übersetzt. Stuttgart: Strecker
           und Schröder.

Siméon, Remi
1889   Annales de Domingo Francisco de San Antón Muñón Chi-
           malpahin Quauhtlehuanitzin, sixième et septième Relations.
           Paris: Maissoneuve.

Spores, Ronald
1980   New World Ethnohistory and Archaeology, 1970–1980. An-
           nual Reviews of Anthropology 19: 575–603.

Sturtevant, William C.
1966   Anthropology, History, and Ethnohistory. Ethnohistory 13:
           1–51.

Zorita, Alonso de
1891   Breve y sumaria relación de los señores y maneras y diferencias
           que había de ellos en la Nueva España, Nueva Colección de
           Documentos para la historia de México. García Icazbalceta,
           pub. Vol. 3, pp. 71–227. México.

2

Some Problems of Sources

Woodrow Borah

All fields of study often pass from periods of making general statements to carrying out detailed local and topical studies, which in turn facilitate a return to making general statements, but now more nuanced and firmly based. In Mesoamerican ethnohistory we are, it seems to me, moving from an older period of making general statements to cover all of Central Mexico or even northern Mesoamerica, derived from general statements in our sources, to a new period of undertaking detailed studies of specific localities and careful textual examination of our sources. The movement is in itself an interesting phenomenon, for it derives strength from a general increase in number of investigators and from a far greater knowledge of languages and techniques. A much more widespread knowledge of Nahuatl, and increasingly of other Indian languages, permits inspection and analysis of records previously untouched or left to the very few who were able to read them. Further, the development of ethnohistory as a respectable field of endeavor is leading to an interpenetration of techniques and a broadening use of skills.

To give a few examples, anthropologists are becoming aware of what students of history have to learn at the start, namely, that forgery is prevalent in documents and that there are more subtle forms of influencing the case or text through special pleading and mind set. They are also learning how to test for these phenomena. Students trained in history are perceiving the need to move from archives and libraries into the countryside in order to match documents to terrain. They are also learning to be alert for subtle hints of social context. In all fields students are adding new dimensions and new forms of analysis by resorting to quantitative treatments. The result should ultimately be a far more nuanced and exact series of general statements. Let me illustrate this trend through two sets of problems, one fairly specific, one more general.

The first problem concerns classes and their meaning within the sixteenth-century peasantry of northern Mesoamerica. Our view at present comes essentially from Alonso de Zorita, backed by testimony of the mid-sixteenth century. According to Zorita (1942), the peasantry was divided into free and unfree categories. The free peasants were organized into *calpullis* and paid tribute and services to the various upper strata of society, to the Triple Alliance in preconquest times, to their own more local state structure, to the town, and even to officials of the calpulli itself. Some of the free peasants (*tecallec*), relieved of the payment of tribute to the uppermost strata, instead delivered goods and services to specific officials, in a form of payment of salaries and perquisites that substituted for cash in a society with far less ability than ours to handle such matters through money. This system continued until midcentury. The unfree peasants (*mayeque, ·tlalmaitl,* or *terrazgueros*) rented land from private owners and in exchange delivered to them a heavy proportion of the yield as well as direct services. They were subject to the jurisdiction of the proprietor in ways that free peasants were not, and were exempt from tribute to the Triple Alliance because they already delivered so much to the proprietor that little was left over. By the same argument, during the first decades of the Spanish period the mayeque were exempt from payment of tribute to the crown *encomendero*. Below the mayeque was a group called "slaves" by the

Spaniards, as the nearest equivalent they could find in European terminology. They were far less important in agriculture than the mayeque in the highlands, but on the coasts, where the system of mayeque was largely lacking, they became correspondingly far more important. The picture then is of a highly stratified society in the highlands becoming progressively more stratified through centuries of invasion, the insertion of new groups, and the corresponding lowering of the status of older groups; in the lowlands society was much simpler. This difference between highland and coastal areas apparently extended across the Isthmus of Tehuantepec to the Maya regions of southern Mesoamerica.[1]

This picture has been the one used in describing and analyzing northern Mesoamerican society for a number of decades. The late Professor Sherburne F. Cook and I made it the basis of our calculations of population for Central Mexico at various points in the years before the great tribute reform of the 1560s that ended most exemption from tribute (Borah and Cook 1960, 1963: 60–88 esp.; Cook and Borah 1963). What is frequently forgotten is that we tested this picture for its validity and universality. By comparing our calculations of preconquest population for the larger regions into which we divided Central Mexico against statements of preconquest population made in reports of the Spaniards in their first years and in the more systematic inquiry of the *Relaciones geográficas* of 1577–85, we found that our estimates were in remarkably close agreement with reporting based upon questioning the natives (Cook and Borah 1966: 234–39). Secondly, we examined the extent of addition of new tributaries to the rolls as a result of the tribute reform of the 1560s. That testing involved a much more nuanced examination by smaller regions, these being set by the nature of the reporting. We found that the statements of Zorita held up well, but could be extended to regions he did not mention, such as the northern Mixteca Alta and the Cañada-Chinantla. We concluded that regional differences were marked and that "Des analyses différentes et plus poussées restent possible à partir d'une connaissance historique plus détaillée de chaque région" (Cook and Borah 1963: 247).[2]

At the same time that we were carrying out our probes, Pedro Carrasco was engaged in the beginnings of a long-term effort to examine the structure of sixteenth-century native society through highly specific analyses of contemporary records in Nahuatl (Carrasco 1961, 1962, 1963, 1967a, 1970). He has been joined in that endeavor by others, such as Frederic Hicks, who has tended to concentrate upon the nature of divisions among the peasantry in the areas around the Valley of Mexico (Hicks 1974: 244–66), and by scholars like Ronald Spores (1967) who work with non-Nahuatl regions and a broader range of problems. One of the most important contingents of scholars has come from the German-sponsored Puebla–Tlaxcala Basin Project, most notably in the persons of Hanns J. Prem and Ursula Dyckerhoff, with careful studies of the Codex of Huejotzingo as well as other records, and the placement of documents in the terrain (Dyckerhoff 1973; Prem 1974, 1978, with a contribution by Dyckerhoff). In 1974, at the Forty-First International Congress of Americanists, held in Mexico City, interest in the general problem led to a symposium on social stratification in prehispanic Mesoamerica, chaired by Pedro Carrasco. The papers have been published in a special volume (Carrasco et al. 1976).

As often happens, these further inquiries, while shedding much light on local conditions, have to date indicated no clear solutions or explanations. In general the studies by Pedro Carrasco, Frederic Hicks, and others of Nahuatl sources find a puzzling discrepancy between the native records and the statements in Spanish. It would be an exaggeration to say that they find a vast, undifferentiated mass of peasantry with no evidence of the divisions into free and unfree. Rather, they find no mention of the term "mayeque," and that rental arrangements were far more complex than the sharp distinctions indicated by Zorita. The relation of such differences to the payment of tribute, and in what forms, also remains baffling.[3]

On the other hand, the studies by Hanns J. Prem and Ursula Dyckerhoff, using as their prime source the Codex of Huejotzingo, a document prepared under Spanish aegis, but supplementing it with much further work in local and other archives and locating documents exactly in the terrain, uphold the essential validity of Zorita's statements as of the middle of the sixteenth century. The two German scholars also offer a detailed examination of changes in landholding in Huejotzingo, a town with perhaps more perturbation in such matters than most. They indicate massive change in kinds of title to land as the Indians tried to justify their ideas and forms in European concepts and as they tried to adjust their structures to the new forms being imposed upon them. The two scholars indicate a substantial transfer of lands from those earmarked for various forms of community allocation or attached to the performance of official duties, to the new European titles of simple ownership. They suggest that in the process the local nobility at first usurped a great deal, but in the end was forced by pressure from the Franciscans and the viceregal government to come to a compromise. In the final settlement much land was allocated to the peasantry, although with requirements of delivery of goods and services that may have meant less change than the Spaniards supposed (Dyckerhoff and Prem 1976; Prem 1978: 220–32).

Clearly there is a substantial discrepancy between what one finds in records in Nahuatl and in Spanish. How may one account for the discrepancy? One explanation would simply hold that the Spanish knew little of native society and that their descriptions of the peasantry greatly exaggerated distinctions or were simply wrong. Such an explanation may satisfy an extreme Nahuatlist, but it quickly runs up against the reflection that Zorita himself had spent years as an *oidor* (judge) of the Audiencia of Mexico, and that he was close to the Franciscans, who had worked in Central Mexico for decades and certainly knew a great deal about the native population.[4] The explanation further supposes two closed societies with relatively little intercommunication, whereas what is emerging rapidly from recent studies is that there was far more rapid and far greater interpenetration of the two societies than had been supposed (Anderson, Berdan, and Lockhart 1976). Accordingly, the chances of deceiving the Spaniards, particularly after their years of study and examination, must have been low.

Another explanation, which certainly accords with the evidence so far, is that there were marked regional differences that have yet to be explored sufficiently (see Carrasco's introduction in Carrasco et al. 1976). Yet another would hold that native society was hardly static, that the conquest, by changing balances of power and pressures, brought rapid change even in the earliest years, so that what native records and Spanish inquiries reveal is a situation in which much change already had taken place through the replacement of elites, the vacating of allocations of land and peasantry for such purposes as native cults and imperial and state functions, and the moving into the niches and lands thus vacated of members of the old nobility as well as new people who were able to make themselves useful to the Spaniards. The development of new intermediaries to meet the new needs brought by the conquest and the changes in native society would be expected, and certainly took place.[5]

If substantial changes in landholding and social structure occurred by the middle of the sixteenth century, a question arises inevitably as to the extent to which the structure of native society at midcentury might be held to resemble that at the time of the conquest. Carrasco very properly raises it. At this point the problem becomes more complex rather than more simple, for the Spaniards by midcentury were conducting an elaborate series of inquiries into the nature of society, landholding arrangements, and the kinds and nature of tribute at the time of Montezuma.[6]

Indians who knew the preconquest patterns were available in large numbers and could be consulted.[7] I am led to comment that sixteenth-century Spaniards may have had firm ideas on the nature of true and false religion and on the proper forms of society, but they also had intelligence, industry, and knowledge of many techniques for testing evidence. A country-wide conspiracy to deceive them on the part of widely scattered natives, who were badly divided and had much profit to gain from providing information to the Spaniards, seems highly improbable; its potential success seems even less likely. I am also led to comment, in passing, that the idea of a relatively static preconquest society is also untenable; it is related to the human yearning for a Garden of Eden. At the time the Spaniards arrived, societies and polities in northern Mesoamerica were undergoing rapid change, both in the development of more hierarchical structures and in political unification. So the problem remains.

Clearly we have learned a great deal from recent studies; equally clearly they have proved that the problems are more complex than we had imagined. I suggest that a satisfactory explanation which will bring all elements into a coherent picture is yet to come.

The first set of problems I have sketched covers a relatively specific question and is illustrative of others that might be advanced. The second set is a far more general category, covering our major contemporary statements about preconquest and sixteenth-century Mesoamerica, and hence involving our major sources. They may be verified or modified by archaeological, linguistic, documentary, and other evidence, but they still remain the mainstay of all our investigations and speculation. Here the basic difficulty arises from the ways in which the sixteenth century, and indeed most centuries until the Enlightenment, regarded the use of sources and the need to give explicit credit for borrowing or copying. The best-known instance of a difficulty of this nature advanced in our times is, of course, the discovery by Joaquín García Icazbalceta of how much of Torquemada's great chronicle is derived from Mendieta, and the extent to which large sections represent direct copying (in Mendieta 1971: xxx–xlv). Icazbalceta's discovery has given rise to charges of plagiarism, as well as to a remarkably subtle and understanding defense by John L. Phelan (1970: 106–11), which explains the Franciscan need to conceal and modify Mendieta's view at the same time that they did not wish to lose the very real value of Mendieta's memories and scholarship. We should stress, too, the tolerance of the age toward borrowing and copying. Previous ages to ours had not developed the relentless requirement of careful footnoting that we now have because of the development of textual scholarship and historical writing since the Renaissance, and even more since the Enlightenment (León-Portilla 1978–79: 312).

The meaning of this is simply that scholars in previous ages copied each other, very often artlessly and without attribution; they sometimes indicated sources, but more often did not. In an examination of texts, present-day students must always be on guard; we may be dealing with independently concurring testimony or we may be dealing with copying. Descriptions of the systems of landholding in preconquest times, for example, may come from a far smaller number of writers than we have believed at first sight.[8] It behooves us as wary scholars to compare accounts with great caution; should we encounter nearly exact agreement, we must consider the possibility and perhaps near certainty of copying. I should suggest also that we put aside the righteous indignation of the nineteenth and twentieth centuries as irrelevant in dealing with what the sixteenth century regarded as justified and proper procedure.

What we need at our present stage of scholarship to secure a more solidly based advance is clearly a painstaking, methodical examination of such accounts. We need to know much more about the preparation and preservation of the various versions that have come down to us; in short, we need textual histories. The results here may be surprising as, for example, in the proof that Bernal Díaz del Castillo wrote his history with that of López de Gómara in hand to serve as the model for organizing his own reminiscences, and the further demonstration that the various versions of Bernal Díaz, with their very great internal differences, are all true versions that he himself prepared in a long life of writing and revision (Sáenz de Santa María 1956, 1967; Cerwin 1963: 171–211). Another illustration of our need is found in the ongoing debate over the relation of Fray Toribio de Motolinía's *Memoriales* and *Historia de los Indios* to each other and perhaps to a larger work, now lost, from which both may have been drawn (Motolinía 1971: vii–cxxxi).

Beyond textual history of this kind, we need to study correspondences and differences in our sources, through line-by-line comparisons among all of them. It would seem to be the only way at this time to achieve the massive breakthrough we need concerning the relations of sources to each other and the extent to which we are dealing with independent corroborative information, simple copying, or explication.

A serendipitous effect of the careful, wary comparative approach I am suggesting is that we may discover fragments of authors previously thought to be lost. Much of the writings of Andrés de Olmos, for example, may be with us through incorporation in the work of later writers without attribution to him (Garibay 1965: 9–14; León-Portilla 1969: 37–40; Warren 1973: 72–73). The same kind of anonymous survival is almost certainly true of other writers.

We can point to substantial beginnings of this kind of study. The late Howard Cline conceived and carried through a systematic cooperative effort to list and examine our sources for the ethnohistory of Mesoamerica, now completed in the four-volume *Guide to Ethnohistorical Sources* within the *Handbook of Middle American Indians* (Wauchope 1964–76). This marshalling of scholarly forces has meant a great advance in knowledge. We now know considerably more about parts of the problem and their relationships. Another cooperative effort still in progress at the Instituto de Investigaciones Históricas, under the inspiration and leadership of Dr. Miguel León-Portilla, involves a seminar for ascertaining the sources of the history of Fray Juan de Torquemada through a systematic examination, line by line and paragraph by paragraph. An impressive array of Mexican scholars, old and young, have joined in this project (León-Portilla 1978–79: 288–89). In the end, it will probably be necessary to examine in this intensive fashion each of the chronicles, histories, and reports of all kinds that have come down to us, in order to achieve a firmer footing for our studies.

Finally, let me add a few words about forgery. As students of ethnohistory increasingly work in archival deposits and plumb records in Spanish, Latin, and native languages, they must be prepared to keep at the forefront of their minds the possibility of the spurious. In general it will not concern the chronicles, histories, memoires, and so on that I have dealt with so far. Nevertheless, two important sources have had the charge raised against them—namely, the biography of Christopher Columbus purportedly written by his son, Fernando Colón, and the account of the conquest of Central Mexico by the "Anonymous Conqueror." Both works come to us by way of Italian publication, the Spanish originals, if they existed, having been lost. The biography of his father by Fernando Colón bears so unmistakably the stamp of family pride that scholars are inclined to accept it as genuine (Iglesia, in Colón 1947: 10–18; Warren 1973: 46). The account of the Anonymous Conqueror, which, as Federico Gómez de Orozco has pointed out, contains no information not available in other published accounts easily available at the time it was printed, is more likely to be spurious. He even indicates Antonio de Ulloa, the announced translator, as the true author (Gómez de Orozco 1961: 23–33; Warren 1973: 67–68). But longer writings of this kind are less likely to be tainted with false authorship and attribution; the more probable difficulties will lie in the defense of private interest and subtle distortions to advance personal views.

Straight, unblushing forgery is most likely to appear in documents proving title to land or office, or advancing claims for family preference. Documents claiming to indicate the location of lost mines or treasure are so clearly recent and spurious that few scholars will be taken in, although there is a steady trickle of people who

are willing to venture money and time for searches based on forgeries
of this kind. For our purpose perhaps the most important category
of documents in which forgery is an ever-present danger is deeds
to land and papers advanced in law suits over title to preferment
and office.[9]

One may account for this likelihood very simply. Throughout at
least northern Mesoamerica, Indian communities and individuals
held land by possession, with considerable dispute over fringe areas.
Although careful records seem to have been kept of land allocation,
they were fairly rudimentary; in the turmoil of the conquest and
ensuing decades they were often lost. The Spanish, on the other
hand, were used to formal written records, executed by notaries,
and recorded in notarial registers that at least formally were public
holdings. In the Spanish system, all land not actively owned by
individuals and corporations, the so-called *tierras baldías,* was crown
property, as was all land allowed to lie unused, even if owned by
individuals and corporations. So the stage was set for conflicts over
title and usufruct, which became worse as much land fell vacant
through shrinkage of the native population.

In the seventeenth century pressures upon the Indians grew harsher,
as the crown began to investigate titles through general searches in
its demands for revenue through the payment of *composición* to al-
locate or quiet title. Indian communities and families, who had
earlier been under considerable Spanish pressure as well as being
involved in continued quarrels with each other over disputed parcels,
found themselves faced by demands for proof of title to their holdings; in many instances they did not have it, even though they had
been in possession for long periods, perhaps generations. Being
thoughtful people, who understood a good deal about their masters,
they began to accommodate to the European demand by preparing
titles in the form of purported grants by previous Spanish governors,
or in the form of earlier investigations establishing the right of one
native party or the other. The result was a large volume of material
prepared in native workshops. In the first years, errors in dating,
names and titles of officials, terms of office, and handwriting and
seals permitted easy identification of the purported records as spurious by the Spanish officials of the time. However, with each setback

the Indians learned. In the course of time they reproduced seals, dates, officials, styles, and other details so accurately that spotting the documents as spurious became far more difficult. Many of their efforts passed official inspection.

There may have been actual workshops turning out such spurious records on request. Of such origin appear to be the so-called Techialoyan codices, a series of native pictorial manuscripts prepared in a single atelier or series of ateliers in what is now the state of Hidalgo. These codices purport to give evidence of titles to land and boundaries for specific villages and towns. They are clearly spurious because of their artistic style, yet were good enough to deceive Boturini Benaducci in the mid-eighteenth century. They are probably to be connected with the country-wide crown investigations of land titles in the middle and later seventeenth century (Robertson 1973; Glass 1973).

In standing guard against forgeries, students will have to look carefully for consistency with one of the proper styles for the time claimed in terms of handwriting, seals, artistic style where appropriate, and vocabulary. We will have to be on guard for inaccuracy in the use of dates, the presence of officials, and their titles; in short, the normal tests that are taught in, say, medieval European history. Students will also have to be on guard against one other tendency, for should we detect a document as spurious, we must not discard it out of hand. It can still have much value as a source, if it is examined as a record of its true time, including the circumstances that led to its preparation. The Techialoyan codices, for example, are still gems of the codical art and give testimony to their true period.

We are at the point where detailed examination of the nature and mutual relationships of our sources has become indispensable. Such examination is the only way to provide a broader, surer foundation for future scholarship.

NOTES

1. Alonso de Zorita (1942: 27–52, 59, 114–20, 124, 130); Sebastián Ramírez de Fuenleal, bishop of Santo Domingo and president of the Audiencia of Mexico, to the king, Mexico City, 3 November 1532, and

Martín Cortés, second Marqués del Valle, to the king, Mexico City, 10 October 1563, both in *Colección de documentos inéditos* (1864–84, 13: 250–61; 4: 444–51); Gonzalo Fernández de Oviedo y Valdés (1851–55, 3: 535); opinion of Vasco de Puga on the reorganization of the tribute system (1562?), in Scholes and Adams (1958: 43–45); Diego Muñoz Camargo (1892: 103–5); *Relación de las ceremonias y ritos* (1903: 25, 37–38); *Códice Kingsborough* (1912); Fray Toribio de Motolinía and Fray Diego de Olarte to the viceroy, Cholula, 27 August 1554, in Cuevas (1914: 228–31); opinion of Fray Nicolás de San Vicente Paulo, Metztitlán, 27 August 1554, in Paso y Troncoso (1939–42, 16: 56–42); Hicks (1974, 1976); Carrasco (1967b, 1976a, 1978: 24–39); and Borah and Cook (1960: 54–74).

2. I should mention a third form of verification, which we became aware of only when our work was well under way—namely, conformity to epidemiological expectation. Our estimates, when charted against time, do fit remarkably well into the kind of trend that would be expected for lethal elements introduced into a hitherto unexposed population, either in a laboratory or in the real world. See Borah and Cook (1963: 4–5) and McNeill (1976: 77–234 esp.).

3. Hicks (1974: 254–55, 1976); see also the comment by Carrasco (1976b: 117) and his study (1978: 23–39).

4. See the long introduction by Benjamin Keen in Zorita (1963: 1–77), especially pp. 16 et seq.

5. Hicks (1976: 76); Dyckerhoff and Prem (1976); Prem (1978: 220–32); Zorita (1942: 38–49); and Fray Nicolás de Witte to the viceroy, Metztitlán, 21 August 1554, in Cuevas (1914: 223).

6. Zorita's account was prepared in answer to a royal command of 20 December 1553 for information, as were letters and accounts by members of the religious orders. See Zorita (1963: 277–78).

7. In the 1540s and 1550s men of fifty to sixty years of age would have been twenty to thirty or even younger at the time of conquest since the fall of Tenochtitlan did not automatically mean the conquest of all the rest of Central Mexico. Subjugation endured at least until the early 1530s, varying with each subregion and town.

8. One may carry out a simple test by examining the footnotes of such a careful and sophisticated account as Alfonso Caso (1959: 29–54). Such writers as Herrera, Torquemada, Durán, Acosta, and Clavijero were too far removed from the time of the conquest to have had direct knowledge of preconquest conditions; that is, their information must have come from other observers, in oral or, more likely, in written form.

9. What follows is based upon my personal research in the Archivo General de la Nación, Mexico City, in various provincial archives, and in the archive of the Departamento de Asuntos Agrarios; and upon my examination of various native pictorial manuscripts.

REFERENCES

Anderson, Arthur J. O., Frances Berdan, and James Lockhart
1976   Beyond the Codices: The Nahua View of Colonial Mexico. Berkeley: University of California Press

Borah, Woodrow, and Sherburne F. Cook
1960   The Population of Central Mexico in 1548: An Analysis of the Suma de Visitas de Pueblos. Ibero-Americana 43.

1963   The Aboriginal Population of Central Mexico on the Eve of the Spanish Conquest. Ibero-Americana 45.

Carrasco, Pedro
1961   The Civil-Religious Hierarchy in Mesoamerican Communities: Pre-Spanish Background and Colonial Development. American Anthropologist 63: 483–97.

1962   Tres libros de tributos del Museo Nacional de México y su importancia para los estudios demográficos. Actas y Memorias del XXXV Congreso Internacional de Americanistas 3: 373–78.

1963   Las tierras de dos indios nobles de Tepeaca en el siglo XVI. Tlalocan 4:97–119.

1967a   Relaciones sobre la organización social indígena en el siglo XVI. Estudios de Cultura Náhuatl 7:119–54.

1967b   Don Juan Cortés, cacique de Santa Cruz Quiché. Estudios de Cultura Maya 6: 251–66.

1970   Las clases sociales en el México antiguo. Verhandlungen des XXXVIII. Internationalen Amerikanistenkongresses, Stuttgart-München 2: 371–76.

1976a   Los linajes nobles del México antiguo. *In* Estratificación social en la Mesoamérica prehispánica. Pedro Carrasco et al. pp. 19–36. México: SEP-INAH.

1976b   Estratificación social indígena en Morelos durante el siglo XVI. *In* Estratificación social en la Mesoamérica prehispánica. Pedro Carrasco et al. pp. 102–17. México: SEP-INAH.

1978   La economía del México prehispánico. *In* Economía política e

ideología en el México prehispánico. Pedro Carrasco and Johanna Broda, eds. México: CIS-INAH, Editorial Nueva Imagen.

Carrasco, Pedro et al.
1976   Estratificación social en la Mesoamérica prehispánica. México:
            SEP-INAH.

Caso, Alfonso
1959   La tenencia de la tierra entre los antiguos mexicanos. Memoria
            de el Colegio Nacional 4: 29–54.

Cerwin, Herbert
1963   Bernal Díaz, Historian of the Conquest. Norman: University
            of Oklahoma Press.

Códice Kingsborough
1912   Códice Kingsborough. Memorial de los indios de Tepetlaoxtoc
            al monarca español. Francisco del Paso y Troncoso, ed. Madrid:
            Hauser y Menet.

Colección de Documentos Inéditos
1864–84   Colección de documentos inéditos, relativos al descubrimiento
            . . . sacados de los archivos del reino, y muy especialmente
            del de Indias. Madrid: Manuel B. Quirós.

Colón, Fernando
1947   Vida del almirante don Cristóbal Colón escrita por su hijo don
            Hernando. Ramón Iglesia, ed. México and Buenos Aires: Fondo
            de Cultura Economica.

Cook, Sherburne F., and Woodrow Borah
1963   Quelle fut la stratification sociale au Centre du Mexique durant
            la première moitié du XVIᵉ siècle? Annales, économies, so-
            ciétés, civilisations 18: 226–58.
1966   On the Credibility of Contemporary Testimony on the Pop-
            ulation of Mexico in the Sixteenth Century. *In* Summa an-
            thropologica en homenaje a Roberto J. Weitlaner. pp. 234–
            39. México: INAH.

Cuevas, Mariano, comp.
1914   Documentos inéditos del siglo XVI para la historia de México.
            México: Porrúa.

Dyckerhoff, Ursula
1973   Patrones de asentamiento en la región de Huexotzingo. Co-
            municaciones (Fundación Alemana para la Investigación Cien-
            tífica) 7:93–97.

Dyckerhoff, Ursula, and Hanns J. Prem
1976   La estratificación social en Huejotzingo. *In* Estratificación so-

cial en la Mesoamérica prehispánica. Pedro Carrasco et al. pp. 157–80. México: SEP-INAH.

Fernández de Oviedo y Valdés, Gonzalo
1851–55   Historia general y natural de las Indias, islas y tierra-firme del mar océano. 4 vols. Madrid: Imprenta de la Real Academia de la Historia.

Garibay K., Ángel María, ed.
1965   Teogonía e historia de los mexicanos. Tres opusculos del siglo XVI. México: Porrúa.

Glass, John B.
1973   A Catalog of Falsified Middle American Pictorial Manuscripts. *In* Handbook of Middle American Indians. Robert Wauchope, ed. 14: 297–310. Austin: University of Texas Press.

Gómez de Orozco, Federico
1961   Estudio. *In* Relación de algunas cosas de la Nueva España y de la gran ciudad de Temestitán México, hecha por un gentilhombre del Señor Fernando Cortés. Jorge Gurría Lacroix, ed. México: Robredo.

Hicks, Frederic
1974   Dependent Labor in Prehispanic Mexico. Estudios de Cultura Náhuatl 11: 243–66.

1976   *Mayeque y calpuleque* en el sistema de clases del México antiguo. *In* Estratificación social en la Mesoamérica prehispánica. Pedro Carrasco et al. pp. 67–87. México: SEP-INAH.

León-Portilla, Miguel
1969   Ramírez de Fuenleal y las antigüedades mexicanas. Estudios de Cultura Náhuatl 8:9–49.

1978–79   New Light on the Sources of Torquemada's Monarchia Indiana. The Americas 35: 387–316.

McNeill, William H.
1976   Plagues and Peoples. New York: Anchor Press.

Mendieta, Gerónimo de
1971   Historia ecclesiástica indiana, obra escrita a fines del siglo XVI. México: Antigua Librería.

Motolinía, Toribio de Benavente
1971   Memoriales o libro de las cosas de la Nueva España y de los naturales de ella. Edmundo O'Gorman, ed. México: Universidad Nacional.

Muñoz Camargo, Diego
1892   Historia de Tlascala. México: Edit. A. Chavero.

Paso y Troncoso, Francisco del, ed.
1939–42   Epistolario de Nueva España, 1508–1818. 16 vols. México:
           Robredo.
Phelan, John Leddy
1970   The Millenial Kingdom of the Franciscans in the New World.
           Berkeley: University of California Press.
Prem, Hanns J.
1974   Matrícula de Huexotzinco (Ms. mex. 387 der Bibliothèque
           Nationale Paris). Edition, Kommentar, Hieroglyphenglossar.
           Graz: Akademische Druck-u. Verlagsanstalt.
1978   Milpa y hacienda. Tenencia de la tierra indígena y española
           en la cuenca del Alto Atoyac, Puebla, México (1520–1650).
           With a contribution by Ursula Dyckerhoff. Wiesbaden: Franz
           Steiner Verlag.
Relación de las Ceremonias y Ritos
1903   Relación de las ceremonias y ritos y poblaciones y gobernación
           de los indios de la provincia de Mechuacán hecha al illmo.
           señor don Antonio de Mendoza. Morelia: Tip. Alfonso Aragón.
Robertson, Donald
1973   Techialoyan Manuscripts and Paintings, with a Catalog. *In*
           Handbook of Middle American Indians. Robert Wauchope,
           ed. 14: 253–80. Austin: University of Texas Press.
Sáenz de Santa María, Carmelo
1956   Bernal Díaz del Castillo, historia interna de su crónica. Revista
           de Indias 16: 585–604.
1967   Introducción critica a la "Historia verdadera" de Bernal Díaz
           del Castillo. Madrid: Inst. "G.F. de Oviedo," C.S. de I.C.
Scholes, France V., and Eleanor B. Adams, eds.
1958   Sobre la manera de tributar los indios de Nueva España a su
           majestad, 1561–1564. México: José Purrúa e Hijos.
Spores, Ronald
1967   The Mixtec Kings and Their People. Norman: University of
           Oklahoma Press.
Warren, J. Benedict
1973   An Introductory Survey of Secular Writings in the European
           Tradition on Colonial Middle America, 1503–1818. *In* Hand-
           book of Middle American Indians. Robert Wauchope, ed. 13:
           42–137. Austin: University of Texas Press.
Wauchope, Robert, ed.
1964–76   Handbook of Middle American Indians. 16 vols. Austin: Uni-
           versity of Texas Press.

Zorita, Alonso de

1942   Breve y sumaria relación de los señores de la Nueva España. México.

1963   Life and Labor in Ancient Mexico. The Brief and Summary Relation of the Lords of New Spain. Benjamin Keen, trans. and intro. New Brunswick: Rutgers University Press.

3

Royal Marriages in Ancient Mexico

Pedro Carrasco

Historical sources from sixteenth-century Mexico provide a wealth of case materials about marriages contracted by the rulers of the main political units in the Valley of Mexico. However, although scholars from Morgan on have speculated about the kinship organization of ancient Mexico, there has been little systematic analysis of this material in terms either of kinship organization and marriage rules or of other aspects of social and political organization.

In a study of the Tenochca, Monzón (1949: 65–69) pointed out that different types of marriage among consanguineal kin were documented in their ruling dynasty. On this basis he concluded that patrilineal exogamy was out of the question, and he interpreted the *calpulli,* or ward, as an ambilateral clan with a preference toward endogamy. On the other hand, Espejo and Monzón (1945: 486) noticed that the rulers of Tlatelolco regularly married women from other ruling dynasties, and they suggested the possibility of exogamous rules in that area. Their analysis showed important differences in the marriage practices of different dynasties. However, from my examination of the information available about kinship in ancient Mexico, I do not think that an understanding of the various marriage types is to be found in strict rules of exogamy or endogamy.

This essay will examine the different types of marriage found in the dynasties of ancient Mexico, in terms of the kin relationship and rank of the contracting parties, and will relate each type to other features of the social organization—specifically, kin-group structure, polygyny, political alliances, transmission of rank and property (especially dowry lands), and succession to office.

Material has been examined from the entire Nahuatl-speaking area of the central highlands, but the emphasis here will be on the dynasties of the realms of Tenochtitlan and Tetzcoco, for which the best information is available. Even there treatment will not be exhaustive; my purpose is simply to define the major types of royal marriages. Some areas, especially Chalco and the Puebla region, need to be studied in more detail, and comparison with the Mixteca material would also prove fruitful (see Spores 1967; Caso 1977).

A few general features of ancient Mexican society should be mentioned as background for our discussion. In regard to kin-group structure, no clear-cut rules of patrilineal exogamy seem to have existed among the Nahuatl-speaking groups. Reports clearly state that kinship was no impediment to marriage, except between parents and children and between siblings (Motolinía 1971: 324–25; Pomar 1941: 26; *Origen de los mexicanos* 1941: 274). Furthermore, I believe that the membership of the chiefly house, *teccalli* (or *tecpan*, "palace"), can be considered a lineage, since it was a corporate group formed by descendants of a common ancestor. The corporate nature of the teccalli was based on the existence of a title and an office with attached lands and peasants; the title holder, or *teuctli* (pl. *teteuctin*), controlled the resources of the teccalli and could count on the joint efforts of its members.

Each teuctli had a number of dependents who were the descendants of a previous teuctli of the house. Also, one teuctli could have several such chiefly houses under his control. In the absence of full genealogical information, neither the descent rules determining membership nor the definition of the boundary of the group are fully clear. Because of this I have suggested that the concept of stem kindred might also be considered (Carrasco 1979). Note that we are not concerned here with kinship among the commoners; the teccalli organization basically concerns the nobility. Although some commoners attached to the teccalli may have been distant descendants of nobles, there is no clear information on this point.

One problem is that the best material reporting the common ancestry of the nobles of the teccalli comes from the Puebla region. I think that the teteuctin of the Basin of Mexico, their palaces, lands, and retainers, formed a similar type of organization, but significant differences may have existed. Since I will not discuss here in detail the question of the structure of the possible lineages or stem kindreds, I will use as far as possible the term "dynasty" to mean not only the succession line of title holders, but also their children and other descendants with possible rights to succession.

Two basic types of succession practices are described. In one there is a lineal succession from father to son, or occasionally to son's son or daughter's son. In the absence of a lineal descendant a collateral would succeed. The second type preferred collateral successors; this is sometimes described as succession going first from elder to younger brother until all had occupied the office, and then going to the sons of the elder brother. In fact, not all brothers succeeded, and an office could be transmitted to other collaterals, such as cousins. Other succession usages mentioned are: previous selection by the dying ruler of the son who would succeed, especially where lineal succession was practiced; qualification for the office as shown in personal qualities and advancement in the military hierarchy—in Tenochtitlan, in particular, attainment of the position of *tlacatecatl* or *tlacochcalcatl;* selection at a gathering of high officials and the people; and, in the case of subordinate rulers, confirmation by their sovereign (see Gibson 1971: 389).

Offices were held by men. But a man's rights to rank and office were clearly influenced by his mother's or wife's status. As mentioned above, the rulership is said to have been transmitted at times to a daughter's son, and the son of a high-ranking wife was also preferred.

Only occasionally is a woman said to have held an office or title. Thus in Chalco, Xiuhtoztzin is described as having the title of *tlailotlacteuctli* and as being *cihuapiltlahtohuani* ("queen") of the Tenanca of Tzacualtitlan (Chimalpahin 1889: 64). In Tenochtitlan, Atotoztli—the daughter of the fifth king, Moteuczoma Ilhuicamina—is often considered a link in the succession line as the mother of Axayacatl, but there is also a report that she herself succeeded her father (see below); in a *probanza* supporting the privileges claimed from the Spanish crown for doña Isabel de Montezuma (Moteuczoma's daughter), one of the witnesses declared that "if there were no males who were close relations and most worthy, females could succeed to the rulership" ("en el señorío bien sucedían las hembras faltando los varones parientes más cercanos e más valientes hombres"; AGI: Patronato 181, r.9, f.31v).

The general descriptions in the sources do not state in detail in which places one or another type of descent rule applied. It is obvious that all the different succession criteria mentioned would not always favor the same candidate, and consequently political maneuvers and conflicts could easily develop. Only an examination of detailed case materials will provide a better understanding of this question.

Polygyny prevailed among the rulers and the rest of the nobility. Wives were of different rank, according to their status at birth and the type of marriage contracted. The highest rank went to women of high birth obtained by the process of petitioning and married in a public ceremony. A wife of high rank could bring with her a retinue of other noble women or servants, who became additional wives or concubines (Ixtlilxóchitl 1977: 164). Sisters could be joint wives, as in the case of Teotihuacan mentioned below (see table 3.2 below). Children of wives of high rank (*tlazopilli*) had higher status than children of concubines (*calpanpilli*).

In some cases we know the names of a ruler's different wives and their children, such as those of Axayacatl (Tezozomoc 1949: 135–39; Chimalpahin 1889: 146–48), and Moteuczoma Xocoyotzin (Tezozomoc 1949: 150–58) of Tenochtitlan, and those of Quetzalmazatzin of Chalco (Chimalpahin 1889: 213–14). The names of some queens are in effect toponyms that probably refer to their place of origin or to the palace or lands connected with them. The data suggest that each of the different wives of a king represented an alliance with a different ruler or city, and her sons were preferred for positions connected with their mother's background.

A king's widow could marry only a man of the same rank as her first husband, with the consequence that most did not remarry. But the king's successor (even when a son) could take as many wives of his predecessor as he wanted, except his own mother.[1]

It is possible to define many of these marriages as different types of unions among consanguineals, but the main criteria I have followed in this classification of marriage types are the social status of the partners and the political significance of their marriage.

In the first place I have determined whether marriages are *interdynastic*—that is, where the partners stem from separate dynastic lines—or *intradynastic,* that is, where both are members of the same dynasty. To the extent that a dynasty has the characteristics of a lineage this dichotomy may coincide with marriage practices stated in terms of kinship.

A second criterion concerns the relative rank of the marriage partners—whether a woman of lower rank marries a man of higher rank (hypergamy), a woman of high rank marries a husband of lower rank (hypogamy), or the rank of both partners is the same (isogamy).

We shall also consider whether these marriages are related to succession practices; in particular, whether the offspring of such unions are preferred to succeed to high office. In order to ascertain this, the rules as given in the sources are not adequate; special attention must be given to identifying the mothers of the rulers.

By following this classification, each type of marriage among consanguineals will be seen as the consequence of a series of marriages in succeeding generations, made in order to maintain the alliance established according to the basic criteria as here defined.

Outlined in table 3.1 is the classification of marriage types.

INTERDYNASTIC HYPOGAMY

Interdynastic hypogamy is a type of marriage alliance that is clearly defined in our sources as a general rule and that can be documented with a number of examples. It relates two dynasties of unequal rank: the superordinate ruler gives a daughter in marriage to a subordinate king or other ruler of lower status.

This type of union is described by Motolinía (1971: 337) as the general practice in the provinces of Mexico and Tetzcoco:

Table 3.1. Types of Royal Marriage Alliances in Ancient Mexico

	INTERDYNASTIC	INTRADYNASTIC
HYPOGAMOUS	Subordinate ruler marries daughter of superordinate ruler and their son succeeds to subordinate rulership. When repeated in successive generations leads to matrilateral cross-cousin marriage. Occurs with lineal succession.	Marriage of male and female descendants of previous ruler. Both are agnates from different collateral lines of the dynasty. Occurs with collateral succession. The distinction between hypogamy and isogamy is difficult to establish.
ISOGAMOUS	Occasional marriage alliances between dynasties. No repetitive pattern develops.	
HYPERGAMOUS	Superordinate ruler marries woman of subordinate dynasty; son does not succeed to either rulership. No consanguineal marriage develops even if this type of marriage is repeated in successive generations.	Superordinate ruler marries daughter of subordinate ruler and their son succeeds to rulership in mother's town. When repeated, agnatic marriages result, with collateral succession in subordinate town.

Although the lords [*señores*] succeeded in direct line, many things
were considered to decide which son would succeed. The first was
to see whether the deceased lord had a son born of a wife who
was a Mexican lady or daughter of the lord of Mexico, or—in the
provinces subject to Tetzcoco—of the lord of Tetzcoco, and they
made that one the lord even if there were other elder sons by
other ladies. And thus it was that in Tetzcoco, where I am
writing this, when the lord called Nezahualcoyotzin died he was
not succeeded by one of his brothers nor his eldest son, although
he had such; Nezahualpiltzintli succeeded because he was the son
of the wife who was a Mexican lady. And it was the same when
Nezahualpiltzintli died. He was succeeded by none of his many
brothers nor his eldest sons, although they were the sons of ladies
who were legitimate wives . . . ; the son of the Mexican lady
succeeded. And if it was thus in Tetzcoco it was much more so in
other domains [*señoríos*] that acknowledged greater dependence.

Of special interest is Motolinía's more complete statement, in
another part of his work, that this kind of marriage was the general
practice binding the great king of Tetzcoco to the kings of the
fourteen subject towns of the realm, to whom he gave his daughters
in marriage (Motolinía 1971: 394):

> Each town had a lord [*señor*] after they married a daughter of the
> lord of Tetzcoco. That is why these women are depicted here;
> they were all daughters of a great lord of Tetzcoco named
> Nezahualcoyotzin who, together with his daughters, gave the
> lordship [*señorío*] to their husbands.

The Spanish text seems to be the explanation of a lost pictorial
document in which the towns subject to Tetzcoco were depicted.
Another Tetzcocan source explains that "the daughters of kings
married kings or lords; they brought great dowries of towns, houses,
lands, slaves, and many other goods and wealth" (Pomar 1941: 29).

The marriage connections between the kings of Teotihuacan and
their superior, the great king of Tetzcoco, are well known; I have
analyzed the data elsewhere (Carrasco 1974). This material shows
that the position of the king of Teotihuacan was enhanced and
confirmed by means of this type of hypogamous marriage and that
the Tetzcocan princesses married to the Teotihuacan kings took as
dowry extensive landholdings, the *ciuatlalli* ("woman's lands"), that

became an important part of the royal lands of the Teotihuacan kings; their continuing possession of these lands was confirmed at subsequent marriages of the same type. The son of the Tetzcocan princess became the Teotihuacan king's successor. There is only one exception to this type of marriage. When king Cotzatzin died without leaving sons from his marriage to a Tetzcoco princess, he was succeeded by his younger brother, who then married his predecessor's (elder brother's) daughters. This is an example of intradynastic marriage, to be discussed later. Shown in table 3.2 are the succession and marriages of the kings of Teotihuacan.[2]

The predominance of Tenochtitlan over Tetzcoco was expressed in the fact that this type of interdynastic hypogamy also related the rulers of these two cities. The general point is mentioned in the quotation from Motolinía, above (cf. also Torquemada 1969[2]: 356). The detailed genealogical information available contains some gaps and conflicting reports, but it supports the statement that during the period of the Triple Alliance, the Tetzcoco kings who succeeded their fathers were sons of Tenochca princesses.

Ixtlilxóchitl, the sixth king of Tetzcoco, ruled when Tenochtitlan and Tlatelolco were part of the empire of Tezozomoc of Azcapotzalco, and when they were helping Tezozomoc to extend his control over Acolhuacan. Ixtlilxóchitl had been engaged to a daughter of Tezozomoc, but when the latter opposed his succession to the rule of Tetzcoco he chose as his wife Matlalcihuatzin, a daughter of the second Tenochca king, Huitzilihuitl, who became the mother of Ixtlilxóchitl's successor, Nezahualcoyotl.[3]

During the reign of the seventh king of Tetzcoco, Nezahualcoyotl, the Triple Alliance with Tenochtitlan and Tlacopan was established. Nezahualcoyotl, like his father, married a Tenochca princess. The sources vary as to names and circumstances, but she is usually described as a daughter of Temictzin, prince (*tlatocapilli*) of Tenochtitlan, a son of Huitzilihuitl and therefore Nezahualcoyotl's mother's brother. Chimalpahin (1889: 128) gives her name as Huitzilxochitzin. In the *Historia chichimeca*, Ixtlilxóchitl gives her name as Azcalxochitzin, with a highly anecdotal account of how Nezahualcoyotl obtained her in marriage, although she had been given for this purpose to the king of Tepechpan. Nezahualcoyotl arranged to have this king killed and then married Azcalxochitzin as his

Table 3.2. Kings of Teotihuacan and their Alliances with Tetzcoco

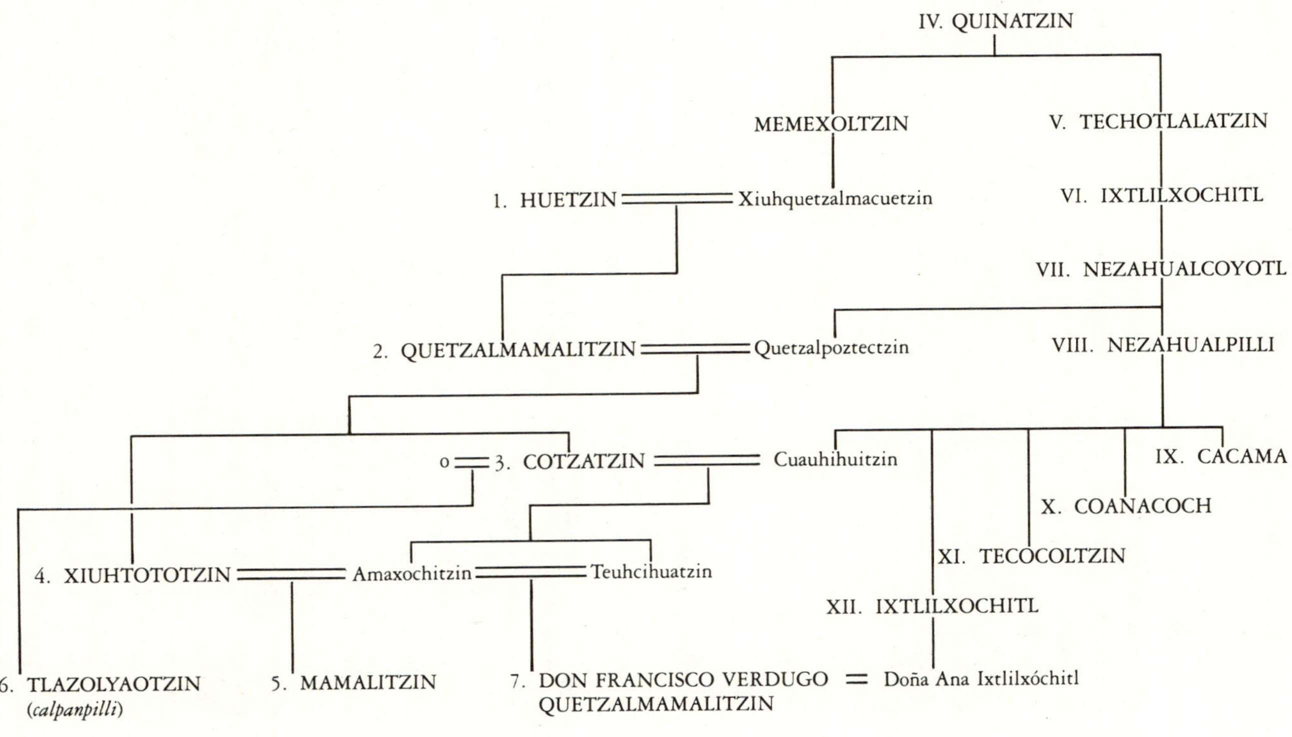

principal wife (Ixtlilxóchitl 1977: 117–18). In another version of
this story (Ixtlilxóchitl 1975: 544–45), the princess is called
Tenancacihuatzin.[4]

Further insight into the usages related to royal wives can be
gleaned from accounts of events that preceded Nezahualcoyotl's
marriage. Ixtlilxóchitl describes a confict that took place between
Itzcoatl, the king of Tenochtitlan, and Nezahualcoyotl after the
formation of the Triple Alliance. Itzcoatl disputed the title of *Chichimecateuctli* held by Nezahualcoyotl, asserting that he was the one
who should have it and that Nezahualcoyotl should only be his
subordinate and king of the Acolhua. Nezahualcoyotl, who traced
his right to the title of Chichimecateuctli from his direct ancestors,
prepared to march on Tenochtitlan. Itzcoatl then sent to him, together with other presents, twenty-five maidens of the Tenochca
royal lineage, but Nezahualcoyotl returned them, continued his
march on Tenochtitlan, and defeated Itzcoatl's army. Peace was
restored, and Nezahualcoyotl obtained the right to the tribute of a
number of places in the *chinampa* region (Ixtlilxóchitl 1977: 86–
88). Later, although Nezahualcoyotl had for a long time had many
concubines who bore him sons, the point is stressed that he had
not yet taken a principal wife to provide him with heirs. He thought
of marrying a woman from the royal houses of Huexotla or Coatlichan, from which his predecessors had taken wives, but the bride
he decided upon was married by one of his nephews, who did not
know that she was being brought up to be the king's wife. Nezahualcoyotl then married a Tenochca princess, as related in the various
accounts given above (Ixtlilxóchitl 1977: 117–18).

This story of a conflict between Nezahualcoyotl and Itzcoatl has
raised doubts in a number of historians. I am tempted to think that
the sending of Tenochca princesses did result in a royal marriage,
which defined the subordinate standing of Tetzcoco in relation to
Tenochtitlan; that the Chinampaneca places whose tribute Tetzcoco
obtained were the lands given together with the Tenochca wife
(*cihuatlalli*); and that the tradition as reported by Ixtlilxóchitl was
a reinterpretation of the facts, aimed at presenting Nezahualcoyotl
in a more favorable light.[5]

There are also conflicting reports concerning the wives of Nezahualpilli, the eighth king, and about which of them were the

mothers of his different sons, several of whom ruled in succession after him. All reports, however, describe them as Tenochca princesses. According to Ixtlilxóchitl's most detailed account, Nezahualpilli's principal wife was the daughter of Prince Xoxocatzin, lord of Atzacualco, and of Teycuhtzin ("younger sibling"), daughter of Temictzin and consequently the sister of Azcalxochitzin, Nezahaulpilli's mother. They were thus cousins, and for this reason she was selected as his legitimate wife.[6] Together with this princess came other Mexican ladies, daughters of kings, among them the lady of Xilomenco, elder sister of Moteuczoma, who was the mother of Nezahualpilli's son Cacama, the first successor to Nezahualipilli (Ixtlilxóchitl 1977: 152).

According to Torquemada (1969[1]: 184), Nezahualpilli married two sisters, nieces of the Aztec King Tizoc and daughters of Tzotzocatzin, lord of the houses of Aticpac. The elder sister became the mother of Cacama; the younger, Xocotzincatzin, was the mother of the other royal children. The *Crónica mexicayotl* (Tezozomoc 1949: 122) states that Nezahualpilli married a daughter of Cacama, the son of the famous *cihuacoatl* Tlacaelel, and she became the mother of Cacama, Nezahualpilli's successor. There are also accounts of Nezahualpilli's marriage to a daughter of Axayacatl, whom he put to death for adultery; she had no children (Chimalpahin 1889: 148; Ixtlilxóchitl 1977: 164–65; Pomar 1941: 31).

Some of these reports can be reconciled, since we clearly have variant spellings of the same name (e.g., Xoxocatzin and Tzotzocatzin). It should also be realized that when a princess is described as a sister, niece, or grandchild, these terms should probably be understood as in Nahuatl usage, in which the terms for siblings apply also to cousins, the terms for nephews and nieces apply also to cousin's children, and the terms for grandchildren also apply to the children of nephews and nieces. Nevertheless some problems remain, and for this reason I have refrained from attempting to draw a genealogical chart. The important point is that all the women concerned are Tenochca princesses and, as Ixtlilxóchitl (1977: 152) remarks, together with the main wife "came other Mexican ladies, daughters of kings." In another passage he states that King Axayacatl of Tenochtitlan and other Tenochca lords sent their daughters to Nezahualpilli so that he could choose from them the one who was to be his legitimate wife and keep the others as concubines, so that if the legitimate wife left no heir a son of one of the other ladies could succeed, according to her nobility and the seniority of her lineage (Ixtlilxóchitl 1977: 164).

According to Pomar (1941: 25), the adulterous daughter of Axayacatl had been Nezahualpilli's principal wife, and the fact that she left no children was the reason why Nezahualpilli's seven sons by other women ruled, one after the other. This report, however, was disputed by Torquemada (1969[2]: 357), who accused Pomar of playing down the importance of legitimacy in order to increase his own status; although his mother was a daughter of King Nezahualpilli, her mother had been only a slave.

In any case, the selection of Nezahualpilli's successor, Cacama, is stated by several sources to have been based on the fact that he was the son of a Tenochca lady. The later succession by his brothers took place under Spanish rule. There is little information about the marriages of these brothers, but in two cases we know of, they are of a different type, which will be discussed below.

The situation in the third city of the Triple Alliance, Tlacopan, is more difficult to assess. During the period under consideration Tlacopan was ruled by two kings—Totoquihuatzin the elder and Chimalpopoca—about whose marriage we have no information. Don Antonio Cortés Totoquihuatzin, governor (*tlatoani*) under Spanish rule, was married to a daughter of don Diego Huanitzin, a member of the Tenochca ruling lineage, who became governor of Tenochtitlan when the Spanish reintroduced the royal line of succession into the governorship (Tezozomoc 1949: 170–71). A later governor, don Gabriel, was married to a daughter of Nezahualpilli.[7]

In the relations between the kings of Tenochtitlan and the subordinate kings of cities subject to them, we also find examples of interdynastic hypogamous marriages. Thus Moquihuix was brought from Acolhuacan and installed as king of Tlatelolco by Moteuczoma Ilhuicamina because he was his nephew, the son of his sister (Tezozomoc 1949: 111; Chimalpahin 1889: 122). Moquihuix was given in marriage a sister of Axayacatl, successor of Moteuczoma as king of Tenochtitlan (Tezozomoc 1949: 114; *Historia de los mexicanos* 1941: 237). This Tenochca princess brought to the marriage lands in the ward of Aztacalco in Mexico (Torquemada 1969[1]: 162–63). According to other reports, Moquihuix's wife was not a sister but a daughter of Axayacatl (Códice Chimalpopoca 1945: 55; cf. Durán 1967[2]: 256, 258). Perhaps they were both his wives. Moquihuix also took in marriage a daughter of King Nezahualcoyotl of Tetzcoco, and their daughter—a wife of Ahuitzotl—became the mother of Cuauhtemoc (Ixtlilxóchitl 1977: 177).

In other reported cases of Tenochca royal women married to kings or princes of towns subject to Tenochtitlan, the marriages formed alliances between Tenochtitlan and Cuauhtitlan (Códice Chimalpopoca 1945: 61), Cuitlahuac (Códice Chimalpopoca 1945: 62; Tezozomoc 1949: 153), Colhuacan, Tiliuhcan Tlacopan (Tezozomoc 1949: 154), and Chalco (Tezozomoc 1949: 153). In the latter case, after a successful campaign by Moteuczoma Xocoyotzin against Chalco, he gave one of his daughters as a wife to Necuametzin, *teohuateuctli* and king of Opochhuacan; "two wards of Otomi accompanied the princess to serve her in Tlalmanalco" ("ome tlaxillacaltin yn Otomi quinhualhuicac cihuapilli, ynin nican Tlalmanalco quitlaecoltico"; Chimalpahin 1889: 181).

In some cases a royal Tenochca woman was given in marriage to the first ruler of a new kingdom. Thus a daughter of Itzcoatl married a commoner of Atotonilco, who became the ruler because of this marriage; a new kingdom (*tlahtocayotl*) was begun (Chimalpahin 1889: 108). A daughter of Moteuczoma Ilhuicamina went to Tepexicmixtlan as the wife of a local noble (*pilli*); they also started a new kingdom (Tezozomoc 1949: 112).

Since the sequence of rulers and their marriages in all these subject kingdoms are not known in detail, we do not know whether a consistent hypogamous pattern developed, as in the marriage alliances between Tetzcoco and Teotihuacan, or between Tenochtitlan and Tetzcoco. There is one case, however, in which this is clearly seen. In Xaltocan, King Coatzinteuctli married a daughter of King Itzcoatl of Tenochtitlan, and the following three kings, until conquest times, also married Tenochca women, although the precise position of two of them within the Tenochca lineage is not known (Nazareo 1940: 125).

Outside the three capitals of the Triple Alliance, there are other examples of hypogamous interdynastic marriages. A clear pattern appears in the dynasty of Tochimilco, whose rulers repeatedly took

wives from Acapetlahuacan (*Historia de los mexicanos* 1941: 239–40).
The usage of giving a woman of high rank from the ruling group
to a dependent ruler is also seen in the *Historia tolteca-chichimeca.*
The two rulers of Cholula, Icxicoatl and Quetzaltehueyac, gave
women in marriage to the leaders of the Chichimeca whom they
installed as rulers in Cuauhtinchan (*Historia tolteca-chichimeca* 1976,
pars. 278, 303).

Thus hypogamy has been identified as part of the relationship
between superordinate and subordinate rulers. If these hypogamous
marriages were to continue through several generations, a pattern
would develop in which two dynasties, one the political dependent
of the other, would be related by hypogamy and matrilateral cross-
cousin marriage, with a substantial dowry in land being brought
by the bride. The concrete case material from Teotihuacan, Tetzcoco,
and Tenochtitlan provides a very close approximation to this model.
The rulers of Teotihuacan marry princesses from Tetzcoco and the
rulers of Tetzcoco marry princesses from Tenochtitlan. The offspring
of these unions succeed to the throne. We have a downward (hypogamous) movement of brides from the highest-ranking dynasty
of Tenochtitlan to that of Tetzcoco and from that of Tetzcoco to
that of Teotihuacan. The rulers of Teotihuacan and Tetzcoco marry
wives who are the agnates of their mothers, i.e., we are dealing
with "matrilateral cross-cousin marriages."

Although data are lacking, one is tempted to think that lesser
rulers, such as the kings of Teotihuacan, may have followed a similar
practice, giving their daughters in marriage to their own dependents, such as lords (*teteuctin*) and ward heads.

INTERDYNASTIC HYPERGAMY

If the previous marriage type is characterized by hypogamy, we
also find its logical opposite, hypergamy, in which a ruler takes a
woman of lower rank. As a general example of this practice, there
is the tradition that the founder of the Tenochca dynasty, Acamapichtli, took wives from all the leading families, and from them
descended the nobility of the country.[8]

A hypergamous marriage may produce a son as the starting point
of a new dynasty. Thus, according to one version, Acamapichtli,

the founder of the Tenochca dynasty, was himself the offspring of a Colhua prince and a Tenochca woman (Davies 1973: 59–61), and, as will be pointed out below, a number of Tenochca princes were installed as rulers of subject towns and married to local women. Members of new dynastic lines thus established may enter into all the various types of marriage alliances.

The kings of Tenochtitlan took wives from the dynasties of Tetzcoco and Tlacopan. Moteuczoma Xocoyotzin had as one of his wives a daughter of King Totoquihuatzin of Tlacopan, named Tayhualcan.[9] Of Nezahualcoyotl it is said that he gave some of his daughters, together with lands as dowry, to the kings of Tenochtitlan and Tlacopan (Ixtlilxóchitl 1977: 123). Another Tetzcocan princess, daughter of Nezahualpilli, married two Tenochca royal princes who were strong candidates for the rulership, first Macuilmalinaltzin and then Atlixcatzin (Ixtlilxóchitl 1975: 450, 1977: 177). The important thing about these cases is that in no instance did the son of a Tenochca ruler and a Tetzcocan princess succeed in Tenochtitlan, whereas in Tetzcoco the opposite obtained: it was a son of a Tenochca princess who was preferred to succeed. This clearly defines the higher rank of the Tenochca dynasty.

It appears that the sons of hypergamous unions did not normally succeed to office, because the offspring of a mother of higher rank were preferred. We may assume that they became part of the lesser nobility; probably this is the reason why information about these marriages and their offspring is not abundant.

Even if such hypergamous marriages were repeated in succeeding generations, because the succeeding kings taking women from the subordinate dynasty were sons of women from the superordinate dynasty, no type of marriage among consanguineals developed that would be relevant in determining succession. Hypergamous marriages become associated with consanguineal marriage types and succession practices only when they take place within the same dynasty in marriages among agnates.

INTERDYNASTIC ISOGAMY

Long-term relationships between dynasties of equal rank are difficult to document. Political relations among the major dynasties in Chalco or among those of other petty states, each with several kings, may have been considered as among equals, and the same situation may have prevailed among some of the city-states before the formation of the Triple Alliance. The three powers of the alliance were considered ideally as equals, at least in some respects, but this is not borne out by the types of marriage alliances formed.

Theoretically intermarriage between two dynasties of equal rank, with succession going to the offspring of interdynastic marriages, would give rise to a pattern of bilateral cross-cousin marriage. No such situation can be documented. Political relations that may have begun as among equals seem to turn into patterns of domination that become manifest in the forms of marriage and succession. When this does not happen what results is an unstable balance among various independent powers, with diverse interdynastic marriages that do not lead to regular patterns of marriage among consanguineals connected with succession.

INTRADYNASTIC ISOGAMY

Another major type of union is that of intradynastic marriages in which both parties are descendants of a ruler of the dynasty. Given the fact that only males occupied offices, marriages within the dynasty turn out to be marriages among agnates.

In intradynastic marriages the rank of the contracting parties appears to be roughly equal. Differences in rank between husband and wife are difficult to define because of the close agnatic relationship. Also, the practice of succession in which the rulership is attained by going through a series of previous ranks and offices makes a man's status somewhat variable throughout his life. One would have to know what stage in his career a man had achieved when the marriage was contracted, and this information is usually not available. Thus these marriages seem basically isogamous when the man has not yet achieved high office. They are clearly hypergamous when an already established ruler marries the daughter of a subordinate.

Well-defined patterns of succession and marriage among agnates appear in the Tenochca dynasty at the time of its political predominance. The number of such marriages is high; I have recorded about twenty of them. Although there are not enough data available in all cases about the political circumstances of these marriages, we may assume that they were contracted to strengthen the solidarity of the dynasty and in the expectation that the husband or the offspring of such a marriage would be in an improved position to aim at an office or a kingship. As an old source puts it apropos of the succession of Moteuczoma Ilhuicamina, "relatives married each other so that the rulership would not go elsewhere" ("casábanse los parientes unos con otros porque no saliese el señorío de entre ellos"; *Relación de la genealogía* 1941: 254; cf. *Origen de los mexicanos* 1941: 274).

Let us examine the marriages connected with succession to the position of the great king of Tenochtitlan. The pattern of intra-dynastic agnatic marriages and collateral succession does not appear with the first kings of the dynasty; instead, the recorded marriages are of the interdynastic type. However, all the information concerning the entire succession line will be considered in order to examine the change from one type to another. Provided in table 3.3 is the genealogy from Acamapichtli, the founder of the dynasty, to the last independent ruler, Cuauhtemoc, who was defeated by the Spaniards.

The ancestry of Acamapichtli is confusing. There are several different traditions that cannot be reconciled (Davies 1973: 55–64), and it is possible that various sources, rather than reporting known facts, attribute to the starting point of the dynasty one or another of the marriage types prevalent in later years. One might also suspect that the uncertainty of Acamapichtli's origin helped to mark clearly the beginning of a new dynastic line and to make it difficult for any other dynasty to claim a well-established right to the rulership. Most reports assigned to Acamapichtli a combination of Mexica and Colhua ancestry, as befits the fact that the Tenochca king held the title of *colhuateuctli,* as ruler of the Colhua domain.

The identity of Acamapichtli's principal wife, usually called Ilancueitl, is also obscure. Significantly it is said that various leaders of the city (or of the region) gave Acamapichtli their daughters and from them descended the later Tenochca nobility (*Códice Ramírez* 1975: 36; Durán 1967[2]: 56; *Origen de los mexicanos* 1941: 270; *Relación de la genealogía* 1941: 250, 251). Many close descendants of Acamapichtli were later known as "old noblemen" (*huehuepipiltin*),

Table 3.3. Kings of Tenochtitlan

1. ACAMAPICHTLI

2. HUITZILIHUITL   TLATOLZACATZIN   4. ITZCOATL

3. CHIMALPOPOCA   CAHUALTZIN   TLACAELEL   5. MOTEUCZOMA ILHUICAMINA

XIHUITLEMOC   IQUEHUAC   Atotoztli = TEZOZOMOC   HUEHUE CUITLAHUAC

7. TIZOC o = 8. AHUITZOTL = o   6. AXAYACATL = o

Teccalco cihuapilli = 9. MOTEUCZOMA XOCOYOTZIN   10. CUITLAHUAC

11. CUAUHTEMOC   ATLIXCATZIN = Tecuichpotzin   AXAYACATL

although their exact parentage was not known (Tezozomoc 1949: 86–87).

The first three kings of Tenochtitlan ruled during the period of Tepaneca supremacy. Acamapichtli was succeeded by his son Huitzilihuitl, born according to one tradition of Ilancueitl (Ixtlilxóchitl 1975: 409), and according to another of the daughter of a Tenochca leader (Cuauhtloquezqui, in Durán 1967[2]: 56; Acacitli, in Chimalpahin 1889: 74). Another son of Acamapichtli, born of a woman of low estate, was Itzcoatl, who was to become the fourth king.

Huitzilihuitl married a princess of Tiliuhcan Tlacopan (Tezozomoc 1949: 89; in a slightly different version, a Tlacopan princess, Ixtlilxóchitl 1975: 409), of whom was born his son and successor, Chimalpopoca. In another tradition Huitzilihuitl is said to have married a daughter of Tezozomoc of Azcapotzalco, Ayauhcihuatl, and she was the mother of Chimalpopoca (Durán 1967[2]: 64; Códice Ramírez 1975: 40; Tezozomoc 1975: 237, 239). In both traditions Chimalpopoca's mother is a Tepaneca princess. Another wife of Huitzilihuitl was a daughter of the king of Cuauhnahuac, and legend tells us that he caused her to become pregnant from a jade placed in a cane, which he shot at her with a bow. Thus was born Moteuczoma Ilhuicamina, the fifth king of Tenochtitlan (Tezozomoc 1949: 90–95; *Historia de los mexicanos* 1941: 229; Nazareo 1940: 122). The story is similar to the myth of the birth of Huitzilopochtli.[10]

Chimalpopoca, the third king, married a daughter of Cuacuauhpitzahuac (Ixtlilxóchitl 1975: 409, 1977: 37–38), king of Tlatelolco, who according to most sources was the son of Tezozomoc of Azcapotzalco (Tezozomoc 1949: 98; *Unos annales* 1939: 121; Nazareo 1940: 123; Chimalpahin 1889: 72), although according to Ixtlilxóchitl (1975: 322, 1977: 25), he was the son of Epcoatl (or Mixcoatl), previous king of Tlatelolco, who was Tezozomoc's brother. Perhaps Chimalpopoca also married a daughter of the king of Azcapotzalco, since the relation between Tezozomoc and Chimalpopoca is described as that of father-in-law and son-in-law (Tezozomoc 1975: 237, 239). The Spanish text, however, might be a faulty translation of the Nahuatl terms *moncolli* ("grandfather-in-law") and *ixhuiuhmontli* ("grandchild-in-law").

Chimalpopoca was killed in the conflict with the Tepaneca, following which Tenochtitlan became the supreme power, allied to Tetzcoco and Tlacopan. A son of Chimalpopoca, Xihuitltemoc, is said to have reigned for sixty days (Tezozomoc 1949: 104), but is usually not included in the list of kings.

It is said that when the Triple Alliance was formed under the leadership of Itzcoatl, the fourth king and a son of Acamapichtli, the Mexica then decided that the descendants of Chimalpopoca would not rule but would be commoners (Nazareo 1940: 118; Códice Chimalpopoca 1945: 66). In this way was abandoned the descent line of kings who had made alliances with Tepaneca princesses according to a pattern of interdynastic hypogamy.

On his mother's side Itzcoatl was not of royal ancestry, but was the son of a slave woman (Durán 1967[2]: 56); or, according to another version, an illegitimate son (*ichtacaconetzintli*) born of a greens seller (*quilnamacac*) from Azcapotzalco Cuauhcaltitlan (Chimalpahin 1889: 106). Itzcoatl had achieved the rank of *tlacatecatl*, but since Chimalpopoca's son is mentioned as king, it does not seem that Itzcoatl would have attained the kingship were it not for the power shift that broke the Tenochca subjection to Azcapotzalco. Under these conditions his maternal ancestry was not decisive.

With Itzcoatl a new succession pattern is clearly established (unless sources describing Huitzilihuitl and Chimalpopoca as brothers are preferred). From this time on no king is succeeded by his son but always by a collateral relative, agnatically considered; in one case (Moteuczoma to Axayacatl) he is also a daughter's son. Itzcoatl and Moteuczoma, leaders of the war against the Tepaneca, had already married and begotten sons under the previous regime, but after the fifth king, Moteuczoma, the preferred wife is always an agnate and the successor is the son of a Tenochca woman. Itzcoatl (like Huitzilihuitl) had married a princess from Tiliuhcan Tlacopan, named Huitzilxochitzin, who became the mother of Tezozomoc.[11]

Itzcoatl was succeeded by Moteuczoma Ilhuicamina, his brother's son, who had been *tlacatecatl* and whose wife was the Chichimecacihuatzin, daughter of the king of Cuauhnahuac, whence Moteuczoma's mother had also come (Nazareo 1940: 122).[12]

In the next generation, Itzcoatl's son Tezozomoc is described as a king's son (*tlatocapilli*) and a great lord (*huey teuctli*); he never ruled, but fathered three sons, who were the next three kings. The

wife of Tezozomoc was Atotoztli, daughter of Moteuczoma Ilhuicamina and, according to some reports (as mentioned above), her
father's successor (Tezozomoc 1949: 114; *Relación de la genealogía*
1941: 253–54; *Origen de los mexicanos* 1941: 274). Had Tezozomoc
ruled, Moteuczoma would then have been succeeded by his father's
brother's son (who became also his daughter's husband), and the
new king would have been marrying his predecessor's daughter.
This is a pattern that is found later in the succession of Moteuczoma
Xocoyotzin by Atlixcatzin and Cuauhtemoc. Thus we may think
that Tezozomoc was probably a presumptive successor, although we
do not know why he did not reign.

The marriage of Tezozomoc and Atotoztli represents the union
of the descendants of the two kings Itzcoatl and Moteuczoma Ilhuicamina, and it is a son of this marriage, Axayacatl, who became
the next, sixth king. Another candidate had been the *cihuacoatl*
Tlacaelel, who had been and continued to be a most influential
personage during the reigns of Tezozomoc's sons. Axayacatl was the
youngest of the three brothers, and was young when selected. Tlacaelel's special position in history and his power, greater than that
of succeeding cihuacoatls, can be understood by the fact that he
was probably the coadjutor of Axayacatl, a position reported to exist
in some Mesoamerican societies to assist a king too young to rule
alone.

Of the various wives of Axayacatl, the mother of sons who later
became kings was a daughter of his father's brother Huehue Cuitlahuac (Tezozomoc 1949: 137–38; Chimalpahin 1889: 147).

During the reign of Axayacatl, Moteuczoma Ilhuicamina's son
Iquehuac held the title of *tlacatecatl* (Tezozomoc 1949: 111; Chimalpahin 1889: 129), and he was probably a candidate to the
succession. It is said of him that "he was killed, he would have
been king" ("quimictique yqueuacatzi ye tlatoani yezquia tenoch-
titla" [*Unos annales* 1939: pars. 138, 275]). Had he reigned after
Axayacatl, the kingship would have gone to the male line of Moteuczoma Ilhuicamina.

Axayacatl was succeeded by his elder brother Tizoc. Tizoc's wives
are not known; his sons achieved high positions but did not rule.
Only his son's son, don Diego de San Francisco Tehuetzquititzin,
later became *tlatoani* (*gobernador*) under Spanish rule.

Tizoc was succeeded by his younger brother Ahuitzotl, who married a daughter of Cahualtzin, grandson of Acamapichtli (Tezozomoc 1949: 105). She was consequently his father's father's brother's son's daughter, and must have been his principal wife, since she was the mother of the Teccalco *cihuapilli* who married the next king, Moteuczoma Xocoyotzin, and of Atlixcatzin, who at the time of the conquest was Moteuczoma's *tlacatecatl* and his presumptive successor (Tezozomoc 1949: 144, 164). Thus Moteuczoma Xocoyotzin, the ninth king, succeeded his father's brother, whose daughter he married.

Another wife of Ahuitzotl was the daughter of Moquihuix, the last king of Tlatelolco, defeated by Axayacatl. She was not a close agnate, and her son Cuauhtemoc probably would not have ruled but for the turmoil caused by the war against the Spanish.

When the Spanish arrived, Ahuitzotl's son Atlixcatzin was *tlacatecatl* and had married Tecuichpotzin, the daughter of Moteuczoma and the Teccalco *cihuapilli* (AGI: Patronato 181, r.8, f.15). She was thus his father's brother's son's daughter, as well as his sister's daughter.[13] Atlixcatzin was probably the strongest contender for succession, but he perished early during the struggle against the Spanish, and Moteuczoma was succeeded by his brother Cuitlahuac, who is said to have taken as wife Moteuczoma's daughter Tecuichpotzin (Gómara 1954[2]: 381–82). Ciutlahuac ruled for only eighty days. Earlier he had been king of Itztapalapan (see below) and had married a Tetzcoco princess (Tezozomoc 1949: 160).

After Cuitlahuac the next ruler was Cuauhtemoc, son of Ahuitzotl. Cuauhtemoc also took as his wife Moteuczoma's daughter Tecuichpotzin (*Origen de los mexicanos* 1941: 277; Gómara 1954[2]:381–82). Thus this lady, later known as doña Isabel de Montezuma, was the wife first of the presumptive successor of her father and then of the two following kings, Cuitlahuac and Cuauhtemoc. This may be simply an example of the practice that, because of her high rank, a royal widow could marry only another king (Pomar 1941: 25). But it also seems that her high status as the descendant of Moteuczoma and Ahuitzotl gave her the right to be the main wife of her father's successors. According to the *Origen de los mexicanos* (1941: 277), Cuauhtemoc married Moteuczoma's daughter Tecuichpotzin so that he could be the legitimate king in the same way that Itzcoatl had married Moteuczoma Ilhuicamina's daughter.[14]

After the execution of Cuauhtemoc in Honduras, Cortés appointed as *tlatoani,* or *gobernador,* of Tenochtitlan the *cihuacoatl* Juan Velásquez Tlacotzin, a grandson of Tlacaelel, who died before the return to Mexico. The next two governors after him were not noblemen and in Nahuatl received only the title *cuauhtlatoani* (military ruler) (Tezozomoc 1949: 166–68; Chimalpahin 1889: 207, 209, 266–67).

The dynastic succession was restored with don Diego Huanitzin, a grandson of Axayacatl who had been king of Ecatepec (see tables 3.4 and 3.5). Huanitzin married a daughter of Moteuczoma (Tezozomoc 1949: 157–58). The next gobernador was don Diego de San Francisco Tehuetzquititzin, Tizoc's grandson, who had married his father's brother's daughter (Tezozomoc 1949: 142).

After a short period with a *juez de residencia,* the post of gobernador went back to the line of Axayacatl in a son of Huanitzin, don Cristobal de Guzmán Cecetzin (Tezozomoc 1949: 170; Chimalpahin 1889: 267). His marriage is not recorded. After him the governorship went back to the line of Ahuitzotl; his grandson, don Luis de Santa María Nanacacipactzin, the son of Acamapich, was the last gobernador of the dynasty (Tezozomoc 1949: 174; Chimalpahin 1889: 264, 268). He married doña Magdalena Chichimecacihuatl, described as "daughter of the late don Diego" (Garibay 1945: 233), which I assume means she was the daughter of the don Diego Tehuetzquititzin mentioned in the same document, or perhaps of don Diego Huanitzin.

The connection of agnatic marriage and collateral succession is functionally related to the dominant position of the Tenochca dynasty. In the hypogamous chain relating the rulers of Mexico, Tetzcoco, and Teotihuacan we find no outside source of wives for the highest-ranking Tenochca kings. The principal wives of the Tenochca rulers, and consequently the mothers of their successors, were women of their own dynasty and very close agnates, in some cases daughters of former kings. In this way collateral succession does not result in a separate descent line; the descent lines of past kings are brought together by these agnatic marriages. Thus after the marriage of Tezozomoc, son of Itzcoatl, and Atotoztli, daughter of Moteuczoma (that is, the children of the first two kings who ruled after Tenochtitlan became the dominant power in the basin),

Table 3.4. Tenochtitlan Governors of Royal Rank Under Spanish Rule

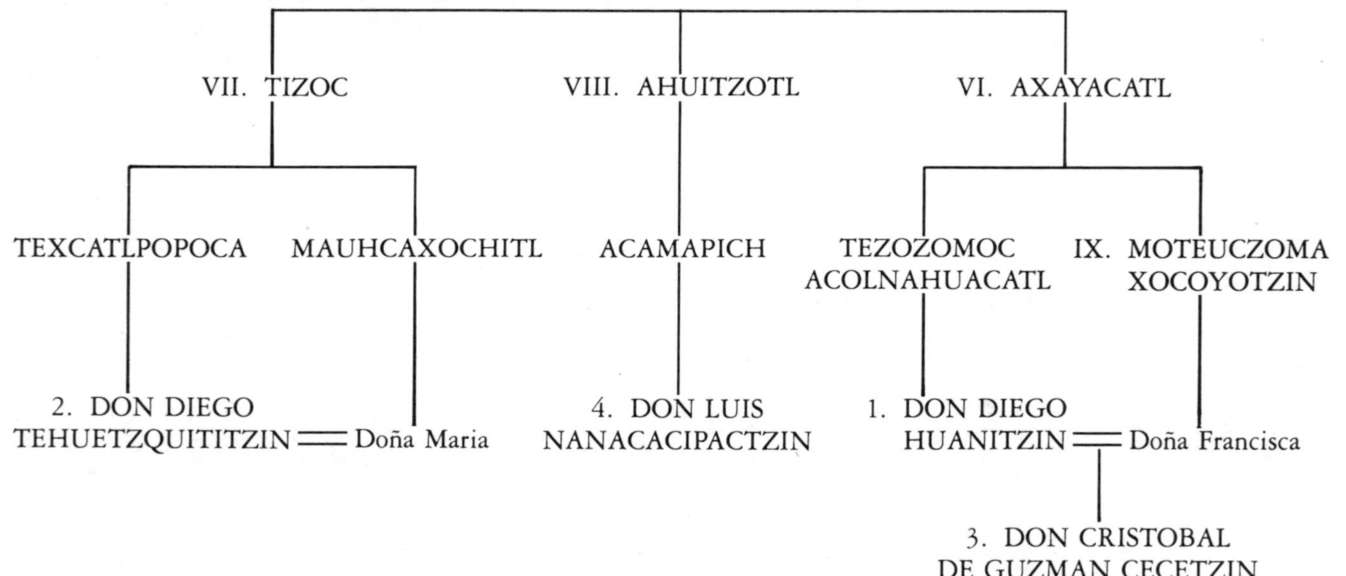

Only governors of royal rank are included—their sequence is indicated by Arabic numbers; the sequence of pre-Spanish kings is indicated by Roman numerals

Table 3.5. Kings of Ecatepec and their Alliances with Tenochtitlan

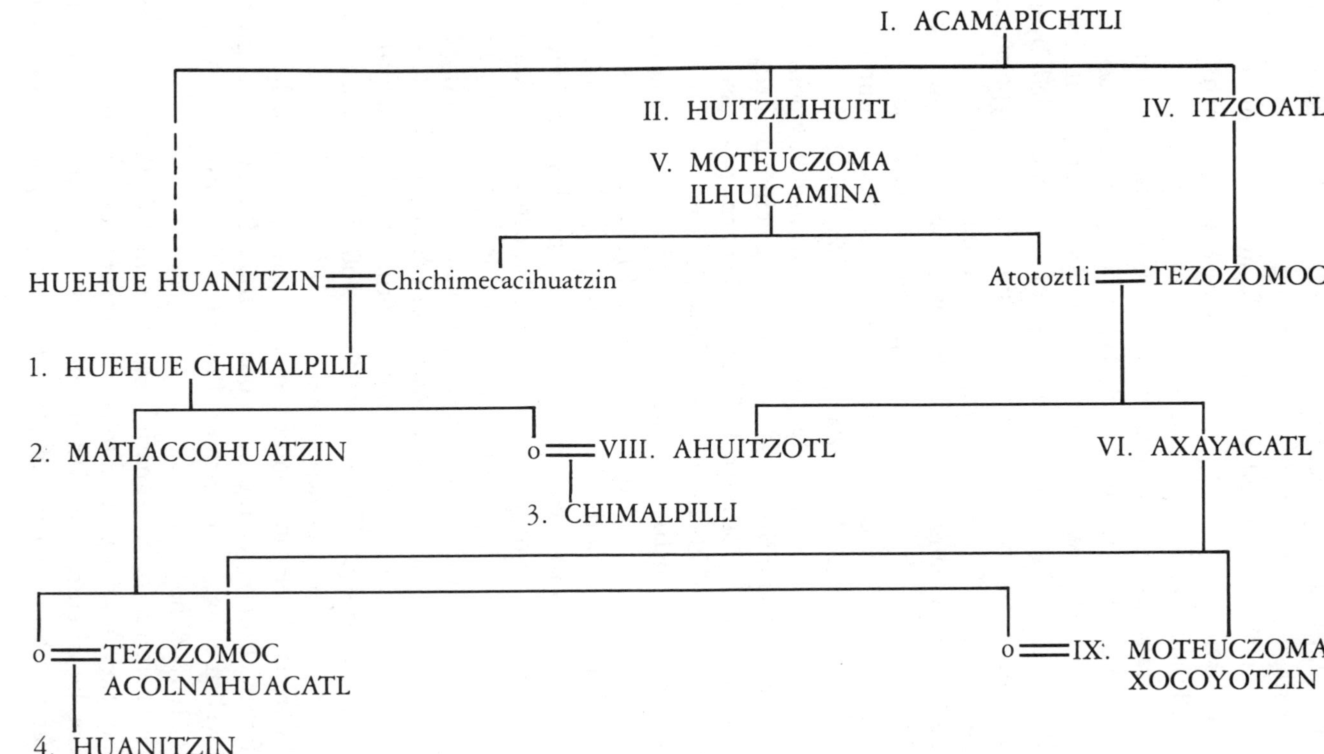

every king is succeeded by a collateral and the prevailing type of marriage is one between close agnates that unites the divergent descent lines of actual or potential participants in the succession line. This is especially true of marriages in which a ruler or a candidate marries the daughter of a previous king.

Intradynastic marriages are found in exceptional instances in other dynasties where the norm is lineal father-to-son succession and marriage to a princess of another dynasty. As an example, in Teotihuacan the second king, Quetzalmamalitzin, was succeeded by his son, Cotzatzin. Following the pattern of interdynastic hypogamy, he was the son of a Tetzcoco princess, a daughter of Nezahualcoyotl, and he married a daughter of Nezahualpilli, who was thus his mother's brother's daughter. Cotzatzin apparently had no sons born of this marriage. His successor was his own brother, Xiuhtototzin, who married Cotzatzin's two daughters, and it is said that "the kingship went to him because of the princesses, his nieces, whom he married" ("ytech ompouh in tlatocayotl ipampa in cihuapipiltin ymachhuan quimocihuati"; Carrasco 1974: 238). Had the princesses been males, clearly one of them would have been the rightful successor; as women, they married the nearest male claimant, their father's brother (see table 3.2; cf. Carrasco 1974: 238).

In Tetzcoco, after the death of the eighth king, Nezahualpilli, several of his sons reigned in sequence, by this time under Spanish rule, when the higher status of the Tenochca kings was no longer operative. One of them, don Hernando Ixtlilxóchitl, married Papantzin (baptized as doña Beatriz and the widow of King Cuitlahuac of Tenochtitlan), who was his father's brother's daughter (i.e., the daughter of Cuauhtlahuanitzin, brother of Nezahualpilli; Ixtlilxóchitl 1975: 492; Tezozomoc 1949: 160–61). Another case is documented in which the children of two of the brothers married: don Pedro de Alvarado, son of the tenth king, Coanacoch, married his father's brother's daughter, doña Antonia Pimentel, daughter of the twelfth king, don Antonio Pimentel Tlahuitoltzin (AGI: Mexico 121, r. 2, no. 37).

There are other agnatic marriages in the Tetzcoco ruling line, but they are not related to collateral succession in Tetzcoco and will not be discussed here in detail. However, they do show that we cannot think of rules of patrilineal exogamy as an explanation of the prevailing lineal succession (see the marriages of Quinatzin and Cuauhcihuatzin, Ixtlilxóchitl 1975: 312, and of Tlacateotzin to Tezcocatihuatzin [*sic*], Ixtlilxóchitl 1975: 305, 310).

Postconquest Tlaxcala also offers an instance of agnatic marriage among the descendants of Xicotencatl, ruler of Tizatlan at the time of the conquest, similar to what we have just seen for the grandchildren of Nezahualpilli in Tetzcoco. Leonardo Xicotencatl married his father's brother's son's daughter, Francisca de la Cerda (Gibson 1952: 100–101).

The data from Chalco are numerous and important. The situation there offers distinctive features in that there were within the same political unit a number of different dynasties connected with different *teuctli* titles whose holders were kings (*tlatoani*) of the various towns of Chalco, and their political relations do not show the clear pattern of super and subordination found in the core area of the Triple Alliance as discussed above. In addition, the Mexica conquest forced some significant changes in the political organization. A number of agnatic marriages are documented in Chalco, and rights to the rulership could be transmitted through women (cf. Rammow 1964: 111–12). I will single out here marriages among agnates connected with succession along lines similar to the examples already discussed.

There is one example in the line of the *tlailotlacteuctli* who were kings (*tlatoani*) of Tzacualtitlan Tenanco. The fourth tlailotlacteuctli, Itztlotzin, had two sons. Of one of them, Chimalpaintzin, it is said that "he would have ruled but he withdrew" ("tlahtocatizquia, . . . zan mocauh"; Chimalpahin 1889: 93). His younger brother, Cuauhtlehuanitzin, became the fifth tlailotlacteuctli, and his son Xiuhtzin married Chimalpaintzin's daughter, i.e., his father's brother's daughter, named Iztacxochitzin. Although Xiuhtzin held the title of tlailotlacteuctli, he did not become tlatoani because of the Mexica conquest (Chimalpahin 1889: 130, 160, 188, 295).

Other examples are found in the line of the *chichimecateuctli,* a title held in Chalco by the chiefs of the Chichimeca Totolimpaneca who were kings of Itztlacozauhcan. The first chichimecateuctli, Atonaltzin, married his father's brother's daughter; his marriage thus united the children of the two sons of the first leader of the Totolimpaneca. Later, the fifth chichimecateuctli, Huehue Quetzalmazatzin, married Tlacocihuatzin, daughter of the second *teo-huateuctli* of Tlailotlacan and sister of the third, a title held by another Totolimpaneca line. Their son was the next teohuateuctli, while the title of chichimecateuctli went to the son of the third teohuateuctli (Chimalpahin 1965: 132, 1889: 215–16).

In all these cases, intradynastic agnatic marriages bring together two individuals with rights of succession to a title or to its transmission. The difference in rank between the marrying parties is not great. When a king's daughter marries a candidate to the succession the marriage could be described as hypogamous, but when, after succeeding, a king marries the daughter of a previous ruler or other agnate, it should rather be seen as hypergamous. Not enough details are known about the circumstances at the time of each of these marriages, but the point seems to be to unite the two highest ranking claims to succession, and thus the unions are basically isogamous.

INTRADYNASTIC HYPERGAMY

A different pattern appears when the intradynastic marriage is connected with succession to a subordinate office. In this type the superordinate ruler marries the daughter of the ruler of a subject town who is himself also a member of the dynasty, previously installed as local ruler. The marriage in this case can be clearly considered hypergamous. A son of this marriage will then be installed as the next ruler in the subject town. Hypergamous agnatic marriage is therefore connected with collateral succession in the subject town by a son of the superordinate ruler and a local princess.

Thus Cuitlachtzin, one of the "old noblemen" (*huehuepipiltin*), descendants of the first Tenochca king, Acamapichtli, was made king of Tollan, where he married a local woman. One of their descendants, Mizquixahualtzin, became a wife of the sixth Tenochca king, Axayacatl, and their son Ixtlilcuechahuac was made king of Tollan "because his mother was from there" ("ipampa in inantzin ompa ichan"; Tezozomoc 1949: 152). A daughter of Ixtlilcuechahuac married her father's half-brother Moteuczoma Xocoyotzin and held considerable lands in Tollan; their son was Tlacahuepantzin, later also known as don Pedro Tlacahuepantzin, or don Pedro de Montezuma (Tezozomoc 1949: 152). The Spanish made him lord (*señor*) of Tollan at the request of the local authorities (*principales*), because Tollan "belongs to him from his mother's side, who stems from there, and is the daughter of the late lord."[15]

Another example comes from the kingdom of Itztapalapan. One son of the fourth Tenochca king, Itzcoatl, called Huehue Cuitlahuac, became king of Itztapalapan. His daughter married Axayacatl (her father's brother's son), and their son Cuitlahuac became king of Itztapalapan. During the conquest he succeeded his brother Moteuczoma as king of Tenochtitlan (see tables 3.3 and 3.7).

One more example is found in Ecatepec (table 3.5). A daughter of Moteuczoma Ilhuicamina, Chichimecacihuatzin, married Huehue Huanitzin, a "great leader" (*huey tiacauh*) of Itztapalapan, and their son Chimalpilli became the first king of Ecatepec (Tezozomoc 1949: 88, 111–12). He was succeeded by his son Matlaccohuatzin, who in turn was succeeded by a son (also called Chimalpilli) of the eighth Tenochca king, Ahuitzotl. Of this Chimalpilli it is said that "because of his mother he was installed there as king by his father, Ahuitzotzin" ("ypampa ynantzin in ynic ompa contlahtocallica ythatzin Ahuitzotzin"; Chimalpahin 1889: 191). Since it was common usage to name a man after his father's father or mother's father (*Origen de los mexicanos* 1941: 276), we may assume that Chimalpilli's mother was the daughter of Chimalpilli the elder and the sister of Matlaccohuatzin. Matlaccohuatzin had two daughters, one of whom married Moteuczoma Xocoyotzin and the other Moteuczoma's brother Tezozomoc. A son of the latter marriage, Huanitzin, was installed by Moteuczoma as king of Ecatepec when Chimalpilli died as a young man. Again it is given as a reason for his ruling at Ecatepec that it was "because his mother was a princess there" ("ipampa yn inantzin ompa cihuapilli"; Chimalpahin 1889: 237).

It is reported that a number of Tenochca royal princes were installed as kings in other dependent cities. Thus sons of Itzcoatl were estabished as kings of Xilotepec, Apan, and Tiliuhcan (Chimalpahin 1889: 108; Tezozomoc 1949: 110), a son of Axayacatl became king of Xochimilco (Tezozomoc 1949: 137), Moteuczoma Xocoyotzin installed a son as king of Tenayocan (Tezozomoc 1975: 697), and a son of Diego Huanitzin became king of Azcapotzalco Mexicapan (Tezozomoc 1949: 164–65).

Sons of royal princes were also introduced as kings of dependent cities. Thus a son of Huehue Tlacahuepan ruled in Tenayocan (Tezozomoc 1949: 134), although he is also described as a son of Axayacatl (Tezozomoc 1949: 138). A son of Huehue Zacatl became king of Huitzilopochco (Tezozomoc 1949: 133). For all these cases there is no information as to whether marriages were made according to the pattern described for Tollan, Ecatepec, and Itztapalapan, but such a system is to be expected.

Another, better documented case is the installation of Miccacalcatl Tlaltetecuitzin as king of Tecuanipan Huixtoco in Chalco. He was the son of the *cihuacoatl* Tlilpotoncatzin and grandson of the famous cihuacoatl Tlacaelel. His mother was Xiuhtoztzin, daughter of Yaopaintzin, military ruler (*cuauhtlato*) of Tecuanipan Huixtoco at the time of the Tenochca conquest. Miccacalcatl was installed as king by Ahuitzotl "because of his mother" ("ipampa ynantzin"; Chimalpahin 1889: 9, 105, 121, 125–26, 150, 165–66, 187–88; Tezozomoc 1949: 146).

The kingships of dependent cities were not the only positions occupied by members of the Tenochca ruling lineage. There are strong indications that the various titles created after the war against Azcapotzalco and the estabishment of Tenochca supremacy were also held by close relatives of the reigning king and were not allowed to be transmitted along separate descent lines. A separate line is known to have developed only in the case of the *cihuacoatl* (table 3.6). The titles of *tlacatecatl, tlacochcalcatl, tlilancalqui,* and *ezhuahuacatl* were steps in the advancement toward the position of *tlatoani,* and thus were not held by separate succession lines (Durán 1967[2]: 99, 125; Monzón 1949: 75).

The data about the transmission of other titles are extremely meager. One suggestive case is that of a certain Achicatzin, *huitznahuatl tlailotlac* and nobleman of Tlatelolco, whose daughter Iyazcuetzin was a wife first of Axayacatl and then of his two successors. Her son by Axayacatl, don Juan Achica, was also huitznahuatl (Nazareo 1940: 121–23; AGI: Patronato 181, r.8, f.52r, 65v).

In all these cases, best exemplified in the ones from Tollan, Ecatepec, and Itztapalapan, the local line of succession in a subject city or office can be traced through a female line, as for instance from a ruler to his daughter's son. Native sources make the point

Table 3.6. Succession of the *Cihuacoatl* of Tenochtitlan

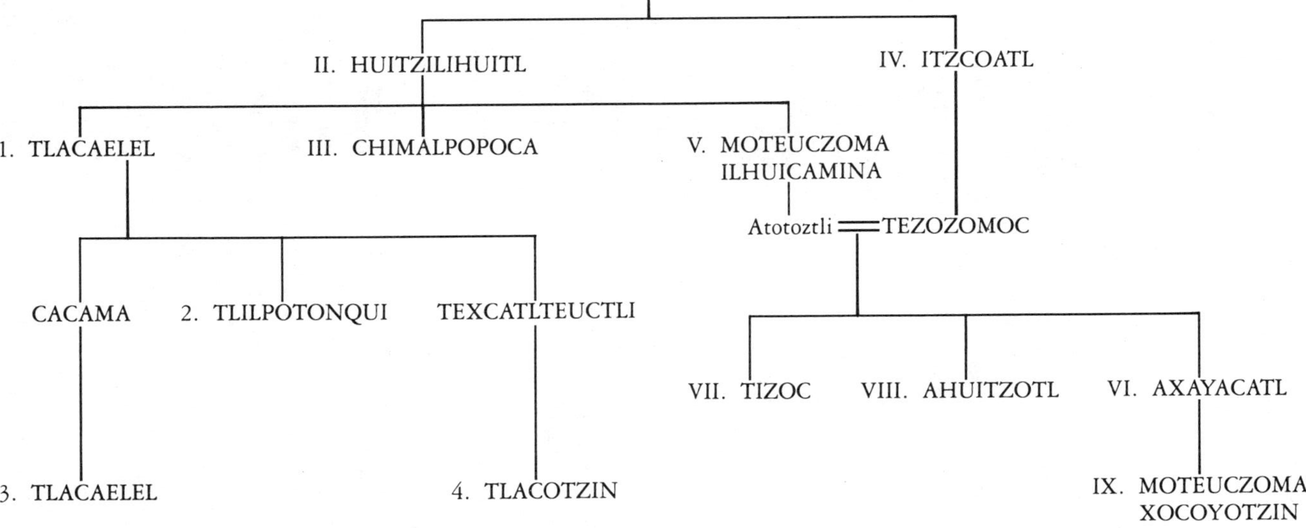

Roman numerals denote the sequence of kings, Arabic numbers that of the *cihuacoatl* (after Tezozomoc 1949)

that a given prince is made king of a town "because of his mother," but the new ruler is also an agnate of his predecessor and of the great king of Tenochtitlan. We thus have a system of collateral succession in which a direct male descendant of the local ruler is discarded in favor of a daughter's son or a more remote collateral who is a close agnate of the king of Tenochtitlan. No separate local descent line is formed to succeed to the local rulership. Instead, the local office is one of several occupied by children of the Tenochca kings, and a single lineage controls all positions.

This seems to have been a procedure by which a ruling dynasty "captures" additional titles and rulerships for the use of its members. From the point of view of the subordinate group it is a way of incorporating members of the superordinate dynasty bound to them by maternal descent. This is how, according to one version, the Tenochca acquired their own first king, of Colhua ancestry, who was the founder of their dynasty and eventually gained supremacy over Colhuacan itself.

In the succession line of a given town it is possible to observe that marriage alliances are established with more than one superordinate dynasty. Thus the material from Itztapalapan shows that while their rulers were close agnates of the Tenochca kings because of intradynastic hypergamy after the establishment of a Tenochca prince as first king, they also married princesses of the Tetzcoco dynasty. These connections are shown in table 3.7.

CONCLUSIONS

We have identified different types of marriage alliances among consanguineals, practiced by the ruling dynasties of ancient Central Mexico. Examples of all these types of marriages can be found throughout the area, but certain configurations appear with particular social concomitants and a definite geographical and historical distribution. A major contrast appears between the agnatic marriages prevailing among the Tenochca and the marriages of the matrilateral cross-cousin type of the kings of the Acolhua, where the kings of Tetzcoco take their wives from the Tenochca and give their own daughters to their subordinates.

Agnatic marriages (including parallel-cousin marriage) develop

Table 3.7. Kings of Itztapalapan and their Alliances with Tenochtitlan and Tetzcoco

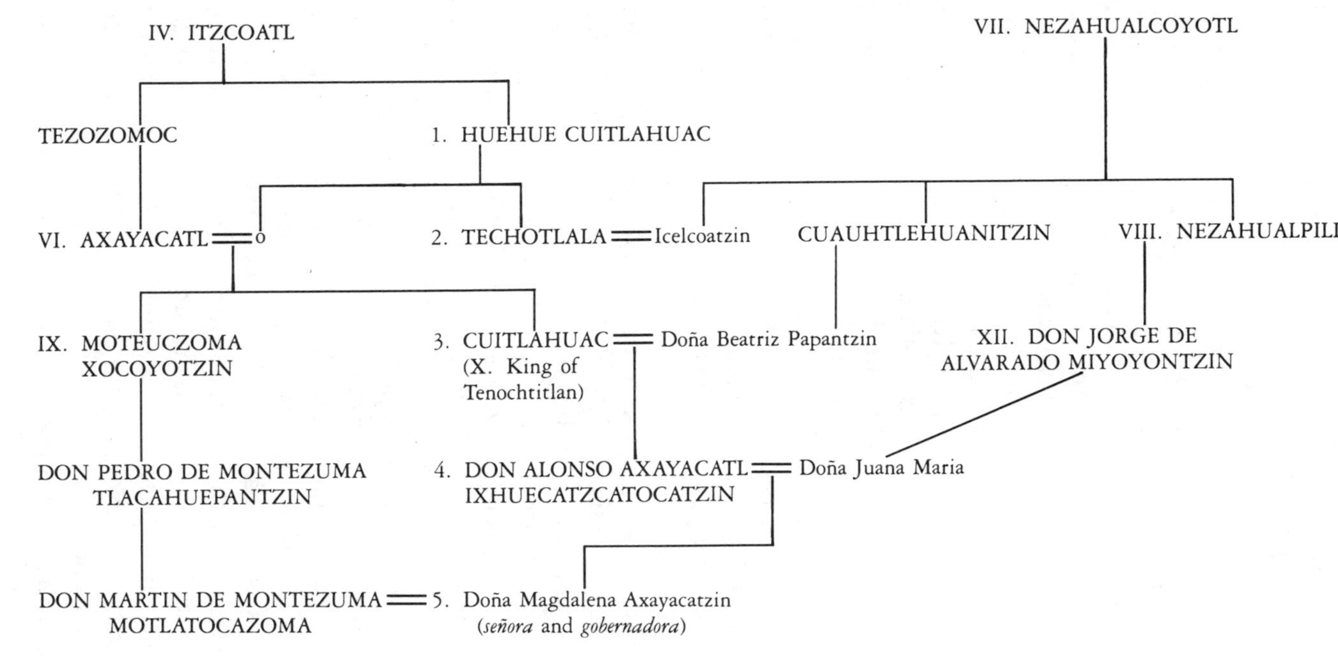

(Tezozomoc 1949: 137–38, 160–61; Ixtlilxóchitl 1975: 492, 1977: 146, 154, 178)

in the presence of collateral succession as a way of binding by marriage the different agnatic lines with a claim to succession. When the offspring of one such marriage succeeds to the rulership, the succession line can also be traced either collaterally or lineally through a female link. Instances of this type of intradynastic agnatic marriage appear in the dynasties of Teotihuacan, Tetzcoco, and Chalco; it became the dominant pattern among the Tenochca after they became the supreme power in the basin. Starting with Itzcoatl, there was no longer father-to-son succession, and from the marriage of Itzcoatl's son with Moteuczoma Ilhuicamina's daughter, whose three sons ruled in sequence, all successive rulers were sons of Tenochca mothers. The kingships of Tenochca subject towns, and other titles, were also transmitted by collateral succession to close agnates of the great king of Tenochtitlan. Thus agnatic marriages and collateral succession appear related to the control of most high offices in the realm by close agnates of the supreme ruler; no separate descent lines were formed, thus preventing the rise of new dynasties that might develop separate and conflicting interests.

From the point of view of kinship, agnatic marriages and collateral succession create and reinforce the bilateral structure of the dynasty as a lineage-like group and prevent the development of permanent fissions. Collateral descent without a strict definition of succession along kinship lines increases the number of suitable candidates for office and reinforces the importance of achievement through a series of grades toward the rulership. This pattern is clearly related to the position of supreme power held by the Tenochca dynasty. Although it is best documented as a recent phenomenon in Mesoamerican history, it is probable that it represents a continuation of Colhua and Toltec practice.

Marriages of the matrilateral cross-cousin type develop as the result of continuous hypogamous marriage alliances between dynasties of unequal rank. They appear related to lineal father-to-son succession, with the new ruler marrying a woman of the superordinate dynasty. In this pattern each dynasty is a clearly distinct agnatic line. Succession is defined by or reinforced through female links only in exceptional cases, and matrilateral relatives are normally to be found in the superordinate dynasty.

The existence of polygyny with marriages of different types creates the conditions for the formation of different political alliances simultaneously and even for the reinterpretation of a given marriage alliance when the power balance shifts. Thus the Tenochca rulers preferred agnates as wives, to bear the sons who would be the best candidates for the rulership and other high offices. Other wives, whether agnates or not, would give birth to sons who could succeed to office in their mother's places of origin. Still other sons, born of women of lower rank, would normally reach lesser offices, but could also rise to the rulership when changing political conditions favored abandoning the selection of the sons of the preferred marriages, as happened with Itzcoatl and Cuauhtemoc.

Because of multiple marriages and a large number of sons, a ruler had on reserve, so to speak, candidates suitable to whatever situation might arise. Had the Tenochca increased their power over Tetzcoco, the offspring of a Tenochtitlan king and a Tetzcoco princess would have been a candidate to the rulership of Tetzcoco, thus introducing a Tenochca prince with local matrilateral connections. Vice versa, had Tetzcoco been able to establish its supremacy over Tenochtitlan, the same prince would have been a suitable candidate to rule in Tenochtitlan as a subordinate of his mother's agnates in Tetzcoco.

On the other hand, while Cacama's succession in Tetzcoco is explained as having been favored because of his Tenochca mother, he would have been the ideal Tetzcocan candidate to establish himself in Tenochtitlan as a Tetzcocan prince with maternal ancestors in Tenochtitlan.

The dynastic succession in Itztapalapan shows how relations could be maintained with both Tenochtitlan and Tetzcoco, according to different marriage types, so that two different alliances could be kept in balance for a time.

It is clear that the different types of marriage we have been discussing cannot be explained in terms of a basic difference in descent-group types or of prescriptive marriage rules defined in terms of kinship categories. These various types of marriage among consanguineals are the consequence of stable, repeated marriage alliances among dynasties, determined by their political relations and succession rules. A given group could change from one type of marriage to another, following shifts in political relations or succession practices.

NOTES

1. Pomar (1941: 25–26). There are instances of royal ladies married
to several kings in a row. Iyazcuetzin was the wife of Axayacatl, Tizoc,
and Ahuitzotl (Nazareo 1940: 122); Tecuichpotzin (doña Isabel de Mon-
tezuma), mentioned below, was married to Atlixcatzin, Cuitlahuac, and
Cuauhtemoc. Papantzin (doña Beatriz) was first married to Cuitlahuac.
When Tenochtitlan fell to the Spaniards, she was captured together with
Cuauhtemoc, whose wife she was to be, and was then married to don
Hernando Ixtlilxóchitl of Tetzcoco (Ixtlilxóchitl 1977: 479).

2. After Carrasco (1974). Succession lines are known for some other
towns subject to Tetzcoco, but data concerning the royal marriages are
deficient (cf. below, table 3.6, on Itztapalapan). In Chiauhtla the local
king was installed by his father, Nezahualcoyotl (Ixtlilxóchitl 1977: 89).
Unfortunately there are no data on his marriage or those of his descendants.
This case is more like the Tenochca practice of installing royal princes as
rulers of dependent towns (see below).

3. Chimalpahin (1889: 101; Ixtlilxóchitl 1975: 326, 1977: 37, 39).
According to Durán (1967[2]: 73), Ixtlilxóchitl was married to a daughter
of Itzcoatl, the fourth king of Tenochtitlan; in any case, he married a
Tenochca princess.

4. I favor this latter account, which follows data from both Ixtlilxóchitl's *Historia chichimeca* and Chimalpahin (1889). The "Mapa Tlotzin"
(Aubin 1885: 65) also reports the marriage of Nezahualcoyotl to a daughter
of Temiccin (*sic*) of Tenochtitlan. Statements without personal names from
Motolinía (1971: 337, quoted above) and Torquemada (1969[2]: 365) say
that the mother of Nezahualcoyotl's son and successor, Nezahualpilli, was
a Mexican princess.

Other reports about the marriage of Nezahualcoyotl use some of the
same names given above, but with differences as to their parentage and
place of origin. In the *Compendio histórico*, Ixtlilxóchitl (1975: 447) mentions as Nezahualcoyotl's legitimate wife and the mother of Nezahualpilli,
Matlacihuatzin, daughter of Temictzin, here identified as a brother of the
king of Tlacopan. In still another passage (Ixtlilxóchitl 1975: 404), Temictzin is lord of Tlacopan. An account by Torquemada (1969[1]: 154–55)
gives the same names in a story similar to Ixtlilxóchitl's tale of Azcalxochitzin and the king of Tepechpan, but the princess, here called Matlalcihuatzin, is the daughter of Totoquihuatzin, king of Tlacopan; Temictzin,
the noble to whom she had been given to marry, is described as one of
Nezahualcoyotl's captains in Tlatelolco and a friend (*amigo*) of Totoqui-

huatzin, king of Tlacopan. *Amigo* is a common translation of Nahuatl *icniuhtli,* which also has the meaning of brother.

For a partial solution of these contradictions, it is probably relevant that the first king of Tiliuhcan Tlacopan, Tlacacuitlahuatzin, gave two of his daughters in marriage to Huitzilihuitl, king of Tenochtitlan, and his brother Tlatolzacatzin, and this is how the royal lineage of Mexico entered Tiliuhcan Tlacopan (Tezozomoc 1949: 89–90; I disagree here with A. León's translation).

There is also a later Temictzin, king of Tiliuhcan Tlacopan (Tezozomoc 1949: 154). Given a common naming practice, he may have taken his name from an ancestor, probably a previous Tenochca king of Tiliuhcan Tlacopan, who could have been the Temictzin named by Ixtlilxóchitl as son of Huitzilihuitl and father of Nezahualcoyotl's wife. Daughters of the king of Tiliuhcan Tlacopan are also reported as wives of the kings Itzcoatl of Tenochtitlan (Chimalpahin 1889: 108) and Acolnahuacatl of Tlacopan (Tezozomoc 1949: 101). Thus I think there is a strong basis for supporting the interpretation that Nezahualcoyotl's wife's father was not from Tlacopan but from Tiliuhcan Tlacopan, where a Tenochca ruler had been installed.

5. Compare the story of a prearranged defeat of Tetzcoco by Tenochtitlan, according to the Tenochca history in Durán (1967[2]: 127–31) and Tezozomoc (1975: 282–84).

6. In one passage Ixtlilxóchitl states that Xoxouchcatzin (*sic*) was a grandson of Moteuczoma Ilhuicamina, and the name of his daughter is given as Azcaxochitzin (1975: 549). In another passage her name is Tlacoyehuatzin ("the middle born"), lady of Azcapotzalco, daughter of Atocatzin and a descendant of Moteuczoma I (1975: 449).

7. AGI: Patronato 245-1. He was a son of Totoquihuatzin according to this document, but a son of don Pedro Tetlepanquetzin according to sources cited in Cline (1969: 85, 87).

8. Perhaps it was in accord with such a practice that the native chiefs of Tlaxcala gave women to the Spaniards, so that the Spaniards would leave their descendants with them (Muñoz Camargo 1948: 207), and that the kings of the Triple Alliance—Moteuczoma, Cacama, and Totoquihuatzin—gave some of their daughters and sister to Cortés (Ixtlilxóchitl 1977: 225–26). We have here the idea that a group of lower rank may incorporate through its women an outside element of higher rank.

9. Ixtlilxóchitl (1977: 177–78; cf. *Origen de los mexicanos* 1941: 276). She was the mother of doña Isabel de Montezuma according to these sources, although more detailed reports say that doña Isabel's mother was a daughter of Ahuitzotl.

10. According to some other accounts, Chimalpopoca was a younger brother, not a son, of Huitzilihuitl (*Historia de los mexicanos* 1941: 229; Códice Chimalpopoca 1945: 35), while Itzcoatl and Moteuczoma Ilhuicamina were sons of Chimalpopoca (Códice Chimalpopoca 1945: 35). None of these variant versions report who their mothers were.

11. Chimalpahin 1889: 107–8. Tezozomoc (1949: 109) gives her name as Tlacuitlaatzin, without stating her ancestry.

12. According to other versions, Moteuczoma Ilhuicamina was a son of Chimalpopoca (Códice Chimalpopoca 1945: 35; Ixtlilxóchitl 1975: 409).

13. An alternate version, however, makes her the daughter of a Tlacopan princess. See Note 9.

14. According to some reports, Cuauhtemoc was instrumental in the death of Axayacatl, a son of Moteuczoma who was probably a candidate to the succession and who had been in the opposing faction in the conflict over how to react to the Spanish presence (Tezozomoc 1949: 163–64).

15. *Relación de la genealogía* 1941: 255. This is a very simplified account. The documentation on Tollan is abundant in Archivo General de la Nación, México, and the Archivo de Indias, Seville, See also Barlow (1949) and Rosas Herrera (1946).

REFERENCES

AGI (Archivo General de Indias, Seville)
>   Patronato 181, Ramo 8; Patronato 245, Ramo 1; México 121, Ramo 2, no. 37.

Aubin, J. M. A.
1885   Mémoires sur la peinture didactique et l'écriture figurative des anciens Mexicains. Mission scientifique au Mexique et dans l'Amérique Centrale. Recherches historiques et archéologiques. 1 ptie. Histoire. Paris.

Barlow, Robert
1949   Anales de Tula, Hidalgo. Tlalocan 3: 2–13.

Carrasco, Pedro
1974   Sucesión y alianzas matrimoniales en la dinastía teotihuacana. Estudios de Cultura Nahuatl 11: 235–41.

1979   The Chiefly Houses of Ancient Mexico. Actes du XLIIe Congrès International des Américanistes, 2–9 Sept. 1976. IX-B: 177–85. Paris: Société des Américanistes.

Caso, Alfonso
1977   Reyes y reinos de la mixteca. 2 vols. México: Fondo de Cultura Económica.

Chimalpahin, Domingo F.
1889   Annales. Rémi Siméon, trans. Paris: Maisonneuve et Ch. Leclerc.
1965   Relaciones originales de Chalco Amaquemecan. Silvia Rendón, trans. México: fondo de Cultura Económica.

Cline, Howard F.
1969   Hernando Cortés and the Aztec Indians in Spain. The Quarterly Journal of the Library of Congress 26: 70–90.

Códice Chimalpopoca
1945   Códice Chimalpopoca: Anales de Cuauhtitlan y leyenda de los soles. Primo Feliciano Velásquez, trans. México: Universidad Nacional.

Códice Ramírez
1975   Códice Ramírez. *In* Crónica mexicana. H. A. Tezozomoc. pp. 9–149.

Davies, Claude Nigel
1973   Los mexicas: Primeros pasos hacia el imperio. México: Universidad Nacional.

Durán, Fray Diego
1967   Historia de las Indias de Nueva España. 2 vols. México: Porrúa.

Espejo, Antonieta, and Arturo Monzón
1945   Algunas notas sobre organización social de los tlatelolca. Memorias de la Academia de la Historia (México) 4: 484–89.

Garibay K., Ángel María
1945   Un cuadro real de la infiltración del hispanismo en el alma india en el llamado "Códice de Juan Bautista." Filosofía y Letras (México) 9: 213–41.

Gibson, Charles
1952   Tlaxcala in the Sixteenth Century. Stanford: Stanford University Press.
1971   Structure of the Aztec Empire. *In* Handbook of Middle American Indians. Robert Wauchope, ed. Vol. 10, pp. 376–94. Austin: University of Texas Press.

Gómara, Francisco López de
1954   Historia general de las Indias. 2 vols. Barcelona: Iberia.

Historia de los mexicanos
1941   Historia de los mexicanos por sus pinturas. *In Nueva colección* 1941: 209–40.

Historia Tolteca-Chichimeca
1976   Historia Tolteca-Chichimeca. Paul Kirchhoff, Lina Odena Güemes, and Luis Reyes García, eds. México: Instituto Nacional de Antropología e Historia.

Ixtlilxóchitl, Fernando de Alva
1975   Obras Históricas. Vol. 1. México: Universidad Nacional.
1977   Obras Históricas. Vol. 2. México: Universidad Nacional.
Motolinía, Toribio de Benavente
1971   Memoriales o libro de las cosas de la Nueva España y de los
            naturales de ella. Edmundo O'Gorman, ed. México: Univer-
            sidad Nacional.
Monzón, Arturo
1949   El calpulli en la organización social de los tenochca. México:
            Universidad Nacional.
Muñoz Camargo, Diego
1948   Historia de Tlaxcala. México: Talleres Gráficos Laguna.
Nazareo, Pablo
1940   Carta al rey don Felipe II. *In* Epistolario de Nueva España.
            Francisco del Paso y Troncoso, ed. Vol. 10, pp. 109–29.
            México: Porrúa.
Nueva colección
1941   Nueva colección de documentos para la historia de México:
            Pomar. Zurita. Relaciones antiguas (siglo XVI). México: Sal-
            vador Chávez Hayhoe.
Origen de los mexicanos
1941   Origen de los mexicanos. *In Nueva collección* 1941: 256–80.
Pomar, Juan Bautista
1941   Relación de Tezcoco. *In Nueva colección* 1941: 1–64.
Rammow, Helga
1964   Die Verwandschaftsbezeichnungen im klassischen Aztek-
            ischen. Beiträge zur mittelamerikanischen Völkerkunde VI.
            Hamburg: Museum für Völkerkunde und Vorgeschichte.
Relación de la genealogía
1941   Relación de la genealogía y linaje de los señores que han
            señoreado esta tierra de la Nueva España. *In Nueva colección*
            1941: 240–56.
Rosas Herrera, Gregorio
1946   Verba Sociorum Domini Petri Tlacauepantzi. Tlalocan 2: 150–
            62.
Spores, Ronald
1967   The Mixtec Kings and Their People. Norman: University of
            Oklahoma Press.
Tezozomoc, Hernando Alvarado
1949   Crónica mexicayotl. Adrián León, trans. México: Universidad
            Nacional.

1975   Crónica mexicana. México: Porrúa.
Torquemada, Juan de
1969   Monarquía indiana. 3 vols. México: Porrúa.
Unos annales
1939   Unos annales históricos de la nación mexicana. Ernst Mengin, trans. Baessler-Archiv 22(2–3). Berlin: Dietrich Reimer.

4

Aspects of Land Tenure in Ancient Mexico

H. R. Harvey

It has been just over one hundred years since Bandelier published his famous essay *On the Distribution and Tenure of Lands, and the Customs with Respect to Inheritance, among the Ancient Mexicans* (1878). Ignoring the fairly obvious complexity of Aztec society presented in his sources, Bandelier saw in the Aztecs something analogous to the Iroquois tribal model. Over time, his analysis has been seriously challenged by a number of scholars drawing upon essentially the same sources (Moreno 1931; Kirchhoff 1954; Caso 1963; Katz 1966; Freund 1968; Castillo F. 1972).

In reviewing the whole matter of Bandelier's interpretation of the socioeconomic structure of Mexican society at the time of the conquest, Kirchhoff singles out land tenure "to be the very core of the problem" (1954: 351). Kirchhoff restricted his examination to sources which most pointedly touched upon land tenure as a system and to generalizations for the region as a whole, while acknowledging the need for seeking out those sources which describe "individual instance," i.e., case studies of localities, families, and social groups (1954: 352). In this essay I shall discuss some questions pertaining to interpretation of sources and present information relating to the community of Tepetlaoztoc, which has a bearing particularly on the issue of landholding among the commoners.[1]

The sources most often cited to describe prehispanic land tenure essentially agree upon several named categories of land (Kirchhoff 1954: 356; Caso 1963: 874; Gibson 1964: 257–70). Among them were lands assigned to the support of temples (*teopantlalli*), office holders (*tlatocatlalli* and *tecpantlalli*), and the army (*milchimalli*). There were also the patrimonial lands of the rulers and the nobility (*pillalli*), and finally, the lands of the commoners (*calpullalli*). All these categories of lands were often found within the bounds of a single community. At the most general level, lands pertained to either public or private domains.

The legal status of lands in prehispanic times also emerges in colonial period descriptions, but sources are sometimes vague or contradictory regarding essential details. As a result, considerable controversy has arisen from the comparison and interpretation of general descriptions of the land-tenure system that prevailed before the Spanish conquest. Such differences of interpretation have serious consequences for determining how the land-tenure system actually functioned within the social and economic institutions of the times.

One important deficiency in the general descriptions of land tenure in the sixteenth century is that there is rare mention of the locality or region to which a description applied. Thus, in the aggregate, such sources yield a somewhat generalized impression of an undefined area. Alonso de Zorita, the most comprehensive source on land tenure, acknowledged with respect to his own work (1963: 86), that

> I must say at the outset, however, that it is impossible to state a general rule as concerns any part of Indian Government and customs, for there are great differences in almost every province. . . . Consequently, if what I say here appears to contradict some other information, the cause must be the diversity that exists in all things in every province.

Another problem with the general sources emanates from the exchange of information and of written manuscripts between scholars in the sixteenth century. That is, they frequently drew upon each other's writings, often without specific citation, and sometimes utilizing different versions. Zorita's work, for example, may have been widely circulated, judging from the number of copies that have come to light.[2] As Calnek (1974: 52) discovered, a later version of this work contained a note indicating that the source of Zorita's information on the role of the *calpulli* in the distribution of lands derived from Fray Francisco de las Navas, who lived in Huexotzingo. Unfortunately, modern scholars have relied exclusively on published versions which do not contain this important annotation.

Perhaps more serious for most purposes is that the sources do not permit much determination of the difference between what might be termed the "normative" as opposed to the "behavioral" aspects of the land-tenure system. What was, in other words, the degree of latitude in the application of general rules or principles? Were there some rules that were inviolable and others that were case-made? We know that there were courts, which perhaps resolved land disputes, but case records have not survived.

For case materials, we must turn to colonial period records. Records of land litigation in the early colonial period are extensive, but they are more indicative of the process of accommodation of the native system of land tenure rather than the defense of that system. Although Spanish courts were inconsistent in their rulings, all categories of Indian lands fell under their scrutiny, and the points of stress in the system clearly emerge. In Tepetlaoztoc in 1559, the Indians contended that palace lands (*tecpantlalli*), on which their cacique had his house and from which he received the produce, were not his private holdings but rather belonged to the community and therfore could not be alienated. It was left to the court to decide whether title rested with the community or with the *principal,* whose office was supported by such lands but which was also hereditary (Gibson 1964: 78–80). Such an issue may well not have arisen in precontact times, but it was common in early colonial litigation and the courts often, but not invariably, ruled in favor of community title for palace lands.

The most neglected sources of material that have a direct bearing on land-tenure questions are those that involve land transfers—bills of sale and wills. Unfortunately, the record is thin for the very early postconquest years, and it is not until well after midcentury that materials become abundant. Some of these records are to be found in the general archives, but the bulk of them are in local archives and in the archives of the notaries. Little attention has been paid to these classes of materials; one difficulty, apart from dispersion and access, is that for the central valleys many of these records are in Nahuatl. These hold promise for clarifying the relationship between a community and the lands within its bounds, between the lands and the people that worked or benefited from them (cf. Cline, this volume).

In terms of their own legal concepts, the early Spaniards perceived two classes of Indian lands: private and communal. The native land-tenure system, as described by them, seemed both to reflect and support the major distinction in social class between the nobility on the one hand and the commoners on the other. The exception to a clear-cut division was in the case of commoners who had distinguished themselves in war and were rewarded by grants of special privileges, including tribute-exempt lands for their personal benefit. *Pillalli,* the private lands of the nobility, did not fit Bandelier's conception of tribal society and he explained them away. While Kirchhoff, Caso, and others were forceful in their rejection of Bandelier's tribal model of Aztec society, they nevertheless accepted without challenge the tribal model as it applied to land-holding commoners (*macehualtin*) (Caso 1963: 874–75; Kirchhoff 1954: 359–61). This idea holds that in contrast to pillalli, which were private, alienable, and tribute-exempt lands of the nobility (*pipiltin*), title to *calpullalli* rested with the community. Those members of the community who held such lands only possessed usufruct rights, but they were heritable. Thus, *calpulli* lands were communal, and for the individual member, inalienable but heritable. Zorita (1963: 106) noted that when a *macehual* abandoned his lands or did not work them for a specified period, the calpulli could reassign these lands to another. It is primarily this attribution of power to the calpulli to reassign lands that has led to the inference that calpullalli were communal lands; this also fits the early Spanish concept of "town lands." It is likewise from this contention that a rather egalitarian image of the macehual level of Aztec society has emerged. This is the image that Zorita (1963: 105–11) conveys, and his has been the principal description of the land-tenure system upon which most scholars in the past have relied.

One of the most serious challenges to Zorita's thesis, and to many reconstructions of the prehispanic land-tenure system, is the record of the range in size of landholdings of macehualtin. In Tepetlaoztoc's barrio of Santa María Asunción Cuauhtepoztla, for example, some families are shown to possess a dozen or more parcels of land totaling in excess of six thousand square *quahuitl* (3.75 ha), while some possess only one parcel of less than four hundred square quahuitl (0.25 ha). The same holds true for lands depicted in the "Codex Vergara." Carrasco's data (1976: 45–64) for Molotla show a range of from twenty to more than two hundred units. The tax schedule reported for Otlazpan covers a range of from two hundred square units to sixteen thousand (*Códice Mariano Jiménez* 1967; Harvey and Williams 1980: 503).[3] Hicks's analysis (1976: 72) of the Oztoticpac Lands Map indicates that the range in macehual landholdings was from 92 to 8701 square meters, with an average of 1865 square meters. Witnesses in Coyoacan testified that some individuals held more land and some less (Carrasco and Monjarás Ruiz 1976).

Thus, as Gibson (1964: 268) observed, "All texts indicate a wide variation, both within single communities and between one community and another, in the form and size of tlalmilli plots. Certain colonial commentaries do refer to plots of equal size, but they indicate that some individuals held one, others two, and others three or more." Analyzing the landholdings depicted in one small community of the barrio of Santa María Asunción, Williams (1980: 171–72) noted that "one would expect that the larger the household, the more land available to it for cultivation. And conversely, the smaller the household the less land it would have. The per capita data from Teçontla indicate the smaller the household, the greater the per capita size of holdings, that is, the reverse of the expected pattern."

Some commoners had sources of income other than agriculture. There were, for example, merchants, artisans, renters, and laborers (e.g., see Dyckerhoff and Prem 1976: 157–80). The high death rate following the Spanish conquest no doubt had its impact on landholdings even within a generation of the Spanish appearance, so that an increase in per capita landholdings might be expected. Nevertheless, the imbalance so shortly after the conquest and so widely reported suggests it to be a reflection of the prehispanic pattern. By whatever social and economic mechanisms, some macehual families controlled more of the means of production than others.

The assessment of tribute based on landholdings confirms such a range among the commoners. Pomar (1975: 22) noted that they paid according to what they possessed.[4] Hernán Cortés (1538: 542) reported that "sus tierras, que son, como he dicho, repartidas por una medida; y destas medidas tiene uno 100, y otro 200, y otro 1000, y otro 2000 . . . y el que las tiene, puede pagar el tributo porque cada medida se les carga tanto tributo." Martín Cortés (1563: 443) reasserts the levy of tribute by measure: "El que tenía una suerte de tierra, pagaba un tributo; y el que dos, dos; y el que tres, tres; y el que tenía la suerte de tierra de regadío, pagaba un doblado que el que la tenía en secano." The Codex Vergara and the Códice de Santa María Asunción serve to clarify what was meant by measure. Both documents contain two cadastral sections of essentially the same lands, one devoted to boundary descriptions, the other to recording the area of the corresponding fields (*tlahuelmantli;* cf. Williams, this volume). In these documents, area is expressed in square quahuitl; the standard areal unit, or "medida," was a parcel 20 by 20 quahuitl or 400 square quahuitl (Harvey and Williams 1980: 503).

A number of factors account for the reported unequal distribution of landholdings. Sahagún (1954: 29) stated that land was among the valuables wagered, so that gambling gains and losses accounted for some land transfers. He also reported (1978: 9) that persons in financial distress might sell their land: "And so he did in connection with whatever land; he did it with calpulli land, the enclosed land, the marshy land, the dusty land, or the planted land on which he worked." Both pillalli and calpullalli could be transferred through time by the mechanism of inheritance (Zorita 1963: 106; Torquemada 1977: 333). For most individuals, commoners and nobles, inheritance must have been the principal way in which lands were acquired in late prehispanic times, when most of the agricultural land of any worth was already under cultivation. The density of population both permitted and required such intensive exploitation of all available lands. Ixtlilxóchitl (1975: 111), referring to pre-hispanic populations, commented that "era de tal manera que hasta los montes y sierras fragosas las tenían ocupadas con sembrados y otros aprovechamientos." Of Tlaxcala, H. Cortés observed (1908: 210): "This province contains many extensive and beautiful valleys, well-tilled and sown, and none are uncultivated."

Both nobles and commoners could add to their landholdings by performing meritorious service, and it was common to redistribute some of the lands of conquered provinces among the nobility and commoners who distinguished themselves in these conquests. Unless such land grants were specifically restricted, they could be disposed of by sale. According to Torquemada (1977), pillalli, including the tax-exempt estates given to knighted commoners, could be sold to other nobility. Lands of knighted commoners could also apparently be passed on to heirs, in which case it would account for some of the observed differences in the range of commoner landholdings. There is no mention in any of the sources that a distinguished commoner would lose his right to whatever calpullalli he had pos-sessed previous to his award. Although the distinguished commoner was explicitly denied the privilege of having renters (*terrazgueros*) work his land, he does not seem to have been denied the ability to hire laborers, a necessity should his aggregate holdings exceed his own family's ability to work them (Torquemada 1977: 333). Most of the land parcels depicted in the Códice de Santa María Asunción appear to be calpullalli, but some are outlined in red, indicating either pillalli of the pipiltin or tax-exempt parcels of distinguished commoners. In one instance a pillalli parcel outlined in red (f. 17v) is specifically glossed, but others are not. Also, the Codex Kings-borough indicates that there were pillalli within the bounds of the barrio which were not included in the cadasters (Paso y Troncoso 1912).[5]

Sources indicate that lands could be assigned to an individual member of a calpulli on the basis of need. Unassigned lands would become available through abandonment or the death of the property holders. The Códice de Santa María Asunción records many instances in which all members of a landholding household died. Such an occurrence, although common in the colonial period with its high mortality and oppressive tribute assessment, must have been relatively rare in prehispanic times. Some of the parcels (*milmanalli*) in the barrio of Asunción were reassigned subsequent to the drafting of the basic land register, and most are small parcels reassigned to individuals with few holdings. If the principle of need were paramount in the reassignment of calpullalli, it is difficult to imagine that individuals with adequate landholdings for their own family maintenance could expect to receive additional lands on this basis, when less fortunate individuals had few or none. Yet there is the reality of the imbalance in aggregate landholdings and the question of how they were acquired.

That there was such an imbalance in landholdings suggests that one man's need did not result in another man's loss. That is, the calpulli does not seem to have had the power to redistribute lands that were held by individuals in proper possession. In Tenochtitlan, Calnek (1974: 52) observed that even when individual calpullalli had been abandoned for decades, they could not be usurped by Indians or Spaniards. A similar situation seems to be reflected in Cholula in the 1590s. Macehualtin petitioned for licenses to sell various parcels of calpullalli to Spaniards, often employing the argument that such lands were of poor quality, that the land(s) in question had not been worked for many years, that they were ancient family possessions, and that they needed the cash to help with the planting of other lands they were working (Reyes García 1973, especially 287). In sanctioning the sale, authorities were recognizing the prior right of the individual to dispose of property acquired by inheritance over the right of the calpulli to prevent alienation of calpullalli. The Cholula land sales are an example of Zorita's observation (1963: 111) that "Because Spanish officials have made no effort to understand this communal system, they have adjudged to many Indians as private property lands which they held from their calpulli, simply because these persons could prove that they and their forebearers had possessed and worked such land."

The Códice de Santa María Asunción provides an example of calpullalli reassignment during the period from 1550 to 1576. What is striking is the small number of reassignments, given the mortality level recorded in the same document. The document supports the impression that the calpulli did not possess unrestricted power to redistribute the lands of individuals whose possession was recognized. The proceedings involved in land transfers among the macehualtin of the same calpulli were no doubt oral, and since they did not involve alienation of lands from the calpulli, the conditions for transfer are not apt to have been recorded in written form. Thus we have no way of knowing whether consent and possibly also indemnification of the original possessor or his heirs had to be secured. The document simply records the completed transaction, but in so doing it is one of our best examples of an active calpulli land register.

The foregoing suggests that macehual lands that had been passed for generations through family lines were viewed differently than those of recent or relatively recent assignment from the collective lands of the calpulli. In either case the approval and recording of land transfers would have been the responsibility of the prehispanic calpulli. In the Cholula cases the authorities were implicitly, if not explicitly, recognizing certain native restrictions on calpullalli transfers (Reyes García 1973). They required the showing of cause and proof of mode of possession. These sales seem to reflect the restrictions on and procedures involved in calpullalli transfers described by H. Cortés (1538: 540–41): "Y los vasallos no las puedan enagenar por venta ni troque ni por otra vía alguna, sin espresa licencia y mandado del señor é sin que el Tequitato de aquel barrio . . . asiente en la matricula o copia que tiene de las tierras y vecinos de aquel barrio."

One of the problems in interpreting Zorita's (1963) statements regarding the communality and inalienability of calpullalli is that the calpullalli often contained, in addition to agricultural tracts, *monte,* or forest, lands which were not individually assigned, but which were used collectively by the members of the calpulli. For these there is no question that title rested with the calpulli, as it did with unassigned agricultural tracts. The calpullalli also contained various tracts which were dedicated to the support of temple and government, for which it claimed title in colonial times. For a geographically extensive area, such as the Tepetlaoztoc barrio of Asunción, the calpulli had unquestionable title to much of the land surface within its bounds. Therefore, in large measure, there is no quarrel with Zorita's generalization. On the other hand, Zorita's flat assertion that calpullalli unworked for two years would be reassigned, seems untenable in terms of whatever fallowing practices may have been in vogue, unless his own recommendations for native agriculture be qualified (that fields be planted and fallowed in alternate years; 1963: 108, 249). From what Zorita observed and from what his understanding of "town lands" were under Spanish law, calpullalli were communal. If there were distinctions within the macehual-held parcels, it did not serve his purpose to recognize them. He was avowedly supportive of the common Indian and protection for the Indian from unbridled Spanish exploitation.

On the surface, Spanish law of the colonial era appears generally to have perpetuated the legal concepts and practices of prehispanic times relative to the calpullalli. That is, under this law the Indian macehual continued to possess and work his lands within the bounds of an Indian town, without the necessity of formal title. Within the community his protection lay in public recognition of his property rights and defense of the community boundaries. The colonial-period quest for formal title, therefore, was directed not at individual holdings but at the level of the community tract. As Gibson (1964: 299) concluded, "the legal advantage for Indians thus lay in a pretense of more communality in pueblo form than was in fact the case." In Tepetlaoztoc, for example, the old distinctions between calpullalli and pillalli seem to have faded after the disappearance of tax-exempt status for the latter. The community closed ranks against the external forces threatening its security.

Under the Spaniards, the barrio of Santa María Asunción Cuauhtepoztla retained its territorial boundaries and its authority over the lands within these boundaries. At some time in the latter half of the sixteenth century, a description of these boundaries was added to the Asunción codex, in effect elevating the old register to the status of title document.[6] The document was used in a later, eighteenth-century land dispute, and the boundaries described are precisely those recognized by older residents of the community today.[7] In 1603 the barrio was congregated and in 1607 it received a *merced* consisting of an *estancia de ganado menor* within its recognized boundaries (AGN: Libro de Congregaciones, Ramo de Mercedes). During that era, throughout Tepetlaoztoc, the economy shifted from primarily crop production to the raising of animals. Its dense population at the time of Spanish contact, reported in one document as thirty thousand tributaries, had severely declined by midcentury; up to the present Tepetlaoztoc has recovered demographically to only a fraction of its former level (Paso y Troncoso 1912).[8] The effects of depopulation and the grazing of sheep and goats are most apparent today in the municipio; many of the former agricultural lands are wastelands, suited neither for agriculture nor grazing.

Through much of the colonial era, with its reduced population, there appears to have been little pressure on the land in Tepetlaoztoc. Well into the nineteenth century surplus lands in the several barrios were being rented, with the proceeds going to the community.[9] In the late seventeenth century Tepetlaoztoc's inhabitants had become prosperous from the operation of mule caravans, since Tepetlaoztoc sits astride an old route to Veracruz (Gibson 1964: 367). Despite its periods of affluence and adaptation to a nonfarming economy, the old concepts of land tenure persisted.

In the mid-eighteenth century, when glimpses of land dynamics show through the documents, *repartimiento* lands were changing hands, contrary to the formal procedures of the community. One woman is reported to have sold various of her parcels to others, which sales were considered void, since she did not first seek authorization and approval from the town government (*cabildo*) and subsequent judicial license.[10] Land sales required official approval, as they had in the sixteenth century, and that the seller show cause determined by need ("necesidad y utilidad"); lands were assigned to individuals with this explicit provision. What is significant about these documents is that they reflect land transfers occurring on an informal basis despite rules to the contrary, and that such transfers might be contested when contrary to community interest, such as a sale to an outsider, or a sale of significant quantities of land.

On July 25, 1856, the "Ley de desamortización de los bienes eclesiásticos" was passed, and its intent was reinforced in Article 27 of the Constitution of 1857 (Huitrón H. 1972: 24). The avowed purpose of the law was to obtain a more efficient tax base by breaking up large institutional landholdings with a "perpetual or indefinite character," particularly those of clerical organizations (Huitrón H. 1972: 24). Since the *ayuntamiento,* however, was specifically cited, the effect of the interpretation of this law was to sever community authority over lands within its jurisdiction. Interpretation and implementation of the law may well have exceeded the intent of its promulgators but, in any case, those who possessed lands of repartimiento hitherto protected by community title could petition for and receive title in fee simple. Under the French, an imperial decree broadened the scope of the property laws of the reform with respect to community and repartimiento lands by specifically establishing the procedures and requirements for procurement of private title by the landholder. Excepted were lands of public use, such as monte and water (Huitrón H. 1972: 118–21). In 1875 the state of Mexico defined, for the first time, "terrenos de común repartimiento" and the procedures and requirements for title procurement (Huitrón H.1972: 27–28). The impact of such laws was to convert the traditional lands of common division to an unrestricted, unencumbered "commodity." Such legislation facilitated growth of the large private estates, haciendas, and ranchos, at the expense of the native community, but its general impact in this regard was perhaps not as great as has frequently been construed.

During this period there were many land transactions in Tepetlaoztoc, the records of which are preserved in the local archives, particularly in the Ramo de Tierras, Ramo de Presidencia, and in the Tesorería. Although quite a number of landholders applied to obtain formal title documents, apparently many did not, and the record contains an abundance of traditional land-transfer transactions. The community continued to receive petitions for the assignment of lands and to deal with the problems involved in requests for reassignment of repartimiento lands. One individual, for example, having cultivated for several years a parcel of land which was not his own, requested the parcel's reassignment to him. His request was frustrated by the possessor's insistence that the latter had been paying him rent for the use of the land and that the possessor had been meeting his tax payments on the parcel. This, and other cases, reflect a common practice of renting lands possessed under traditional community title. Petitions for approval to sell lands included the required show of cause and were often approved, except in instances involving would-be purchasers from other communities or in instances where rights of possession were considered questionable. In cases of extracommunity sales, some were approved and some not, apparently based on the community's assessment of the buyer; that is, whether the buyer could be expected to contribute to the community and would agree to abide by community rules for property transfer. Most notable about sale-transfer petitions is that they were not open ended, but rather were made with reference to a specific purchaser. Interesting also are the frequent petitions for formal approval of property transfers expressing as cause the need to satisfy a debt. In effect this type of transfer amounted to a sale, but one with justifiable and highly acceptable cause.

The foregoing cases illustrate that those who held "good possession" as determined by the standards of the community could not easily be dispossessed, whether they personally worked their lands or not. Secondly, lands of common division, when held in good possession (inherited or acquired by proper procedure), functioned essentially as private lands in the sense that the landholder could rent them, lend them, prevent others from usurping them, dispose of them by sale, trade, or transfer for his own personal benefit, or acquire new holdings by the same means.

In modern Tepetlaoztoc, even though lands are often held in private title, such lands are still referred to as *común repartimiento*. Individuals sometimes petition for and may occasionally expect to receive an assignment of lands from the community land bank (*bienes comunales*). In making the assignment the community in effect informally transfers title from the corporation to the individual. A recent case involved the reassignment of lands which had long been left abandoned by the owner and his heirs. The community exerted strong coercive pressure on the heirs to relinquish claim to the land. Their title was in fact precarious, since the *escrituras* could not be located and were believed to have been destroyed during the revolution. The heirs were unhappy about the community action, but did not contest it, since they live in the community. Such practice is not uncommon in communities with a heritage of común repartimiento, where the customary procedures of the community can often be more potent in land tenure than the formal legal system of which it is a part.

CONCLUSIONS

In recent years there has been a mounting body of evidence from the analysis of early colonial documents that casts doubt on previous interpretations of the prehispanic land-tenure system, interpretations largely based on compilations of general descriptions.[11] One obvious problem with the general descriptions is that the early Spanish observers seldom drew on case materials, most were not lawyers, and many observers generalized from limited geographical experience. Nevertheless, the early observers provide a general outline of a system that is not incompatible with what can be seen in actual practice from local documents. What seems to emerge from individual case studies, however, is that the land-tenure system perhaps varied with locality or region and, in any case, was more flexible than a literal interpretation of Zorita and some other general descriptions seem to allow. Even some of the early general statements, however, are supportive of a certain latitude in land-tenure practice.

There are many details of the prehispanic system of land tenure that need clarification, but the right of commoners to hold and to dispose of or acquire property within their home community has the most consequence for understanding the dynamics of prehispanic society. From the earliest Spanish observers down to the present, the issue has been focused on "communal" versus "private" property, and the issue was clouded from the beginning by the intermixing of native concepts of community authority on the one hand and Spanish views of community jural rights on the other. Because of procedural proscriptions on the transfer of calpullalli indicated by various sources, it does appear that such land was not an unrestricted commodity in prehispanic Mexico; but it also appears that a mechanism for real-estate transfers initiated by the interested parties did exist. Within this frame the prehispanic macehualtin may well have enjoyed considerable freedom in terms of property transactions, as they did later under Spanish colonial law, when their situation was explicitly "communal." The range in aggregate landholdings of the macehualtin recorded in so many localities strongly suggests that it was also individual initiative and ability and not only the collective community that determined who could hold property. Wills, sale documents, and litigation of the early colonial period indicate that the manner in which property was acquired was perhaps the key factor in defining an individual's property rights. Spanish authorities recognized a distinction between inherited lands, purchased lands, and those assigned by the community, and the Spanish attempted, at least, to mediate between the two systems, their own and the native.

NOTES

1. Archival and field research for this paper was conducted in the summer of 1978 under a grant from the Cyril B. Nave Fund, University of Wisconsin–Madison.

2. For a discussion of the manuscript's history, see Zorita (1963: 52–58).

3. For different interpretations, see Leander (1967) and Gibson (1964: 269–70).

4. See also *Relación de Fray Domingo de la Anunción* (1914: 238).

5. One such place was Tlantozcac. Fourteen households, containing seventy-eight members, are recorded for this locality in the Códice de Santa María Asunción, and fifteen renters, or *mayeques,* for this locality in the "Codex Kingsborough."

6. These additions to the basic manuscript were probably made in the final quarter of the sixteenth century, perhaps in relation to the community's petition for a *merced* of an *estancia de ganado menor.*

7. A litigation document involving lands of the Rancho Cuauhte-poztla is preserved in the church of Santa María de la Asunción and is regarded by the members of the modern barrio as a title document. The document centers on the period from 1755 to about 1816, but it contains extracts from earlier documents, among them the boundary descriptions from the "Códice de Santa María Asunción."

8. In 1970 the municipio census is reported to have been 7,068 (*Monografía del municipio de Tepetlaoztoc* 1974: 32).

9. The local archives of the municipio of Tepetlaoztoc contain a substantial record of town finances for the late eighteenth and the nineteenth centuries. The archive has recently been organized, and an index of the documents is being prepared for publication by the state of Mexico.

10. Church document, barrio of Santa María Asunción; see Note 6.

11. Even so fine a scholar as José Miranda (1966) accepted implicitly the interpretation of prehispanic land tenure as propounded by Kirchhoff and Caso. Other scholars, however, began to challenge this viewpoint. Soustelle (1961: 80) summarizes my own viewpoint: "No doubt the *calpulli* retained ownership, but in practice, the citizen who followed his father and his grandfather in the same holding really felt himself at home. At the time immediately before the Spanish invasion it appears that the sale of land was provided for by law. Arising from the traditional collective ownership, private property was in the act of coming into existence." A number of scholars have recently reached the same conclusions. "Commoners as well as noblemen held what was in effect private property in addition to family land still under residual community control. Since all the terms are Nahuatl and the patterns appear in the earliest documents, one may at least wonder if it does not extend back into preconquest times; though proof would be difficult, the question is surely worth thorough investigation and consideration" (Anderson, Berdan, and Lockhart 1976: 5). Calnek (1974: 52), likewise, questions the assumption of communal lands. On the other hand, Carrasco (1978, especially 24–29) argues for communal control not only of the calpullalli but of the pillalli as well.

REFERENCES

AGN (Archivo General de la Nación, México)
          Libro de Congregaciones. Ramo de Mercedes, V.25, f.239.

Anderson, Arthur J. O., Frances Berdan, and James Lockhart
1976   Beyond the Codices. UCLA Latin American Studies Series, 27.

Bandelier, Adolph F.
1878   On the Distribution and Tenure of Lands, and the Customs with Respect to Inheritance, among the Ancient Mexicans. *In* Eleventh Annual Report of the Trustees of the Peabody Museum of American Archaeology and Ethnology II (2): 385–448.

Calnek, Edward E.
1974   Conjunto urbano y modelo residencial en Tenochtitlan. *In* Esayos sobre el desarrollo urbano de México. México: Sep-Setentas, 143.

Carrasco, Pedro
1976   The Joint Family in Ancient Mexico. *In* Essays on Mexican Kinship. Hugo G. Nutini, Pedro Carrasco, and James M.

Taggert, eds. pp. 45–64. Pittsburgh: University of Pittsburgh Press.

1978   La economía del México prehispánico. *In* Economía política e ideología en el México prehispánico. Pedro Carrasco and Johanna Broda, eds. pp. 15–76. México: CIS-INAH, Nueva Imagen.

Carrasco, Pedro, and Jesús Monjarás-Ruiz, comps.

1976   Colección de documentos sobre Coyoacán, visita del oidor Gómez de Santillán al peublo de Coyoacán y su sujeto Tacubaya el el año de 1553. México: CIS-INAH, Colección Científica, I.

Caso, Alfonso

1963   Land Tenure among the Ancient Mexicans. American Anthropologist 65: 863–78.

Castillo F., Victor M.

1972   Estructura económica de la sociedad mexica, según las fuentes documentales. Mexico City: Universidad Nacional, Instituto de Investigaciones Históricas, Serie de Cultura Náhuatl, Monografías, 13.

Códice de Santa María Asunción

Códice de Santa María Asunción. Apeo y deslinde de tierras (de los terrenos) de Santa María de la Asunción. Ms. de Olaguibel. Biblioteca Nacional de México, 1497 bis.

Códice Mariano Jiménez

1967   Códice Mariano Jiménez. Nómina de tributos de los pueblos Otlazpan y Tepexic en geroglífico azteca y lenguas castellana y náhuatl, 1549. México: Instituto Nacional de Antropología e Historia.

Codex Vergara

Codex Vergara. Bibliothèque Nationale, Paris. Ms. Mex. 37–39.

Cortés, Hernán

1538   Carta al Consejo de Indias, 20 September 1538. *In* Colección de documentos inéditos, relativos al descubrimiento . . . , sacados de los archivos del reino, y muy especialmente del de Indias. Vol. 3. pp. 535–45. Madrid: Manuel B. de Quirós.

1908   Letters of Cortes. Francis Augustus MacNutt, ed. Vol. 1. New York: G. P. Putnam's Sons.

Cortés, Martín

1563   Carta al Rey D. Felipe II, 10 de Octubre, 1563. *In* Colección de documentos inéditos, relativos al descubrimiento . . . ,

sacados de los archivos del reino, y muy especialmente del de
Indias. Vol. 4. pp. 440–62. Madrid: Manuel B. de Quirós.

Dyckerhoff, Ursula, and Hanns J. Prem
1976   La estratificación social en Huexotzinco. *In* Estratificación so-
          cial en la Mesoamérica prehispánica. Pedro Carrasco et al. pp.
          157–80. México: SEP-INAH.

Freund, Georg
1968   Derecho agrario y catastro en el México antiguo. *In* Traduc-
          ciones Mesoamericanistas. Vol. 2. pp. 157–78. México: SMA.

Gibson, Charles
1964   The Aztecs under Spanish Rule. Stanford: Stanford University
          Press.

Harvey, H. R., and Barbara J. Williams
1980   Aztec Arithmetic: Positional Notation and Area Calculation.
          Science 210: 499–505. (Reprinted in Ciencia y desarrollo 38
          [1981]: 5–14).

Hicks, Frederic
1976   Mayeque y calpuleque el el sistema de clases del México an-
          tiguo. *In* Estratificación social en la Mesoamerica prehispánica.
          Pedro Carrasco et al. pp. 67–77. México: SEP-INAH.

Huitrón H., Antonio
1972   Bienes comunales en el estado de México. Toluca: Ediciones
          Gobierno del Estado de México.

Ixtlilxóchitl, Fernando de Alva
1975   Obras Históricas. Vol. 2. México: Universidad Nacional, In-
          stituto de Investigaciones Históricas.

Katz, Friedrich
1966   Situación social y económica de los aztecas durante los siglos
          XV y XVI. México: Universidad Nacional, Instituto de In-
          vestigaciones Históricas, Serie de Cultura Náhuatl, Monogra-
          fías, 8.

Kirchhoff, Paul
1954   Land Tenure in Ancient Mexico, a Preliminary Sketch. Revista
          Mexicana de Estudios Antropológicos 14: 351–61.

Leander, Birgitta
1967   Códice de Otlazpan. México: Instituto Nacional de Antro-
          pología e Historia, Serie Investigaciones, 13.

Miranda, José
1966   La propiedad comunal de la tierra y la cohesión social de los
          pueblos indígenas mexicanos." Cuadernos Americanos 6: 168–
          81.

Monografía del municipio de Tepetlaoztoc
1974   Monografía del municipio de Tepetlaoztoc. Toluca: Gobierno
            del Estado de México.

Moreno, Manuel M.
1931   La organización política y social de los aztecas. México: Univ-
            ersidad Nacional, Serie II, No. 1.

Paso y Troncoso, Francisco del
1912   Códice Kingsborough—Memorial de los indios de Tepetlaoz-
            toc al monarca español contra los encomenderos del pueblo.
            Madrid: Hauser y Menet.

Pomar, Juan Bautista
1975   Relación de Tezcoco. Toluca: Biblioteca Enciclopédica del Es-
            tado de México, XLIX.

Relación de Fray Domingo de la Anunción
1914   Relación de Fray Domingo de la Anunción acerca del tributar
            de los índios, Chimalhuacan, 20 de Septiembre, 1554. *In*
            Documentos inéditos del siglo XVI para la historia de México.
            Mariano Cuevas, comp. México: Porrúa.

Reyes García, Cayetano
1973   Indice y extractos de los protocolos de la notaría de Cholula
            (1590–1600). México: Instituto Nacional de Antropología e
            Historia, Colección Científica, 8.

Sahagún, Berardino de
1954   Florentine Codex: General History of the Things of New Spain,
            8. Arthur J. O. Anderson and Charles E. Dibble, trans. Santa
            Fe: School of American Research and University of Utah.

1978   Florentine Codex: General History of the Things of New Spain,
            3. 2nd ed., rev. Arthur J. O. Anderson and Charles E. Dibble,
            trans. Santa Fe: School of American Research and University
            of Utah.

Soustelle, Jacques
1961   The Daily Life of the Aztecs on the Eve of the Spanish Con-
            quest. London: George Weidenfeld and Nicholson.

Torquemada, Juan de
1977   Monarquía indiana de los veinte y un libros rituales . . . Méx-
            ico: Universidad Nacional, Instituto de Investigaciones His-
            tóricas, 4.

Williams, Barbara J.
1980   Aztec Soil Classification and Land Tenure. Actes du XLIIe
            Congrès International des Américanistes, 9-b. pp. 165–75.
            Paris: Société des Américanistes.

Zorita, Alonso de
1963   Life and Labor in Ancient Mexico: The Brief and Summary
            Relation of the Lords of New Spain. Benjamin Keen, trans.,
            intro. New Brunswick: Rutgers University Press.

5

Mexican Pictorial Cadastral Registers:

An Analysis of the Códice de Santa María Asunción
and the Codex Vergara

Barbara J. Williams

In the sixteenth century Alonso de Zorita reported (1963: 110) that Indian *principales* maintained detailed cadastral records of community lands by "pictures on which are shown all the parcels, and the boundaries, and where and with whose fields the lots meet, and who cultivates what field, and what land each one has." Classes of data contained in such pictorial documents would have included the names of individual landholders, number and location of cultivated and noncultivated fields, field forms, linear measurements, and *paraje* (land-tract) names. In addition Spanish sources indicate that land tenure information was conveyed through color conventions: light yellow for commoner lands (*calpullalli*), light red or cochineal for lands of the nobility (*pillalli*), and dark red or purple for palace lands (*tecpantlalli*) (Torquemada 1943: 546; Clavigero 1944: 24). According to Torquemada (1943: 546), cadastral data were painted on *lienzos* "so that on opening one of these rolls, the

103

entire pueblo, its limits and outlines could be seen at a glance." In effect, such manuscripts would have been cadastral maps. One notable example of the genre is the Oztocticpac Lands Map. Although it does not portray an entire community, and perhaps for that reason is classified by Glass (1975: 36) as a property plan, it does show the spatial arrangement of properties, their owners (or renters), field forms, linear measurements, and paraje names (Cline 1966). Other pictorial documents indicate that land records were not maintained exclusively in map format, but also as cadastral registers. The Humboldt Fragment VIII (Seler 1904: 200–209), the Cadastral Fragment of the Ramírez Collection, the Codex Vergara, and the Códice de Santa María Asunción are examples of such cadastral registers. The purpose of this essay is to discuss cadastral information presented in the most extensive documents of this type, the Codex Vergara and the Códice de Santa María Asunción, focusing on the classes of data recorded and the writing conventions.[1]

THE CODICES

The Códice de Santa María Asunción pertains to the modern *barrio* ("ward") of Asunción Cuauhtepoztla in Tepetlaoztoc, located 8 km. northeast of Texcoco, in the Valley of Mexico. The Codex Vergara relates to the nearby barrio of San Gerónimo and adjacent parajes. Drawn in the mid-sixteenth century, these codices together record landholdings of approximately two hundred and fifty households, residing in fifteen localities. For each community there is a household census and two cadastral registers (also by household), one glossed *milcocoli* and the other *tlahuelmantli*. Although the milcocoli and tlahuelmantli registers refer to the same fields, they are discussed separately because they record different data and employ distinct writing conventions.

MILCOCOLI CADASTRAL DATA

In the micocoli sections of the two codices the following glyphic information appears: (1) demographic data on household and family heads; (2) house types; (3) number and shape of household fields; (4) linear measurements of field perimeters; (5) soil types; (6) land subdivisions and transfers; (7) nobles' land; and (8) paraje names.

The kinds of data gathered on landholding and maintained over time were clearly extensive and varied.

The landholders depicted in the two codices were mostly, if not entirely, *macehualtin* ("commoners"), and with few exceptions the lands they held were calpullalli. Landholding household heads are listed in columns, four or five to a page, and are shown with their names in glyphs and Spanish glosses, with the grapheme for house (*calli*). In multiple family households, the glyphic name and Spanish gloss of family heads are also indicated, and the fields pertaining to each family are set apart. Landholders are distinguished by sex, age, and civil status. Hairstyles differentiate men and women, and old age is indicated by wrinkled faces. In some cases widows and widowers are identified glyphically by tears on their cheeks (see table 5.1). Sociological data on age, sex, and household structure were apparently considered a necessary part of the cadastral record. Another item of sociological data is conveyed by a distinction in house types; most households have houses shown in profile with a flat roof (the calli), but a few are shown with conical, thatched roofs, the *xacalli* (see table 5.1). House type may indicate economic status, but there is no apparent correlation between house type and household landholdings. In his analysis of social structure in the Codex Vergara, Offner (this volume) suggested that house type might indicate ethnic differences, perhaps Otomí enclaves within the Nahua population. He concluded that household size and composition does not reflect such a difference, but since a Dominican priest in the monastary of Tepetlaoztoc ministered in Otomí, ethnic difference remains a possible interpretation.[2] Whatever the meaning, clearly the depiction of distinct house types was not arbitrary; if it were, the scribe would not have erased a xacalli and redrawn a calli, as on folio 17r of the Códice de Santa María Asunción.

Measurements

In a line to the right following the names of landholders are drawings of the household fields. Distances along each side are indicated in the Texcocan line-and-dot numerical convention (see table 5.1). One dot equals twenty linear units, a vertical line equals one, and five vertical lines connected by a line on top equal five. The numbers are always in sequence from large to small, and usually

Table 5.1. Hieroglyphic Conventions Depicting Cadastral Data in the Codex Vergara and the Códice de Santa María Asunción

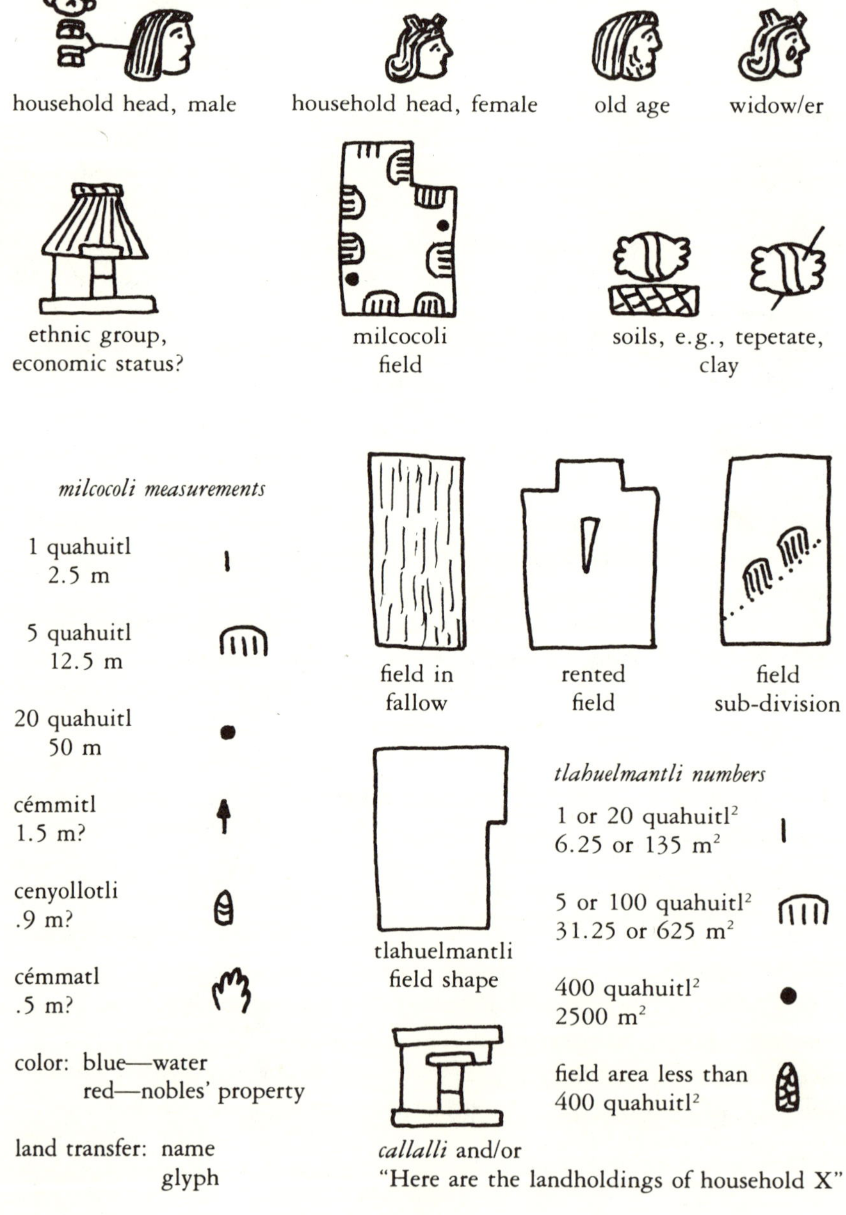

but not always, they are read from right to left. The standard Indian linear unit of land measurement in the Texcocan area was the *quahuitl,* not the *cémmatl,* as inferred by Castillo F. (1972a: 213). Evidence for this interpretation is found in Texcocan property descriptions from the 1580s and 1590s (Papeles de la Embajada Americana). In these documents the term "quahuitl" appears in Nahuatl texts which accompany pictorial representations of fields following the same conventions employed in the two Tepetlaoztoc codices. The length of the quahuitl was 2.5 meters, a figure derived from Ixtlilxóchitl's comparison (1952: 174) of Indian measures (*medidas*) to Spanish *varas.* Field evidence supports this equation. Using the 2.5 meter conversion factor, sixteenth-century field measurements fall well within the range of contemporary field dimensions in the Tepetlaoztoc area, and relic fields measuring approximately 50 meters (20 quahuitl) square have been identified on air photographs (Compañía Mexicana de Aerofoto). Moreover, until recently rope was sold in Texcoco by the *mecate,* a length equal to 2.5 meters.

Field measurements also include distances shorter than the standard quahuitl, and when these occur they are always placed after the last full quahuitl. The fractional linear measures are shown by glyphs for arrow (*cémmitl*), heart (*cenyollotli*), and hand (*cémmatl;* see table 5.1). Nahuatl glosses of similar heart and hand glyphs in the Papeles de la Embajada Americana manuscripts confirm the reading of these two fractions. Modern equivalents of the fractions remain problematical, however. Orozco y Berra (1960: 460) suggested that fractions based on fifths would be consistent with the Nahua arithmetical system, but the same could apply to fourths as well. It is possible that the cémmitl was ½ quahuitl (1.25 m), measured from one elbow to the tip of the other hand; the cenyollotli ²/₅ quahuitl (.9 m), measured from the chest to the hand (Castillo 1972a: 215, 217); and the cémmatl ¹/₅ quahuitl (.5 m), measured from the elbow to the hand, and perhaps to be equated with the *cemmolícpitl* (Castillo 1972a: 217). Since the linear fractions are abundantly recorded, the importance which the Indians attached to precision land measurement is underscored, and greatly contrasts with Spanish practices of the time (cf. Anderson, Berdan, and Lockhart 1976: 5).

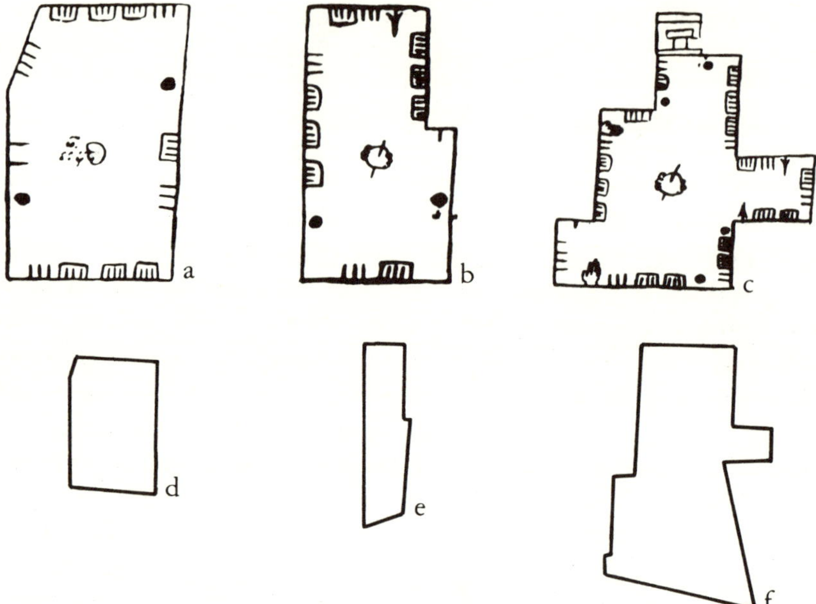

Fig. 5.1 The graphic convention in the milcocoli usually portrays approximate shape but not linear scale of agricultural fields (*a–c* from the Codex Vergara, ff. 23r, v; *d–f* represent the same fields drawn to linear scale)

Fields

Although dimensions are recorded precisely, the fields themselves are not drawn to scale on the manuscripts; they are depicted as roughly the same size, probably for composition purposes. Normally the left margin of each field is drawn as a vertical straight line, which apparently served as a baseline. There is a definite attempt to show approximate field shape, particularly in the case of polygons (see figures 5.1 and 5.2). However, the angular relationships between sides cannot be read in degrees of arc but only as obtuse or acute angles.

Field dimensions and shapes in the two codices suggest that the intent of the milcocoli sections was to record arable land only. For example, many quadrilateral fields have nearly rectangular "cutouts" with modal dimensions of five to ten quahuitl (see figures 5.3a–d).

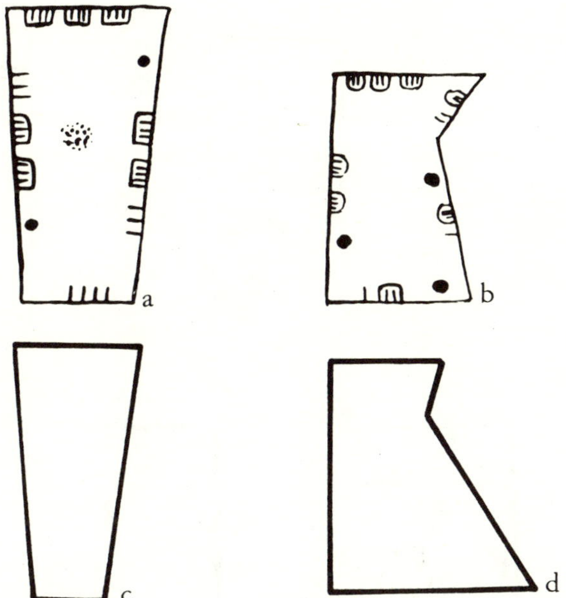

Fig. 5.2. Occasionally both linear scale and shape of fields are depicted in the milcocoli register (*a* from the Codex Vergara, f. 23v; *b* from the Códice de Santa María Asunción, f. 68v; *c* and *d* represent the same fields drawn to linear scale)

These probably were house complexes, since the dimensions correlate well with archaeological and contemporary data (Parsons 1971: 336, tlatel 460 of Tx-A-24). Smaller cutouts of one or two quahuitl might indicate trees or rocks (figure 5.3e) and elongated ones, paths leading to residences (figures 5.3f and g). Thus, features in the sixteenth-century landscape can be reconstructed by interpreting the milcocoli registers for what they exclude as well as for what they portray directly.

The milcocoli data indicate that very few Indian fields were perfectly square or rectangular. Of the nearly six hundred fields in the Códice de Santa María Asunción, for example, only eighteen had similar opposite sides; that is, only eighteen could have been true rectangles or squares. On the other hand, many fields were quadrilaterals, probably trapezoidal shape. Most likely these fields were *metepantles,* or *tablas*—maguey-hedged terraces found on gently

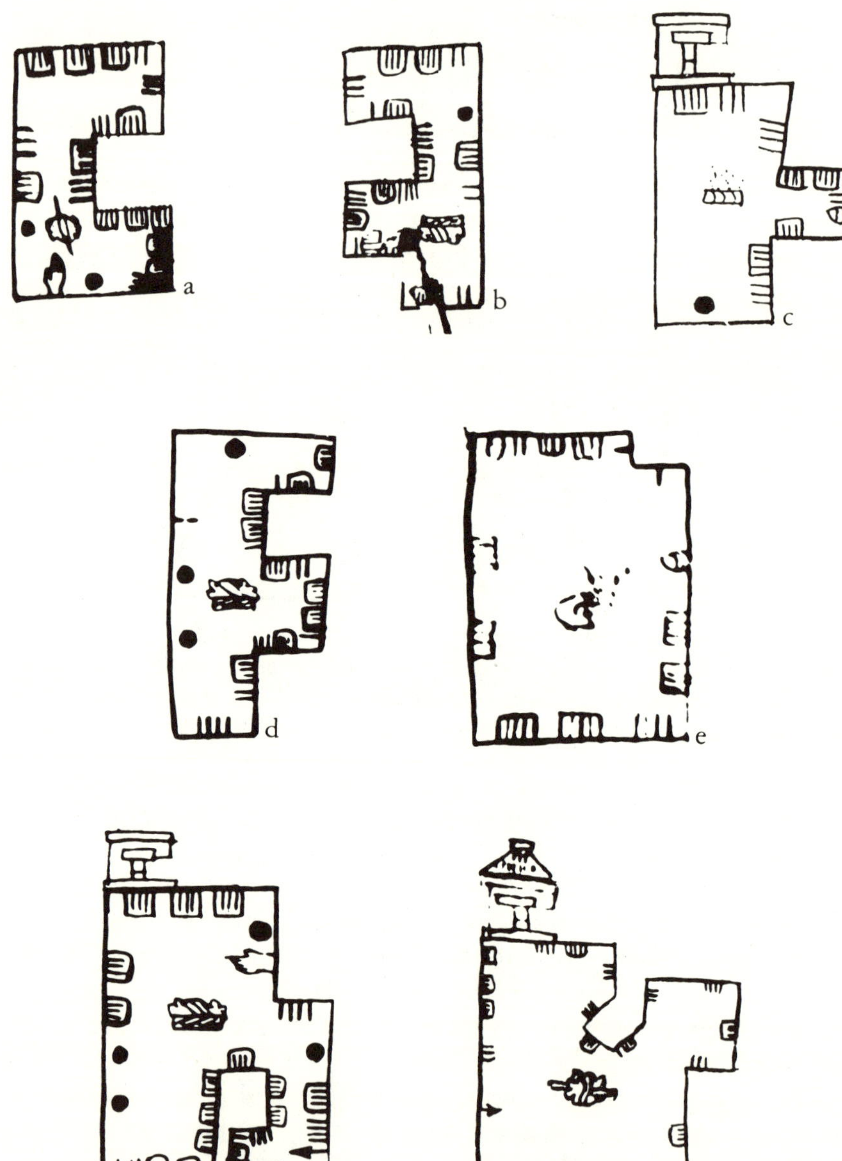

Fig. 5.3. "Cutouts" in milcocoli fields suggest the presence of houses, paths, rocks, and trees (*a* f. 9r; *b* f. 9v; *c* f. 12v; *d* f. 14v; *e* f. 12v; *f* f. 14v; *g* f. 57v, all from the Códice de Santa María Asunción)

to moderately sloping terrain typical of the piedmont and alluvial fans. Thus, the field shapes themselves suggest particular land-use and agricultural practices.

The milcocoli cadastral registers are not cadastral maps, but still their content provides a mental image of the character of the sixteenth-century landscape. The semidispersed *tecorral* settlement pattern, the large number of small fields (most of approximately one acre), irregularly shaped fields, and maguey-hedged terraces suggest an agricultural landscape exhibiting a finely divided, lattice-like structure, orderly but not geometrically precise—in fact, not unlike that of contemporary Tepetlaoztoc.

Soils

In addition to field dimensions, shape, and number, the milcocoli registers indicate soil type by glyphs in the center of each field.[3] The interpretation and implications of these glyphs have been discussed elsewhere (Williams 1980a, b, c). That soil type formed part of the cadastral record is not unexpected, since it is an identifying characteristic of land parcels. More importantly, however, soil quality apparently was considered in assessment of tribute, and it may have been noted for that purpose (see Zorita 1963: 237).

In the Códice de Santa María Asunción some fields have surfaces partially or entirely shaded with drawing ink, usually in addition to a soil glyph.[4] The significance of shading is suggested by its use in other contexts. In the census portion of the manuscripts, many household members are shown with shaded heads, a standard convention for indicating the deceased (Gibson 1964: 203; Prem 1974). And in the milcocoli section of Conçotlan, one household is shown with two houses, the second of which is shaded, implying "dead," that is, unoccupied (f. 67v). By analogy, shading of fields probably signifies "unused," or in fallow. Tribute assessment and identification of land potentially available for redistribution may have motivated the recording of such data.

Finally, in addition to soil glyphs a *uictli de hoja* ("hoe") appears in the center of two fields in the Asunción codex (ff. 37r, 46r). The uictli may relate to the soil glyph, but in other documents, such as the Codex Kingsborough, it appears in association with individuals who are property renters (Paso y Troncoso 1912). This suggests that the Asunción scribe intended to indicate rented fields. Since the fields are not red-lined, the implication is that the land was rented from other macehualtin.

Color

Color is used sparingly in the cadastral portions of both codices, but since I have not examined the Vergara in detail, the observations presented here are restricted to the Códice de Santa María Asunción. In the Asunción, two streams (ff. 8v, 17r) and an aqueduct glyph (f. 15v) are colored blue. Aside from depiction of one *barranca* margin (8v), the streams and aqueduct are the only topographic or cultural features explicitly indicated in the codex, and it is significant that they are both associated with water. The second instance of the use of color relates to land tenure. Some fields are entirely outlined in red, others have one red side, and there is one case of a red xacalli.[5] A Nahuatl gloss, *pilmilli,* next to a red-lined parcel (f. 17v) suggests that the red convention mentioned in Spanish sources was followed in the Asunción codex to indicate nobles' property, both land and houses.[6]

The lack of more extensive color in the Códice de Santa María Asunción is somewhat curious. Kindred documents such as the Ramírez Fragment and the Humboldt Fragment VIII (Seler 1904) employ color more liberally, for example, in the soil glyphs, and therefore they appear to be more akin to the reported native style. Since other Texcocan conventions are followed in the Asunción, this suggests that the codex is a copy of an older document and that in the process of copying, colors were largely omitted.

Other Conventions

Two classes of data in the milcocoli registers relate to the native practice of updating pictorial records. One is the recording of field subdivisions by a dotted line to indicate revised boundaries. Possibly because fields were already extremely small, only three cases occur in the Códice de Santa María Asunción (see figure 5.4), and none in the Codex Vergara. Land transfer is indicated once in the Asunción codex by a name glyph above the field which identified the individual involved (10v). This single glyph among the seventeen or so cases of land transfer probably represents a vestige of the native

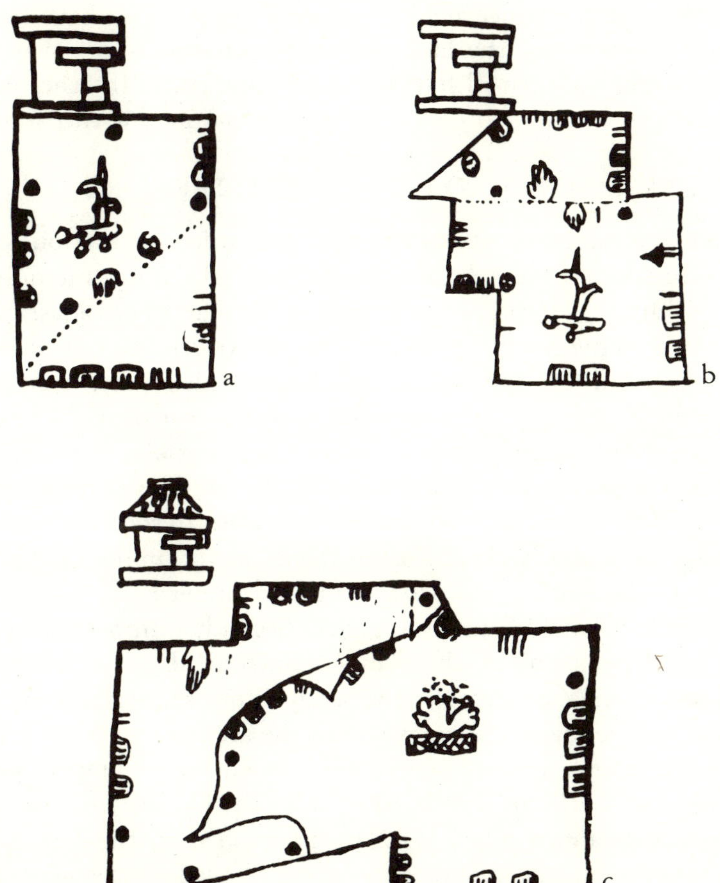

Fig. 5.4.   Land subdivision conventions from the Códice de Santa María Asunción (*a* f. 43v; *b* f. 44r; *c* f. 57v)

convention, which was subsequently replaced by the introduction of script.

In contrast to other native cadastral documents, both codices lack any systematic recording of paraje names. In the Codex Vergara none occur, and in the Asunción only one paraje glyph occurs, three times (ff. 43r, v). Since field location is reported to have been of primary importance, the lack of paraje names suggests that fields listed for each locality all fell within a single tract. In other words, the localities in the two codices were synonymous with parajes.

TLAHUELMANTLI CADASTRAL REGISTER

From the foregoing it is clear that the milcocoli sections of the two codices conveyed a great deal of cadastral data in hieroglyphic form. Additional information is portrayed in another cadastral register of the same fields, glossed "tlahuelma(n)tli," in which household heads and family heads within households are depicted in the same manner and approximate order as in the milcocoli.[7] The number of fields ascribed to each household is essentially the same, and there is a general correspondence in soil glyphs. There are significant differences between the two registers, however. In the tlahuelmantli, all fields are drawn with the same shape, as rectangles of the same size, and most with a protuberance in the upper right-hand corner (see table 5.1); field form is abstract. Second, numbers are placed in selected positions in the tlahuelmantli fields, not around the perimeter, as in the milcocoli. An analysis of the numbers indicates that the tlahuelmantli sections record the area of milcocoli fields in square quahuitl, using a positional line-and-dot notation system (Harvey and Williams 1980: 500–501). In this system lines equal one square quahuitl when they are positioned in the upper right protuberance, and twenty square quahuitl if placed elsewhere. Dots, which only occur in the center of the fields, equal 400 square quahuitl. When the field area is less than 400 square quahuitl a *cintli* glyph (ear of corn) appears at the top field margin. The tlahuelmantli registers, therefore, exhibit a second and completely distinct hieroglyphic convention for portraying cadastral information.

For present purposes it is important to note that native Texcocans included area as an item of cadastral data, whereas Spanish sources are moot on this point. The practice of depicting a field first with perimeter dimensions and approximate shape and then again in the abstract to record area continued at least into the late sixteenth century, as indicated by the Papeles de la Embajada Americana manuscripts. Therefore, it is curious that the practice was not noted by Spanish observers. The terminology does not even appear in dictionaries, such as Molina (1970) or Siméon (1977). For example, tlahuelmantli is defined as "smooth, leveled, or equalized," but not as area, although the semantic range could have included the concept. That tlahuelmantli does translate as "area" is demonstrated by context in figure 5.5; in this figure, drawn from the Papeles de la Embajada Americana, two fields appear, one recorded in the milcocoli convention and the other linked to it by a dotted line and glossed tlahuelmantli. The area of the field shown in the milcocoli convention may be roughly calculated (omitting quahuitl fractions) by multiplying length (17 quahuitl) by width (16 quahuitl). The area is thus 272 square quahuitl. The number depicted in the tlahuelmantli convention is also 272, which confirms the intent of the tlahuelmantli to show area.

The tlahuelmantli record of parcel areas poses several questions. For what purpose was field area recorded, and what might explain the convention of "red-flagging" by a cintli glyph those parcels whose area was less than 400 square quahuitl? For cadastral purposes the tlahuelmantli record is essentially redundant, because the milcocoli portions of both codices record "what land each one has." The function of the tlahuelmantli data more likely related to tribute. Deriving field area provides a mechanism for standardizing size of landholdings upon which to base an equitable tax assessment. For example, consider a hypothetical household **A** which has two plots of land, one 8 by 50 and another 10 by 40, and a household **B** which has one plot, 20 by 40. If assessments were based on number of holdings, household A would be taxed double that of B. On the other hand, if assessments were based on area, then both would be assessed equally, since each had 800 square units. Spanish sources relate that taxes were assessed on the basis of *medidas* (Hernán Cortés 1538: 542) or *suertes* (Martín Cortés 1563: 443) of land. The medida, "measure," may not have referred to numbers of parcels but to a standard areal unit. The base-20 arithmetical system logically sug-

Fig. 5.5.   The tlahuelmantli convention as an expression of field area (redrawn from the Papeles de la Embajada Americana, 3ᵃ Serie, Exp. 2–7, Reg. 10–3, Doc. 3)

gests a medida equivalent to 400 square units (20^2). As such a medida of land could have been of any shape and included several parcels. The hypothesis of a medida as 400 square units is reinforced in the Tepetlaoztoc codices by the use of the cintli glyph to distinguish properties whose area was less than 400 square quahuitl. The cintli glyph in effect denotes parcels whose area was less than the standard measure.

That the native Texcocans recorded the area of their individual fields also raises questions regarding the procedures and methods of cadastral survey. How were measurements taken? By what methods was area determined? There are numerous Nahuatl terms associated with measuring, among them terms for land surveyor (e.g., *tlaltamachiuani, tlalpouhqui*) and for correct or incorrect measurements (Lameiras 1974). However, little is known of native instruments beyond the use of ropes and measuring sticks. Since sophisticated survey techniques are implied by native hydraulic and construction achievements, a systematic review of textual and pictorial sources, similar to Rojas's work (this volume) on agricultural tools, would probably reveal a substantial inventory.

RECONSTRUCTION OF A CADASTRAL MAP

Native land records were produced in both map and register format. If the micocoli register is an accurate portrayal of land dimensions, then it should be possible to transform the data into map format. Chiauhtlan, one of the smallest hamlets in the Códice de Santa María Asunción, was selected to test this hypothesis. The transformation requires the following set of assumptions: (1) all fields were located in the paraje of Chiauhtlan; (2) the orientation of fields on the pages of the register reflects the surveyor's view of the field, so that the left-hand field boundary corresponds to the left vertical line in the drawing; (3) the order in which households appear on the register corresponds roughly to the spatial sequence in the landscape; (4) household landholdings might or might not be contiguous; (5) the shape of the fields in the manuscript is approximately correct; (6) similar soil types were contiguous, with heavier soils on lower slopes and lighter, or eroded soils above; (7) the aggregation of fields into approximately rectangular blocks with the long axis oriented upslope, as in Tepetlaoztoc today, would have been the prevalent field pattern also in the sixteenth century.

According to the census portion of the codex, forty-five people resided in eight households in Chiauhtlan. These households had twenty-six fields totaling 26,633 square quahuitl (16.3 ha). Two fields had sandy soil, seven were of sandy clay, and fourteen were of clay. One field of tepetate was in grass (*zacate*), and two others lack soil glyphs; they are presumed to be of sandy clay. The reconstructed cadastral map of Chiauhtlan is shown approximately to scale in figure 5.6. In the reconstruction the upper slope (top part of the map) is composed of fields of tepetate, sandy, and sandy clay soils, and the lower slope of clayey fields. Fields which have shapes suggestive of terraces are oriented so that the short side is upslope. The fields are aggregated into rectangular blocks. Within these constraints the milcocoli household sequence is only partially preserved in the hypothetical path of the surveyor/scribe. Since some households had properties with distinct soil types, it is highly unlikely that their fields would have been contiguous.

Two problems are apparent in the reconstruction: the lack of fit, and location of house sites. Several factors may explain lack of fit. First, the codex indicates only relative angular relationships between field sides, and thus in reconstruction, a variety of shapes can be generated. Second, on the basis of other sixteenth-century documents and the character of the zone today, it is known that fields were bounded by rows of maguey, nopal, and pirul trees, by paths, and by *zanjas* (channels cut into the soil or tepetate to direct water flow and to collect silt). Probably at least some of the area around the fields was occupied by such features. Also, it is rare to find two fields reported with similar side dimensions, and this suggests that field measurements were taken of the arable land inside the boundary features, rather than by including them or dividing them between contiguous fields.

As suggested above, house sites may have been located in the corners of quadrilateral fields, as well as on the margins of other irregularly shaped parcels. In both codices the grapheme for house is located above the first field in the household register. Many of the "calli" fields are irregularly shaped or have cutouts, suggesting that the household callalli ("house plot") was depicted first in the

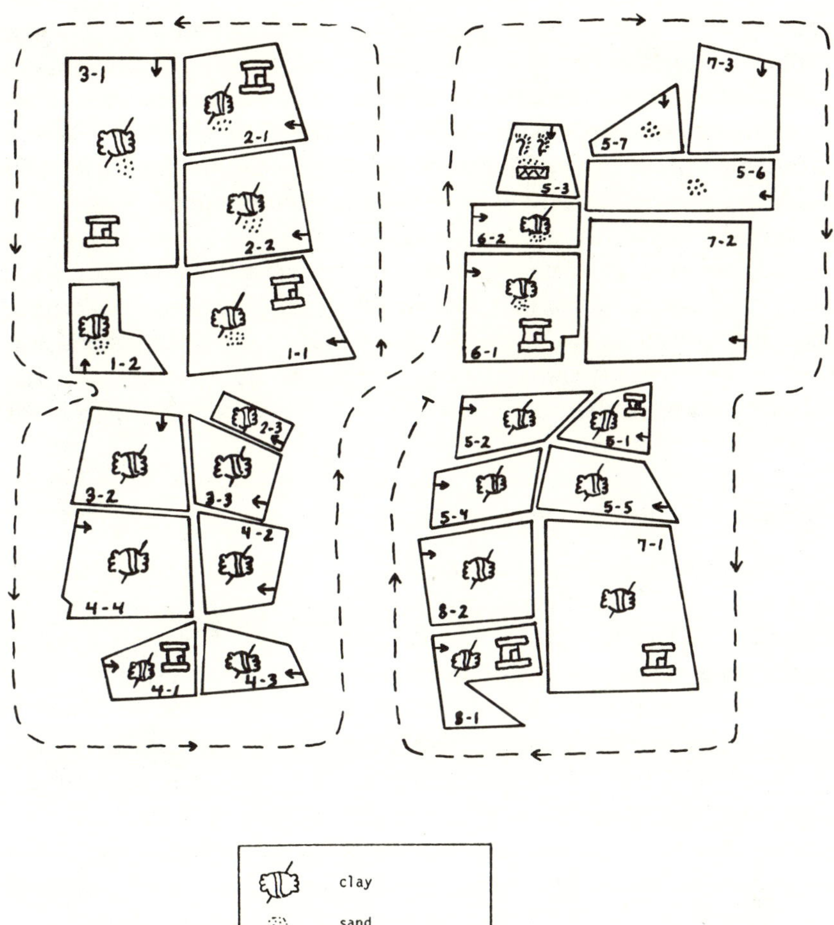

Fig. 5.6.   Reconstructed cadastral map of sixteenth-century Chiauhtlan showing field and settlement pattern and soil types. Households and household landholdings are indicated by numbers assigned according to the sequence in which they appear on the milcocoli register. Arrows indicate the presumed surveyor/scribe's view of each field.

register. One Nahuatl gloss referring to the first plot with a house grapheme includes the term *icalal* (f. 15v, Códice de Santa María Asunción), which strengthens this interpretation. On the other hand, in Chiauhtlan, many plots with the calli grapheme lack a cutout for a house site. Therefore, perhaps in some cases the calli grapheme may read "here are the lands of household X," instead of "here is the callalli of household X."

Since the micocoli data can be arranged spatially into a somewhat realistic field and settlement pattern, the assumptions concerning recording procedures and the distributions of landholdings and soil types underlying the transformation appear to be tenable. Also, the ability to transform the cadastral register into a cadastral map lends credence to the accuracy of the milcocoli data.

CONCLUSIONS

The cadastral portions of the Códice de Santa María Asunción and the Codex Vergara reveal much about native Texcocan methods and practices of cadastral surveying and recording. The measurement of field perimeters was precise to within fractions of a quahuitl. The area of agricultural fields was determined by some method which must have involved either mathematical calculation or grid surveying, the latter in turn requiring a method of accurate angle determination. Soils were classified, and the specific soil type of each field formed part of the cadastral record, which also included sociological, economic, and demographic data gathered on household heads. Glyphic conventions portraying these classes of data are summarized in table 5.1. The early Spanish chroniclers were impressed with the native cadastral records, and had they been aware of the full range of data depicted hieroglyphically, their descriptions of cadastral methods and procedures might have been more comprehensive.

The substantive content of the cadastral registers in the two codices permits the formulation of several generalizations which may apply to the interpretation of other cadastral manuscripts. First, in Acolhuacan there were at least two native pictographic conventions for depicting agricultural parcels—the milcocoli convention and the tlahuelmantli convention. When native drawings show fields in the milcocoli convention, the approximate shape and perimeter measurements are given. When the drawings are based on the tlahuelmantli convention, fields are shown in the abstract, as rectangles, and the numbers record the field area. Second, only the cadasters recorded in the milcocoli convention provide an accurate impression of the agricultural landscape. The milcocoli data from Tepetlaoztoc indicate that perfectly rectangular or square fields were extraordinarily rare in the mid-sixteenth century, and that irregularly shaped properties the norm. The realistic landscape portrayed by the milcocoli convention contrasts totally with fields depicted in the abstract, tlahuelmantli convention. Many land documents which appear to depict the outline and form of real properties may portray properties in the tlahuelmantli convention. Failure to distinguish between the two native cadastral conventions may lead to a misinterpretation of size of landholdings and give a false impression of the configuration of the sixteenth-century landscape. Further, the contrast between the milcocoli and tlahuelmantli conventions underscores the complexity not only of native cadastral abilities and practices, but also of their hieroglyphic writing.

NOTES

1. Research was supported by National Science Foundation Grant BNS 7725659. The facilities and support of the Centro Internacional de Mejoramiento de Maíz y Trigo during fieldwork are gratefully acknowledged.

2. "En el pueblo de Tepetlaoztoc que es de Joan Velazquez de Salazar está un monesterio de la orden de Santo Domingo en el qual rresiden dos rreligiosos sacerdotes y ambos lenguas mexicana y el uno sabe la otomi porque estas dos diferencias de lenguas está dividido" (AGI: México, 336A, Ramo 2, no. 104).

3. These glyphs have been interpreted erroneously by Castillo F. (1972b: 72) to signify crops sown.

4. Shaded fields occur on ff. 10v, 14v, 24r, 28v, 29v, 30r, 38v, 57v, 59r, 62r, 64v, 65r, and 66r of the Códice de Santa María Asunción. None appear in the Codex Vergara.

5. Fields partially or entirely outlined in red occur in Cuauhtepoztla (two cases) ff. 17v, 21r; in Huisnahuac (seven cases) ff. 31r, v; and in Tlanchiuhca (twenty-seven cases) ff. 56r, v; 57r, v; 69r, v; 70r, v. The red xacalli appears in Tlanchiuhca, f. 69r. In addition, the name glyph of Juan Temitl (ff. 12v and 22r) and part of the Tlantozcac place glyph (48r) are colored red. What accounts for this selectivity remains unresolved.

6. An analysis of the amount and distribution of noble lands in the Asunción and Vergara codices and their relationship to the Codex Kingsborough is in progress. Interestingly, Tlanchiuhca, the locality which has the greatest number of noble properties, is not among the Kingsborough place names.

7. An exact transcription of the term as it appears in the codices is "tlahuelmatli," but in the Texcocan document shown in figure 5.5, the term is written "tlahuelmantli." Lack of the nasal in the Tepetlaoztoc codices may reflect a local dialect (Luis Reyes, personal communication). Further, it is found in free variation in place name glosses in the Códice de Santa María Asunción, e.g., Çapontla/Çapotla and Tlantozcac/Tlatozcac.

REFERENCES

AGI (Archivo General de Indias, Seville)
         México, 336A,Ramo 2, no. 104.
Anderson, Arthur J. O, Frances Berdan, and James Lockhart
1976   Beyond the Codices: The Nahua View of Colonial Mexico. Berkeley: University of California Press.
Castillo F., Victor M.
1972a   Unidades nahuas de medida. Estudios de Cultura Náhuatl, 10. México: UNAM, Instituto de Investigaciones Históricas.
1972b   Estructura económica de la sociedad mexica según las fuentes documentales. México: UNAM, Instituto de Investigaciones Históricas.
Clavigero, Francisco J.
1944   Historia antigua de México. Vol. 2. Joaquín de Mora, trans. México: Editorial Delfin.
Cline, Howard F.
1966   The Oztoticpac Lands Map of Texcoco, 1540. Quarterly Journal of the Library of Congress 23: 77–115.

Codex Vergara
>Codex Vergara. Mss. Mexicains 37–39. Paris: Bibliothèque Nationale.

Códice de Santa María Asunción
>Códice de Santa María Asunción. Apeo y deslinde de tierras (de los terrenos) de Santa María Asunción. Mss. 1497 bis. México: Biblioteca Nacional.

Compañía Mexicana de Aerofoto
1977   Compañía Mexicana de Aerofoto, Valley of Mexico Roll 3 (November).

Cortés, Hernán
1538   Carta al consejo de Indias. *In* Colección de documentos inéditos, relativos al descubrimiento . . . , sacados de los archivos del reino, y muy especialmente del de Indias. Vol. 3. pp. 535–45. Madrid: Imprenta Manuel B. de Quirós.

Cortés, Martín
1563   Carta al Rey D. Felipe II, 10 de Octubre, 1563. *In* Colección de documentos inéditos, relativos al descubrimiento . . . , sacados de los archivos del reino, y muy especialmente del de Indias. Vol. 4. pp. 440–62. Madrid: Imprenta Manuel B. de Quirós.

Gibson, Charles
1964   The Aztecs under Spanish Rule. Stanford: Stanford University Press.

Glass, John B.
1975   A Survey of Native Middle American Pictorial Manuscripts. *In* Handbook of Middle American Indians. Vol. 14. pp. 3–80. Robert Wauchope, ed. Austin: University of Texas Press.

Harvey, H. R., and Barbara J. Williams
1980   Aztec Arithmetic: Positional Notation and Area Calculation. Science 210: 499–505. (Reprinted in Ciencia y desarrollo 38 [1981]: 5–14).

Ixtlilxóchitl, Fernando de Alva
1952   Obras históricas. Vol. 2. México: Editorial Nacional.

Lameiras, Brigitte B. de
1974   Terminología agrohidráulica prehispánica nahua. México: INAH Colección Científica, 13.

Molina, Alonso de
1970   Vocabulario en lengua castellana y mexicana. México: Porrúa.

Orozco y Berra, Manuel
1960   Historia antigua de la conquista de México. México: Porrúa.

Papeles de la Embajada Americana
         Papeles de la Embajada Americana, 3ª Series, Exp. 2–7, Reg.
         10–3, Doc. 3. México: Museo Nacional de Antropología–
         Archivo Histórico.

Parsons, Jeffrey R.
1971   Prehistoric Settlement Patterns in the Texcocan Region, Mex-
         ico. Memoirs of the Museum of Anthropology, University of
         Michigan, 3.

Paso y Troncoso
1912   Códice Kingsborough. Memorial de los Indios de Tepetlaoztoc
         al monarca español contra los encomenderos del pueblo. Mad-
         rid: Hauser y Menet.

Prem, Hanns J.
1974   Matrícula de Huexotzinco. Ms. Mex. 387 der Bibliothèque
         Nationale, Paris. Graz, Austria: Akademische Druck- und
         Verlagsanstalt.

Ramírez Fragment
         Cadastral Fragment of the Ramírez Collection, Museo Na-
         cional de Antropología–Archivo Histórico, Col. Antig 213.
         México.

Seler, Eduard
1904   The Mexican Picture Writings of Alexander von Humboldt.
         Bureau of American Ethnology, Bulletin 28: 127–229.

Siméon, Rémi
1977   Diccionario de la lengua náhuatl o mexicana. Josefina Oliva
         de Coll, trans. México: Siglo Veintiuno.

Torquemada, Juan de
1943   Los veinte i un libros rituales i monarquía indiana. Vol. 2.
         México: Salvador Chavez Hayhoe.

Williams, Barbara J.
1980a   Aztec Soil Classification and Land Tenure. Actes du XLIIe
         Congrès International des Américanistes, 9. pp. 165–75. Paris:
         Société des Américanistes.
1980b   Náhuatl Soil Glyphs from the Códice de Santa María Asunción.
         Actes du XLIIe Congrès International des Américanistes, 7.
         pp. 27–37. Paris: Société des Américanistes.
1980c   Pictorial Representation of Soils in the Valley of Mexico: Evi-
         dence from the Codex Vergara. Geoscience and Man 21: 51–
         62.

Zorita, Alonso de
1963   Life and Labor in Ancient Mexico: The Brief and Summary
            Relation of the Lords of New Spain. Benjamin Keen, trans.
            and intro. New Brunswick: Rutgers University Press.

6

Household Organization in the Texcocan Heartland:

The Evidence in the Codex Vergara

Jerome A. Offner

The Codex Vergara, like its companion, the Códice de Santa María Asunción, depicts Aztec domestic organization in unparalleled detail. In a recent study of Texcocan law and politics (Offner 1979: 435–64, Appendix C), I analyzed the genealogical sections of the Codex Vergara and presented them in tabular form. The illustrations of household organization in the Vergara provided a large number of fresh perspectives on Aztec domestic organization and kinship behavior as well as on land tenure and other types of law; some of these new perspectives will be presented in this essay.[1]

THE PROVENIENCE OF THE CODEX VERGARA

The Codex Vergara, located in the Bibliothèque Nationale de Paris, France, consists of fifty-five leaves of European paper measuring thirty-one by twenty-two centimeters; its companion, the Códice de Santa María Asunción, located in the Biblioteca Nacional de México, consists of eighty leaves of European paper measuring thirty-one by twenty-one centimeters. The initial leaf of each is now missing, but the first leaf of the Asunción is preserved on microfilm (e.g., Museo Nacional de Antropología, Archivo Histórico: Serie Biblioteca Benjamin Franklin, rollo 4, exp. 2). The final leaf of each codex contains the signature of one Pedro Vásquez de Vergara, and the first leaf of the Asunción also contains his signature, along with a statement that the order of things contained in the document is to be guarded for a locality named Chimalpan, which does not appear in the Asunción itself. Numerous similarities in style and content also indicate that the documents may have a common origin (Glass and Robertson 1975: 88, 229). In addition, Nicholson (1973: 27–32) has noted that the complex glyphs in both documents are typical of the style of indigenous early sixteenth-century Acolhuacan.

Several pieces of evidence link the Vergara directly with Tepetlaoztoc in Acolhuacan. Tepetlaoztoc is named twice in the Vergara (f. 21r, f. 22r), and Gibson (1964: 543, citing AGN: Mercedes 2, f. 209v–219v) mentions that the Spanish colonial official, Pedro Vásquez de Vergara was ordered to go to Tepetlaoztoc in 1543. Vergara's portrait and name also appear in the Codex Kingsborough, which surely is from Tepetlaoztoc; on f. 229r, it is reported that Vergara came to Tepetlaoztoc to reduce the service and tribute demands of the agents of the *encomendero* upon the native population; further evidence on f. 242v implies that he visited and taxed Tepetlaoztoc more than one time.

Archival data confirm that records such as the Vergara existed in sixteenth-century Tepetlaoztoc; the celebrated legal case which involved Tepetlaoztoc and its rapacious encomendero family (AGI: Justicia 151: 68r–75r; Justicia 159: 41v–45v) contains a detailed description of an indigenous pictorial document which, when "translated," was shown to contain separate population counts of married tributaries, carpenters, single male tributaries, single females, young male and female tributaries, boys and girls, and orphans, along with other information of the type found in the Codex Vergara.

Finally, ethnographic fieldwork and local archival research has recently shown that both the Códice de Santa María Asunción and the Codex Vergara pertain to identifiable barrios in Tepetlaoztoc (Harvey and Williams 1980: 499).

THE STRUCTURE OF THE CODEX VERGARA

The Vergara has fifteen sections which detail the population and landholdings of five territorial units: (1) Callatlaxoxiuhco, (2) Topotitla, (3) Teocaltitla, (4) Patlachiuhca, and (5) Texcalticpac. Each unit has a *tlacatlacuiloli* ("register of people"; ff. 2r–6r; 21v–22r; 26v–27r; 33r–34r; 38v–42r) which depicts the residents of each household in the unit, and two cadastral land registers, one always glossed *milcocoli* (ff. 6v–13v; 22v–24r; 27v–30r; 34v–36r; 42v–49r), the other glossed *tlahuelmantli* (ff. 14r–21r; 24v–26r; 30v–32v; 36v–38r; except for Texcalticpac, glossed milcocoli). Milcocoli sections are concerned with perimeter measurements of land parcels, while tlahuelmantli sections deal with the surface areas of the fields (Williams, this volume; Harvey and Williams 1980: 500).

If attention is directed to the sections glossed tlacatlacuiloli ("register of people"), it is seen that five households are typically depicted on each side of each leaf (see figure 6.1). These are arranged in a vertical column; each row begins with the name glyph of the household head and is followed by a conventional portrayal of a house, the head of the household head, and a variable number of human heads or upper bodies with heads. Red lines indicating genealogical relationship usually connect the household head with some or all of the other figures; Nahuatl glosses sometimes specify what these relationships are. Some figures are not connected to the household head by red lines; this would seem to indicate that they are not consanguineal kin; nevertheless, glosses occasionally specify a consanguineal or affinal relationship to the household head.

The figures of the household members are drawn so that the following types of people may be differentiated (Nahuatl and Spanish glosses support these identifications): (1) old men, shown with wrinkled faces; (2) old women, shown with wrinkled faces and the married woman's hairdo; (3) males, other than children; (4) boys, with hair shorter than that of older males; (5) women with the married hairdo; (6) women without the married hairdo (single women);

Fig. 6.1   Codex Vergara, ff. 2v–3r, with ten households. The names of persons whose faces have been darkened—probably as an indication of death—are underlined. *Folio 2v:1—Marcos Tochtli,* with his wife, *Francisca,* daughter, Ana, son, *Antonio,* and infant son, *Andres.* This nuclear family is a Type 1 household. *Folio 2v:2—Pedro Techin,* with his wife, *Juana,* and daughter, Ysabel. His aunt ("ynahui"), *Ana* is linked directly to the house by a red line. Also a member of the household is *Martin Xochihua,* a single male of tributary age. This household, with a nuclear family, head's aunt, and an (apparently) unrelated male is Type 3. *Folio 2v:3*——Juan Quauhxilotl with his wife, Maria, son, Domingo, unnamed daughter, and infant child "cuemetz." Also depicted is Juan's mother ("ynaçin"), Maria. This household, with a nuclear family and head's mother is Type 3. *Folio 2v:4—*Juan Chiquitl with his wife, Juana. Also shown is Luis Quiauh (with footprint underneath) with his wife, Maria, and and son, Philipe. These two (apparently) unrelated families form a Type 8 household. *Folio 2v:5—*Domingo Coxcox with his wife, Juana, and daughter, Lucia. This nuclear family is a Type 1 household (continued p. 132).

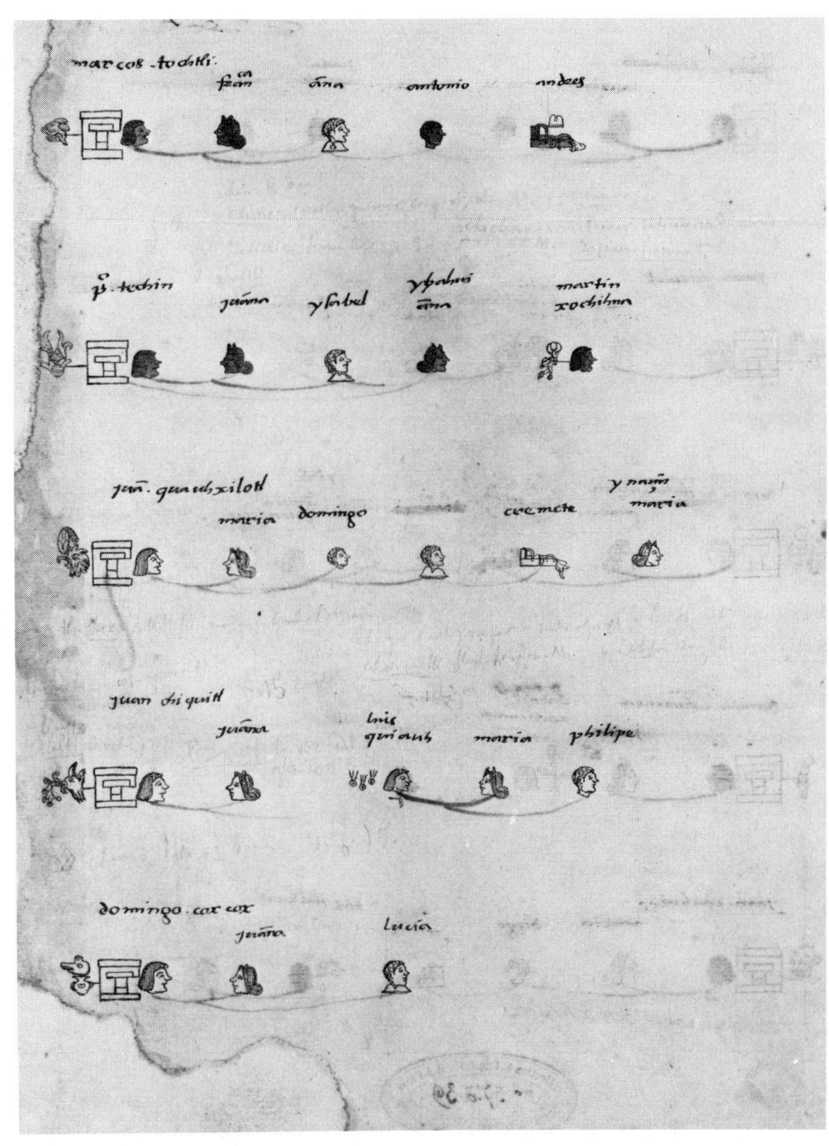

Figure 6.1

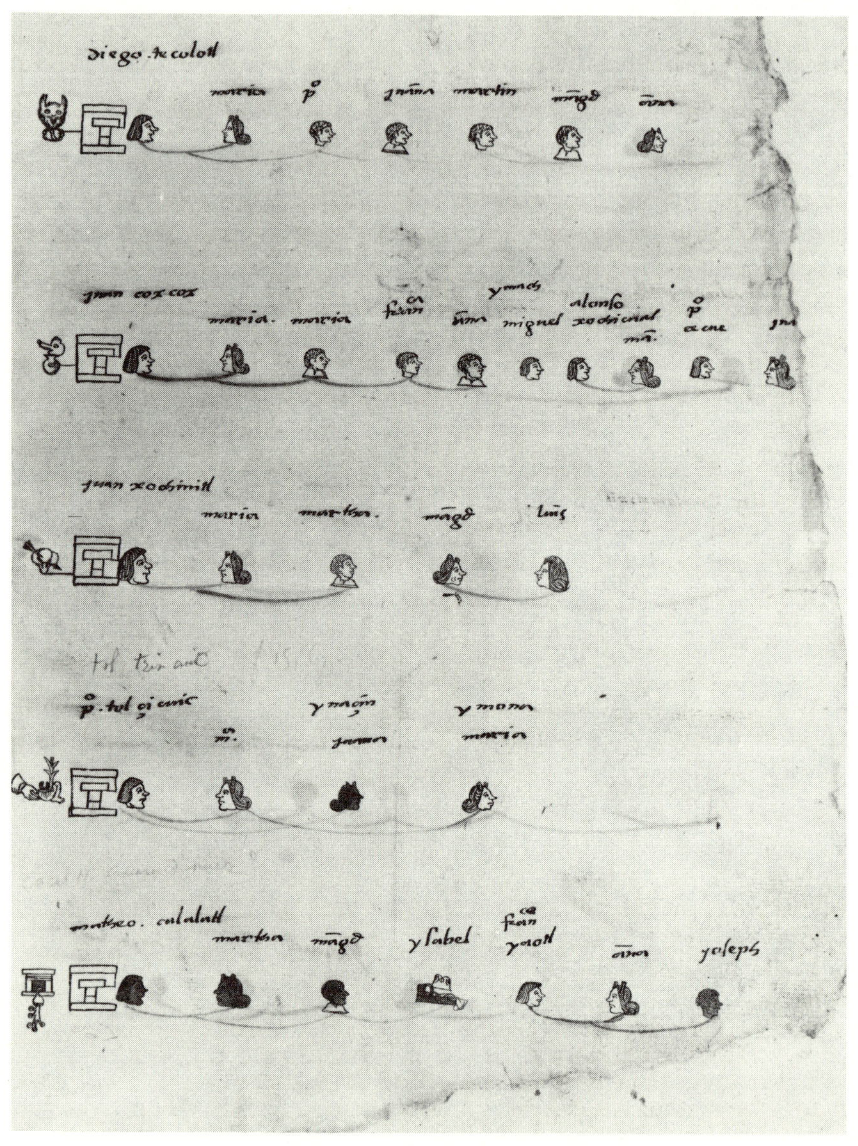

Figure 6.1 continued

Fig. 6.1 (continued) *Folio 3r:1*—Diego Tecolotl, with his wife, Maria, son Pedro, daughter Juana, son Martin, and daughter Magdalena. Also depicted is an (apparently) unrelated old woman, Ana. This nuclear family with an unrelated old woman constitutes a Type 3 household. *Folio 3r:2*—Juan Coxcox with his wife, Maria, daughter Maria, son, Francisco, and daughter Ana. Also shown is his nephew ("ymach"), Miguel, along with two (apparently) unrelated nuclear families— Alonso Xochicual and his wife, Maria, and Pedro Cecue and his wife, Juana. This complex household is Type 2 as well as Type 8. *Folio 3r:3*—Juan Xochimitl with his wife, Maria, and daughter, Martha. Also shown are two figures—one an old woman, Magdalena (with a footprint underneath), the other a young male of tributary age, Luis. These figures may represent a widow and her son, although the fact that they face each other tends to indicate that they are married. This household, made up of a nuclear family and an (apparently) unrelated woman with her son or husband is a provisional Type 3. *Folio 3r:4*— Pedro Tolçicuic with his wife, Maria, mother ("ynaçin"), *Juana,* and mother-in-law ("ymona"), Maria. Note that his mother, Juana, is linked directly to the house by a red line. This household is Type 3. *Folio 3r:5*—Matheo Calalatl with his wife, *Martha,* daughter, *Magdalena,* and infant daughter, *Ysabel.* Also shown is an (apparently) unrelated nuclear family composed of Francisco Yaotl, his wife, Ana, and son, *Joseph.* These two nuclear families make up a Type 8 household.

(7) girls, with short hair and part of their upper torso; and (8) infants of either sex, shown on cradle boards. Spouses are always shown with their mates facing them, and certain figures are glossed as widows, (sing. *icnocihuatl*), old women (*ilamaçin*), and orphans (sing. *icnotl*).

Every household head is also found in each of the two cadastral sections associated with his unit; the first plot of land associated with a household head invariably contains a house; other members of the genealogical section also appear in the cadastral sections, but houses are not depicted on their lands. Still other figures are shown with land in the cadastral sections but do not appear at all in the genealogical sections; their lands do not contain houses (perhaps these are the *renteros,* "renters," mentioned in some land tenure sources). However, no members of the genealogical sections appear as landholders in units other than their own.

TIME DEPTH IN THE CODEX VERGARA

The Codex Vergara was undoubtedly used for a number of years after its composition, as was the Asunción; however, its pictorial content is remarkably stable. Only one significant erasure exists in the document; the house of Juan Ycnotl (26v:5) contained Juan, his mother, Ana, his older brother, Diego Nauhyotl, and Diego's wife and daughter. On ff. 28r and 31r, the house lot of Juan is erased and it reappears in place of an erasure as the first of Diego's plots of land (ff. 29v, 32v). This may reflect fraternal succession to the position of the household head, but it may also be a scribal error which was at once corrected.

There are two other probable indications of time depth in the Vergara: the blackening of faces by pigment and eighteen footprint symbols. The blackening of faces may be an indication of death; it is found also in the Asunción. For example, Diego, the apparent son of tributary age of the household head Martín Miton (40v:1) may have become an orphan (*icnotl*)—as he is glossed—upon the death of his parents, whose faces are darkened. Although of tributary age, he held no land separately at the time of the Vergara's composition; he probably maintained himself and his two sisters with the land allotted to his father. While it seems impossible to demonstrate conclusively that the blackening of faces is an indication of death, it has been interpreted elsewhere as such (Williams 1980: 52).

The footprint symbols are also puzzling; they appear underneath eighteen individuals. Six of these (2r:1; 2r:2; 2v:4; 3v:3; 6r:3; 40r:5) are the male heads of nuclear families within a household, but they are never the household head. One (3r:3) is an old woman apparently not related to the other members of the household; three are male tributaries related in some unspecified way to the household head (21v:3 [two individuals]; 21v:4); three are siblings-in-law of the household head (21v:5, "iuepol"; 26v:4 and 27r:4, "itex"); one is the daughter of a head of a nuclear family within a household (40r:1). Two are sisters of the household head (6r:3; 40v:4); one is a stepson of the household head (41r:3), and one is the niece of the household head (40r:5, "ymachuac"). The footprints certainly do not appear to correlate with rights to land at the time of the composition of the Vergara; some who are marked with the footprint possess land (e.g., 2r:1) but most do not.

The footprints may well indicate a change of residence; Williams (personal communication) has pointed out that one individual marked with a footprint in the Códice de Santa María Asunción (f. 53r, bottom) has a toponymic glyph below him which appears to indicate that he changed his residence to another town or ward. If it is assumed that the footprint symbol has the same meaning in the Codex Vergara, a number of interesting insights into the stability of domestic organization in Tepetlaoztoc result. These will be discussed later; here it should be noted that an additional piece of information in the Vergara argues for the change of residence idea. On f. 3v:3, the gloss "ypalnemi" ("he lives with him") appears over an individual with a footprint; this appears to be a later written correction of the footprint symbol.

In conclusion, although there are substantial indications that the Vergara was used for a number of years after its composition, only a few insights into the diachronic development of household organization are obtainable. In fortunate contrast, the apparent stability of the pictorial content allows for intensive synchronic investigation of household organization for the time of the composition of the document.

HOUSEHOLD ORGANIZATION IN THE
CODEX VERGARA

There are ninety-five households in the Codex Vergara's genealogical sections. The core of each household was the nuclear family of procreation of the household head with adopted and/or stepchildren, or the remnants of such families. Households exhibiting solely these features have been designated Type 1 (see table 6.1); they are twenty-eight in number and constitute 29.5 percent of the sample. Certain other relatives and non-relatives attached themselves to this core. These often included niblings and one of their widowed parents; the arrangements often seem to have amounted to the practice of the levirate.[2] In addition, the ideal of Aztec kinship behavior, reported in the Sahagún (Tenochcan/Tlatelolcan) materials (e.g., Paso y Troncoso 1905–7: VI, 93r, n. 9, and note in left margin; see also Offner 1979: 413–15), that an uncle should house his orphaned nephews and nieces, seems also to have been an ideal of kinship behavior in Tepetlaoztoc. Such households, augmented by the head's brother's wife or sibling and/or their children, will be designated Type 2. Type 2 households, which included the spouse or the spouse and children of a nephew or niece, will be designated Type 2a. Type 2 and 2a households are ten in number and comprise 10.5 percent of the sample.

Nuclear families of heads augmented by unmarried or widowed consanguineal and/or affinal relatives and/or non-relatives, not included in Type 2, will be designated Type 3; they constitute 22 percent of the sample. Type 4 includes households in which the head is single or widowed, and in which there are related and/or unrelated nuclear families; there are only six such households. If the households containing only one or no married couple are extracted from Types 1 through 4, it is found that they number fiftynine, or approximately 62 percent of all of the households in the Codex Vergara; certainly such household organization is radically different from the type of organization reported by Calnek (1972, 1974, 1976) for Tenochtitlan, where groups of married siblings often resided together.

Coresidence by married siblings does occur in at least three instances in the Vergara; these are Type 5 households. Type 6 house-

Table 6.1. Types of Household Organization

	Type 1	Type 2	Type 3	Type 4	Type 5	Type 6	Type 7	Type 8
	2v:1[a]	2r:4	2v:2	3v:5	5r:1	34r:1	2r:3	2r:1
	2v:5	3r:2	2v:3	4r:5	26v:1	34r:4	26v:2	2r:2
	3v:1	5r:3	3r:1	26v:5	27r:1	38v:1	38v:3	2r:5
	3v:2	21v:1	3r:3	27r:2		38v:5		2v:4
	3v:4	21v:2	3r:4	39r:3		40r:2		3r:2[c]
	4r:2	21v:5	5r:4	41v:4		40r:5[a]		3r:5
	4r:3	22r:1[b]	6r:1			41r:4[a]		3v:3
	4r:4	39v:2	21v:3					4r:1
	6r:2		21v:4					5r:2
	33r:2	Type 2a	22r:2					6r:3
	33v:2		22r:3					26v:3
	33v:3	22r:1	22r:4					33r:1
	33v:4	40r:5	26v:4					33v:5
	34r:2	41r:4	33r:3					39v:4
	34r:3		33v:1					40r:1
	38v:2		38v:4					40r:3
	39r:1		39v:1					40r:4
	39r:2		40v:4					40v:5
	39v:3		41r:1					41v:1
	39v:5		41v:2					42r:1
	40v:1		41v:3					
	40v:2							
	40v:3							
	41r:2							
	41r:3							
	41r:5							
	41v:5							
	42r:2							
Total	28	10	21	6	3	7	3	20
%	29.5%	10.5%	22%	6%	3%	7%	3%	21%

[a]2v:1 indicates folio 2, verso, household depicted in row 1, etc.
[b]Also Type 2a
[c]Also Type 2

holds, in which two consanguineally related families live together, number seven; some members of Type 6 may actually be Type 5. Still other households include the household head's nuclear family plus a nuclear family which appears to be related to the head; these three households have been designated Type 7.

Finally, there are some twenty households made up of the head's nuclear family plus a nuclear family which, because it is not connected to the head by a red line, or because there are no glosses which specify its relationship to the head, is assumed to be unrelated to the head; these twenty households are Type 8. Consequently, while the nuclear family was clearly the predominant form of household organization, multifamily organization was not rare at Tepetlaoztoc.

There are an average of 6.0 persons and 1.3 married couples per household in the Codex Vergara. This sort of household organization contrasts strongly with the multifamily organization described by Calnek from Tenochtitlan, as well as with the household organization of Tepetlaoztoc's near neighbor, Acolman, where contact-period households typically contained "six or seven married Indians, not counting the bachelors" (Paso y Troncoso 1905[6]: 211). The Vergara data do, however, compare closely with household organization in Tepoztlan as reported by Carrasco. In Tepoztlan there were an average of 5.4 persons and 1.4 married couples per household (Carrasco 1971: 368–69), and 54 percent of the households were nuclear families. In areas outside of Tepoztlan proper these figures were slightly higher. The Codex Vergara data, then, are not without precedent and seem fully reliable as interpreted.

Available indications of the physical size of houses and houselots in the Tepetlaoztoc region suggest a predominance of nuclear families or small extended families. Williams (personal communication) and Parsons (1971: 336, tlatel 460 of Tx-A-24) have described a small residential structure measuring 2.5 × 1.8 indigenous *brazas* (of 2.5 m), and Williams (this volume; personal communication) has noted that many agricultural fields in the Codex Vergara and the Códice de Santa María Asunción are depicted as quadrilaterals, but with one corner "cut out." These "cutouts" range in size from five to ten indigenous brazas (12 to 25 m) on a side and are probably representations of houselots. Such houselots would allow space for a garden and/or corral, an arrangement often found today in the barrio of Asunción Cuauhtepoztla, where walls commonly enclose the house sites and adjacent gardens and corrals. Obviously, however, intensive archaeological investigation is required to produce a more secure estimation of Tepetlaoztoc house and houselot size in Aztec times.

In closing this discussion of household organization, the individuals mentioned above who were marked with footprints and who thus seem to have left their homes and wards should be recalled, since their actions provide insight into the internal dynamics of Tepetlaoztoc households. The principal motivation for leaving a household may well have been to set up one's own household, free from the domination of the former household head. Thus, six male heads of secondary nuclear families appear to leave to found their own households; four single male tributaries also leave, as do the stepson of a household head and two brothers-in-law of household heads. Male authority relations in Tepetlaoztoc seem to have been quite volatile, and this seems to have led to fissioning of many of the more complex households. A nuclear family household may well have been the goal of younger males in the Tepetlaoztoc area. The Códice de Santa María Asunción provides similar information. Of the eight individuals with footprints in that document (ff. 4r, 33r, 52r, 53r, 54r, 55r), six are males in a subordinate position in their households.

POINTS OF JURISPRUDENCE IN TEPETLAOZTOC

Pomar's (1941: 25–26) description of inheritance and succession among nonnobles in Texcoco accords with what is depicted in the Codex Vergara. In Texcoco the estate of the deceased was divided "equally" among the deceased's offspring, and birth order was unimportant in determining the deceased's successor. In the Vergara there is certainly no indication that groups of siblings lived together to preserve their parents' estates; instead, one child generally appears to have inherited the house while the others married out and founded their own houses. Residence, then, appears to have been predominantly neolocal, although patrilocal residence was no doubt also very common. Patrilocal residence could be patriuxorilocal (34r:1;

38v:1?; 40r:2?) or patrivirilocal (34r:4?; 38v:5?). On the matter of succession, younger (27r:1; 26v:5?) as well as older (41r:1; 5r:1) brothers could be household heads according to what is depicted in the Vergara.

Examination of the types of household heads in the Codex Vergara provides significant insights into domestic, political, and legal organization in Tepetlaoztoc. As Pospisil (1971: 97–126) has pointed out, every functioning subgroup in a society must have a legal system to induce conformity and to assure its cohesiveness and very existence; legal systems of the same scale of inclusiveness together constitute a legal level. Three levels are discernible in the Codex Vergara: nuclear family, household, and ward.

On the level of the household, the household head was usually a male who possessed land and was a member of the household's senior generation. There are, however, notable exceptions to these generalizations. Sons of living mothers were most often (e.g., 2v:3; 3r:4; 5r:3) but not always (40v:3) the head of the household. Widowed (e.g., 4r:4; 4r:5; 5r:4) or even married women (e.g., 33v:1; 38v:3) could also be household heads, although in such cases the household's land tends to appear with the husband's glyph. Finally, consanguineal junior male relations of elderly women could also be household heads (e.g., 2v:2).

In the cadastral sections of the Vergara, land is shown assigned to household heads; this would indicate that they were responsible for the management of agricultural activities and for the payment of tribute (it is known that this is true of other areas in Central Mexico; see Gómara 1826[2]: 205). Household heads apparently supervised the agricultural activities of all other nuclear families or persons in the household, except in a number of cases where heads of nuclear families who are not household heads are shown with land of their own (e.g., 2r:1; 2r:2), and where single males are depicted as landholders (e.g., 21v:3). Thus, in some households the nuclear families of which the household head was not a member appear to have had considerable economic (and therefore probably also legal and political) independence. In some cases, apparently, this independence became absolute, as households fissioned into two nuclear families.

A most intriguing detail of property law is visible in the Codex

Vergara (see figure 6.1, which is f. 2v–3r). In several instances the indigenous artist seems to have been concerned to show that certain individuals had some type of direct linkage to the house in which they resided, which was not mediated through the household head; this is shown by a red connecting line from a given figure directly to a given house. For example, mothers of household heads are shown linked to the house (e.g., 3r:4; 5r:3; 39r:3; cf. also the *ahuitl,* "parent's sister," of 2v:2); this seems to indicate that they had rights in the house upon which the household head could not infringe. Sometimes mothers of heads are not shown linked to the house (e.g., 2v:3); this may indicate that residence was neolocal and that the mother therefore had no absolute rights in the house. Similarly, husbands of female household heads also may not have had any absolute rights to the house in which they resided.

Certainly the gross generalizations about corporate ownership of and individual usufruct rights in *calpullalli* ("ward land") typically found in the sources do not do justice to the complexity of property rights within the *calpultin* ("wards"). For example, the Codex Vergara data just mentioned suggest strongly that possession of housesites and houses was governed by different legal dispositions than was tenure of agricultural lands. Some household heads do not seem to have exclusive or primary rights to the houses or housesites in which they reside, but are the people to whom the household's land is assigned; and husbands of female household heads most often hold the land assigned to the household, while the female household head does not.

A passage in the Florentine Codex (Dibble and Anderson 1950–69[6]: 227) further attests to the complexity of legal rights involving commoners' lands and houses and commoners' readiness to defend those rights. The following saying was reportedly common in Aztec society: "My task is to guard turkeys. Shall I peck at those who peck at one another?" The indigenous informant explains the saying in this manner:

> The turkey guardian does not bring it about that turkeys
> constantly peck at one another, for they simply fight among
> themselves. . . . Hence it was well said when common folk
> contend, when they fight among themselves over perhaps their
> lands, their houses or something. The leaders do not stir them

up; the commoners purely of their own accord contend among
themselves, fight among themselves.

The Aztecs appear to have been a dynamic and litigious people; the
sophistication of their legal systems and the differences between the
legal systems of the various Aztec states have been greatly under-
estimated (see Offner 1979). Monolithic views of a simplistic individual usufruct, communal tenure of land by all commoners in
Central Mexico, now appear to be misleading (see Offner 1981;
Harvey, this volume).

THE LEGAL LEVEL OF THE CALPULLI

Very little of the governing structure of the calpulli ("ward")
corporation is visible in the Codex Vergara. However, in another
work dealing with different data (Offner 1979: 355–473), I have
not only pointed out the utter lack of evidence for a descent principle
in Aztec society—thus ruling out the existence of calpulli-clans—
but I have also demonstrated that the *calpultin* ("wards") were ruled
by officials responsible to higher legal and political levels within
the state. The calpultin were undoubtedly not the center of legal
or political power in Aztec society. Certainly there is no indication
in the Vergara of organization by descent groups or portions of
descent groups, or even of organization by groups of closely related
households.

In contrast, in view of the standard five households per page
found in the Codex Vergara, the report describing the internal
organization of the Aztec society which mentions the existence of
macuiltecpanpixque ("centurions") and *centecpanpixque* ("scorekeepers"),
who were in charge respectively of groups of one hundred houses
and twenty houses each, bears some consideration (Paso y Troncoso
1939–42[14]: 145–48). Four pages of the Vergara would contain
twenty households, so that Tepetlaoztoc might well have had a type
of organization utilizing macuiltecpanpixque and centecpanpixque.

The evidence in the Codex Vergara also indicates that calpultin
were not ethnically unitary, since two different types of houses are
shown in each of two localities. The typical house in the Vergara
is a flat-roofed adobe structure; there are, however, fifteen houses
with a pointed thatched roof (Patlachiuhca 33v:3, 4, 5; 34r:1, 2,

3, 4; Texcalticpac 39r:2, 3; 41r:3, 4, 5; 41v:1, 2, 5). The difference in construction methods may be due to an ethnic difference; the thatched-roof house employed as part of the symbol for the town Otompan on the Mapa Quinatzin, leaf 2, comes immediately to mind; the pointed thatched-roof houses might have been occupied by Otomí.

However, the evidence for this is not conclusive, since the variation in household architecture is not associated with a marked variation in household composition, which one might expect to find among different ethnic groups; there are an average of 6.9 persons and 1.3 married couples per household in the pointed thatched-roof houses, figures which are very close to the overall average for the Vergara. Still, the evidence is strongly suggestive of multiple ethnic groups, perhaps residentially segregated in Tepetlaoztoc (they occur in groups in the Vergara). The internal politics of the calpultin must have been quite complex and volatile.

Finally, the locality of Topotitla in the Vergara appears to have been the property (and perhaps the *pillalli,* "nobles' land") of one don Agustín de Rojas. In Tepoztlan, Carrasco found that households under the authority of the *cacique* (indigenous ruler) were larger and contained more married couples than other households. However, the Topotitla's households do not contain the largest number of tributaries per household, nor the largest number of people per household, nor the largest number of married couples per household in the Codex Vergara (see table 6.2).

CONCLUSION

The Codex Vergara provides one of the most detailed depictions extant of the household and ward organization of an Aztec society. It is this heretofore unexploited information in the Vergara which exposes the inadequacies in much of our current understanding of the legal and political structuring of, and household and family organization within, the Aztec calpulli ("ward"). Traditional published sources provide us only with the general outlines of what calpultin, households, and families were like; available descriptions of household organization, inheritance, land tenure, and other social, political, and legal structures are clearly inadequate and must

Table 6.2. Household Organizational Statistics

Locality	House-holds	Popu-lation	Married Couples	Pop/ hshld	Couples/ hshld
Callatlaxoxiuhco	32	174	43	5.44	1.34
Topotitla	9	59	10	6.56	1.11
Teocaltitla (a)[a]	7	60	14	8.57	2.00
(b)	7	49	11	7.00	1.57
Patlachiuhca	12	62	15	5.17	1.25
Texcalticpac	35	211	44	6.00	1.26
Totals: (a)[a]	95	565	126	5.95	1.33
(b)	95	554	123	5.83	1.29

[a]Row (a), both for Teocaltitla and for the totals, results from an assumption that 27r:2, 3, 4, and 5 are all one household; row (b) is the result of excluding 27r:3, 4, and 5 from the analysis altogether.

be used with considerable caution. Only the study of archival materials, already begun by Calnek, Carrasco, and others, may be able to provide a deeper understanding of the lower political and legal levels of Aztec society.

NOTES

1. Research support for this paper was provided by a National Science Foundation Graduate Fellowship, a Henry L. and Grace Doherty Foundation Fellowship for Advanced Study in Latin America, and an HEW Fulbright-Hays Fellowship for Overseas Research. The International Congress of Americanists kindly provided a travel grant to its 1979 Vancouver meetings. I wish to thank Barbara Williams and Herbert Harvey for their advice, encouragement, and suggestions for revisions.

2. "Nibling" is used here as a non-sex-specific term for niece and nephew, in the same way that sibling is a non-sex-specific term for brother and sister.

REFERENCES

AGI (Archivo General de Indias, Seville).
    Justicia 151, 159. Seville.

Aubin, Joseph Marius Alexis
1886   Mapa Quinatzin, cuadro histórico de la civilización de Tezcuco. Fragmento de la obra de M. Aubin tulada: "Mémoire sur la peinture didactique et l'écriture figurative des anciens Mexicaines," traducido para los "Anales del Museo" por Francisco Martínez Calleja. Anales del Museo Nacional de Mexico, ep. 1, 3: 345–68, 1 folding plate.

Calnek, Edward E.
1972   Settlement Pattern and Chinampa Agriculture at Tenochtitlan. American Antiquity 37: 104–15.
1974   The Sahagún Texts as a Source of Sociological Information. *In* Sixteenth Century Mexico: The Work of Sahagún. Munro S. Edmonson, ed. pp. 189–204. Santa Fe: School of American Research.
1976   The Internal Structure of Tenochtitlan. *In* The Valley of Mexico: Studies in Pre-Hispanic Ecology and Society. Eric R. Wolf, ed. pp. 287–302. School of American Research Advanced Seminar Series. Albuquerque: University of New Mexico Press.

Carrasco, Pedro
1971   Social Organization of Ancient Mexico. *In* Handbook of Middle American Indians. Vol. 10. R. Wauchope, ed. pp. 349–75. Austin: University of Texas Press.

Dibble, Charles, and A. J. O. Anderson
1950–69   Florentine Codex: General History of the Things of New Spain by Fray Bernardino de Sahagún. Monographs of the School of American Research, 14, pts. 2–13. Santa Fe: School of American Research and the University of Utah.

Gibson, Charles, and A. J. O. Anderson
1964   The Aztecs under Spanish Rule: A History of the Indians of the Valley of Mexico, 1519–1810. Stanford: Stanford University Press.

Glass, John B., and Donald Robertson
1975   A Census of Middle American Pictorial Manuscripts. *In* Handbook of Middle American Indians. Vol. 14. R. Wauchope, ed. pp. 81–252. Austin: University of Texas Press.

Gómara, Francisco López de
1826   Historia de las conquestas de Hernando Cortés . . . Juan Bau-

tista de San Anton Muñón Chimalpain Quauhtlehuanitzin, trans. 2 vols. Carlos María de Bustamenta, ed. México: Ontiveros.

Harvey, H. R., and B. J. Williams
1980   Aztec Arithmetic: Positional Notation and Area Calculation. Science 210: 499–505.

Nicholson, Henry B.
1973   Phoneticism in the Late Pre-Hispanic Central Mexican Writing System. *In* Mesoamerican Writing Systems. Elizabeth P. Benson, ed. pp. 1–46. Washington, D.C.: Dumbarton Oaks Research Library and Collections.

Offner, Jerome A.
1979   Law and Politics in Aztec Texcoco. Ph.D. dissertation, Department of Anthropology, Yale University (available through University Microfilms, Ann Arbor, Michigan; a revised edition is forthcoming, from Cambridge University Press).
1981   On the Inapplicability of "Oriental Despotism" and the "Asiatic mode of production" to the Aztecs of Texcoco. American Antiquity 46: 43–61.

Parsons, Jeffrey R.
1971   Prehistoric Settlement Patterns in the Texcoco Region, Mexico. Memoirs of the Museum of Anthropology, University of Michigan, no. 3.

Paso y Troncoso, Francisco del
1905   Papeles de la Nueva España publicados de ordén y con fondos del gobierno mexicano. Segunda serie, geografía y estadística. Vol. 6. Madrid: Est. Tipográfica Sucesores de Rivadeneyra.
1905–7   Fray Bernardino de Sahagún: Historia de las cosas de Nueva España. 4 vols. Madrid: Hauser y Menet.
1939–42   Epistolario de Nueva España, 1505–1818. México: biblioteca Historica Mexicana de Obras Inéditas, Segunda Serie.

Pomar, Juan Bautista
1941   Relación de Tezcoco. *In* Nueva colección de documentos para la historia de México. Vol. 3. Joaquín García Icazbalceta, ed. pp. 1–69. México: Salvador Chavez Hayhoe.

Pospisil, Leopold
1971   Anthropology of Law: A Comparative Theory. New York: Harper and Row.

Williams, Barbara J.
1980   Pictorial Representations of Soils in the Valley of Mexico: Evidence from the Codex Vergara. *In* Geoscience and Man 21: 51–62.

7

Rotational Labor and Urban Development
in Prehispanic Tetzcoco

Frederic Hicks

The purpose of this essay is to contribute to an understanding of certain aspects of urban development in prehispanic Central Mexico, through a study of some features of the labor force of one city, Tetzcoco (modern Texcoco). Tetzcoco was one of the main cities of Aztec Mexico, capital of the kingdom of Acolhuacan, and a partner, with Tenochtitlan and Tlacopan, in the Empire of the Triple Alliance. My principal concern is the role played by rotational labor—that done by people from various parts of Acolhuacan, whose tribute obligations required them to spend part of each year working in Tetzcoco. Mesoamericanists have long known of this form of labor, as it is described in a number of well-known basic sources, and one aspect of it has recently been treated, from a different standpoint, by Rojas R. (1977). However, its significance for an analysis of Aztec urbanism, or indeed of urban settlement in other parts of Mesoamerica, has largely been overlooked. In this essay I will

147

present a general outline of work organization in late pre-Spanish Tetzcoco, with emphasis on rotational labor, and then discuss what I see as some of its possible implications for the development of urbanism. I will omit from detailed consideration members of the nobility and others in supervisory positions, as well as draft labor brought in from conquered areas beyond Acolhuacan. Emphasis will be on the ordinary commoners (*macehualtin*) who were natives of Acolhuacan and were near the bottom of the chains of command.

Rotational labor involved serving in "the palaces of the king" by turns on a regular basis, "por su tanda y rueda," as Pomar (1941: 9) put it. It should be distinguished from the *cohuatequitl,* which was extraordinary corvée labor on a large scale, called for special projects (Gibson 1956). The "palaces of the king" must be understood in a very broad sense. As commonly used in the sources it refers to virtually the whole politico-religious center of the city, which in this redistributional economy (Berdan 1977; Carrasco 1978) was the effective economic center as well. It seems quite possible that at any given time more than half the labor force in the politico-religious center, and perhaps a quarter of the people in the urban nucleus of Tetzcoco, consisted of people doing their rotational labor service.

URBAN SETTLEMENT PATTERN

In prehispanic times, Tetzcoco apparently consisted of a relatively small, tightly nucleated area in the immediate vicinity of the palaces of Nezahualpilli and Nezahualcoyotl, which in themselves were quite extensive (Ixtlilxóchitl 1952[2]: 174–83), but beyond that it was rather open, with clusters of houses, an occasional noble establishment, and a few small subsidiary centers interspersed among cultivated fields for a considerable distance from the politico-religious center. Ixtlilxóchitl (1952[1]: 140) wrote that the city extended from the region of Tetzcotzinco in the east to the "barrio" of Oztoticpac, which was near the lake. This is supported by a number of early colonial documentary sources, in which "barrios" of the city are located as far east as the Tlaixpan region and as far north as San Francisco Acuescomac, both about 7 km. from the center of modern Texcoco (e.g., AGN: Tierras 2726, Exp. 8; Vínculos 234, Exp. 1).[1] Other early sources describe it as a huge city, with from one hundred thousand to one hundred and eighty thousand inhabitants, dispersed over several leagues outward from the royal palaces (Aguilar 1977: 95; Motolinía 1971: 206; Torquemada 1975[1]: 304). The population of the central nucleated area, however, was more likely between twenty thousand and twenty-six thousand (Borah and Cook 1963: 76; Sanders 1970: 414). In his archaeological survey of the area, Parsons (1971: 120) found it to cover approximately 450 hectares.

The focal point of the city was the royal palace, built by order of king Nezahualpilli (r. 1472–1515) and used also by his successor, Cacama, who was king at the time of the Spanish conquest. In addition to the very extensive living quarters, this palace contained most of the institutions through which Acolhuacan was governed. Adjoining it was the palace built by Nezahualpilli's predecessor, Nezahualcoyotl (r. 1431–72), and still occupied, at contact, by junior branches of the royal lineage. Ixtlilxóchitl, who observed its ruins, states (1952[2]: 174–83) that this palace measured 1,234 by 978 varas (about 85 hectares; Castillo F. 1972: 213), and contained some three hundred rooms (Ixtlilxóchitl 1952[2]: 174–83). He describes the palace of Nezahualpilli as somewhat smaller, but more sumptuous. The royal palace also included granaries, an extensive kitchen area, a ballcourt, and a market plaza. Next to it was an extensive temple area which included the dwellings of priests, their assistants, and novices (Pomar 1941; Motolinía 1971: 206; Mapa Quinatzin, in Robertson 1959; Ixtlilxóchitl 1952[2]: 175). The two palaces plus the temple precinct may well have occupied an area almost as large as that of the present urban center of Texcoco.

Many members of the royal family, including the king's many wives or concubines and his children by them, seem to have lived in the royal palace until they were given authorization to build palaces of their own. The king also ordered homes or palaces built for many other nobles who had duties in the politico-religion center (Ixtlilxóchitl 1952[2]: 187). Many of these were doubtless built in the near vicinity of the politico-religious center, but many others evidently were not, as is indicated by some of Ixtlilxóchitl's historical anecdotes referring to the palaces of royal princes in the city (Ixtlilxóchitl 1952[2]: 219, 294–95). A son of Nezahualcoyotl, for example, selected the site of his palace for its setting, around a large

ahuehuete tree. Another prince, Huexotzincatl, was executed by his
father, Nezahualpilli, which so saddened the latter that he renamed
Huexotzincatl's palace Ixayoc, "place of tears." This is probably the
San Pablo Ixayoc that lies east of Huexotla today; in one of a series
of documents dealing with land sales in that general region in the
late sixteenth century there is mention of a Juan de la Cruz Huexotzincatl pilli, a resident of Tetzcoco whose *calpulli* was Ixayoc
(INAH-AH, PEA: Ser. 3, Leg. 30, Doc. 3, ff. 30v–31r).[2] The
"palacios y casas solariegas" of another prince was called Teotlan,
and two nobles of a barrio of Tetzcoco called San Pedro Teotlan
appeared as witnesses in a case heard in 1593 (INAH-AH, PEA:
Ser. 3, Leg. 30, Doc. 8, ff. 3v, 4r). Finally, another prince built
himself a palace without proper authorization; it must have been
reasonably far from the royal palace, since he evidently had it all
built before the king discovered it.

At least since the time of Nezahualcoyotl, the city was divided
into six units generally called *parcialidades* in Spanish sources. They
were Chimalpan, Tlailotlacan, Mexicapan, Colhuacan, Tepaneca-
pan, and Huiltznahuac; the names are derived from six ethnic groups
that arrived in Acolhuacan at various times prior to the fifteenth
century. These names do not survive in Texcoco today, but the
Spanish prefixed saints' names to them, and some of these names
do survive as the names of barrios of the modern city (Vetancurt
1971, Tratado 2, Cáp. 1, Par. 102).[3] At the time of the Spanish
conquest the six parcialidades may have been centered in small,
subsidiary ceremonial centers, not far from the main administrative
center, but each of them also had landholdings distributed in various
parts of the city; the macehualtin who worked these lands gave
service to the nobles of their parcialidad. For example, there were
several calpulli (small communities) of macehualtin in the Tlaixpan
region, working subsistence plots there, who traditionally owed
service to the nobles of Chimalpan (AGN: Tierras 2726, Exp. 8,
ff. 48r–51r; for reference to them as calpulli see INAH-AH, PEA:
Ser. 3, Leg. 30, Doc. 3, esp. ff. 7r, 15r, 16r. Only the small
communities are called calpulli; the parcialidades are not).

Royal princes, and probably other nobles who had palaces in one
or another part of Tetzcoco, also had lands for their own support,
again not necessarily in the immediate vicinity of their palaces. For
example, don Carlos Chichimecatl teuctli, a son of Nezahaulpilli,

was provided during the 1530s with a house in Oztoticpac, Tetz-coco, that was part of the palace estates. He also had landholdings of his own in several regions, and at least one of them in the vicinity of Tetzcotzinco, included plots assigned to macehualtin (Cline 1972). Don Carlos evidently had duties in the palace, and some of his macehualtin may have been called upon to lend assistance there, as well as for service in his house.

Commoners who were attached neither to one of the parcialidades nor to an individual noble household owed service to the king directly. Many of them, but probably not all, were placed by Nezahualcoyotl under the control of a *calpixqui* ("steward") named Matlalaca, whose charge was "la ciudad de Tetzcuco con sus barrios y aldeas" (Ixtlilxóchitl 1952[2]: 168). This was one of eight "cal-pixcazgos" in Acolhuacan which Nezahualcoyotl created, and which had obligations of various kinds to the palace.

The politico-religious center of Tetzcoco was served by an extensive labor force, ultimately under the direction of the king; we do not know how many people comprised it. The basic sustaining area upon which this center drew, for labor as well as for food and other necessities, was the kingdom of Acolhuacan. The heart of this kingdom was in the eastern Valley of Mexico, but it extended beyond this area to the northeast (see Figure 1). The king (*tlatohuani*) of Tetzcoco was the supreme ruler, but there were also other *tlatoque* in Acolhuacan—fourteen, according to most accounts—each ruling semiautonomously over his own local domain (table 7.1, Col. 1). They were clearly dependent on the king of Tetzcoco, who installed or confirmed them in office and who gave them his daughters in marriage, but they participated with him in the highest councils of the kingdom, and they often held important posts in the royal court at Tetzcoco. They thus divided their time between their home palaces and the city (Gibson 1956; Trautmann 1968).

WORK IN TETZCOCO

As we have seen, the parcialidad centers and the various noble households established in the Tetzcoco area had their own macehual-tin to work their lands and provide domestic service. There seems no reason to believe, however, that they received tribute or service from beyond the limits of the city of Tetzcoco, in its extended sense. Our main concern in this paper is with work under the auspices of the royal palace, and this did involve virtually the entire kingdom, as well as some regions beyond it. Among the tasks most frequently mentioned in the sources are sweeping floors, hauling water, providing firewood and charcoal, kitchen service of all kinds, and various activities connected with preparations for ceremonies. There were also errands to be run, messages to be delivered, burdens to be carried, gardens to be maintained, and all kinds of minor repairs to be made. The spinning and weaving of cloth, a domestic skill that all women were expected to have, must also have consumed considerable labor time. The various courts, councils, and other institutions were evidently provided with a staff of helpers, ranging from skilled specialists, such as scribes and constables (*achcacauhtin*), to menial servants. The largest staff mentioned in the sources is the two thousand people that king Axayacatl of Tenochtitlan provided to accompany and serve his young daughter when he gave her in marriage to Nezahualpilli (Ixtlilxóchitl 1952[2]: 285), but most were doubtless much smaller. Skilled craftsmen also worked for the royal court.

There must have been some fluctuation during the course of a year in the number of workers in the politico-religious center, because many of the courts and councils which they served were not in session continually. For example, the principal forum in the "council of government," the *naupohuallatolli,* initiated a new session every eighty days, and usually remained in session for about ten to twelve days each time (Motolinía 1971: 355; see also Ixtlilxóchitl 1952[1]: 326; Pomar 1941: 29–30). In another court sat fifteen judges who came from various parts of Acolhuacan, and who returned to their home areas when the session ended (Ixtlilxóchitl 1952[2]: 177). Many palace officials had lands, homes, and subjects in other parts of Acolhuacan, and were in attendance in Tetzcoco only at periodic intervals. In the time of Nezahualcoyotl, for example, the *tlacochcalcatl* in charge of the war council was the tlatohuani of Teotihuacan, who also had responsibilities in that region.

People on duty in the palace, or otherwise in the service of the king away from their homes, were provided with meals, evidently from the palace kitchens (Pomar 1941: 9; Ixtlilxóchitl 1952[2]: 295). This applied to macehualtin as well as nobles, and members of the royal household, whether on duty or not, were also provided with food from the palace stores. Ixtlilxóchitl (1952[2]: 266) describes the "gran gasto que el rey tenía en sustentar la gente que en estos palacios [of Nezahualpilli] y los de su padre había, así de servicio como de señores, criados, jueces y otros caballeros y allegados."

In Central Mexico generally, nobles ordinarily received the services of commoners through what is often termed the "tribute" system, although the Nahuatl word for it, *tequitl,* might be better translated as "duty." Everyone had a tequitl, from the king down to the lowliest servant, but those of the macehualtin were set for them by their lords. Normally tequitl involved service, although such service might consist of the production and delivery of food or craft items. A different word, *tlacalaquilli,* was used to denote "tribute" in material objects (Carrasco 1978: 29).[4] Technically every commoner was the subject of a lord; those who were not attached to a noble or a noble lineage were considered subjects of the king directly. Indeed, the word for "commoner," *macehualli,* actually means "subject," and the Spanish often glossed it as "vasallo." To enable them to carry out their duties to their lords, the macehualtin were ordinarily provided with lands on which they could grow food for their own subsistence. As Zorita (1941: 100) put it, land functioned as the equivalent of a salary. On a higher level also, when a tlatohuani gave a grant of land to a deserving noble, he also gave him subjects; or he could recruit them by offering subsistence plots. The subsistence plots (*calpullalli*) of those commoners not attached to a particular noble (including, I presume, the nobles of a parcialidad) were considered to have been provided by the king, and it was to the king, directly or indirectly, that they owed service (Hicks 1978).

ROTATIONAL LABOR

Pomar (1941: 9) has stated that the tribute of the "nearest towns and provinces" included personal service by turns in the buildings of the king, but Ixtlilxóchitl provides more detail. From his account and Torquemada's we have a series of lists of what appear to be towns, having obligations of various kinds, including labor, to the king, in Tetzcoco. The sources present this information, which is summarized in table 7.1, in the context of explaining Nezahual-

Table 7.1. Lands for the Support of the City of Tetzcoco

	1	2	3	4	5	6	7
Acolman	*				*		
Achichillacachyocan						*	
Ahuatepec			*	*		*	
Atenco			*				*
Axapochco			*	*		*	
Aztaquemecan				*		*	
Calpollalpan							*
Cempohuallan				*		*	
Cohuatepec		*		*	*		
Cohuatlichan	*				*		
Coyohuac						*	
Cuauhtlatlauhcan						*	
Cuauhtlatzinco			*			*	
Chalco					*		
Chiauhtlan	*				*		
Chimalhuacan	*				*		
Chiucnautlan	*				*		
Huexotla	*				*		
Itztapalocan		*		*	*		
Mazaapan							*
Otompan	*					*	
Oztoticpac				*		*	
Papalotlan		*			*		
Tecpilpan			*				
Teotihuacan	*					*	

Table 7.1 (continued)

	1	2	3	4	5	6	7
Tepechpan	*				*		
Tepeapolco			*	*		*	
Tepetlaoztoc	*				*		
Tetitlan			*				
Tetliztacan						*	
Tetzcoco			*		*		
Tezonyocan	*				*		
Tizayocan				*		*	
Tlallanapan						*	
Tzihuinquilocan							*
Xaltocan		*		*	*		
Yahualiuhcan							*

KEY:

1—Dependent tlatocayotl (the three northernmost, which do not appear on any other lists, are omitted)
2—Taken by Nezahualcoyotl for himself rather than placed in calpixcazgos
3—Calpixcazgos established by Nezahualcoyotl
4—Kept by Nezahualcoyotl for his household
5—Gave palace service first half of each year
6—Gave palace service second half of each year
7—Towns assigned to the king's household

coyotl's restructuring of the kingdom following his assumption of power in 1431. Between that time and the Spanish conquest there must have been many reallocations of land and perhaps some modification in the obligations of specific communities, but there were no changes in the system itself.

Before turning to these lists, it should be noted that although they appear to be lists of towns, they probably do not mean that the whole town, and all of its inhabitants, was obligated in the way specified. Indeed the same town often appears on different lists as having different obligations. What I think was meant was that certain landholdings within the boundaries of these towns, and/or certain barrios of macehualtin, were set aside for the purposes indicated. For example, Ixtlilxóchitl (1952[2]: 210) lists five towns as having been assigned to the king's household ("la recámara del rey"): Calpollalpan, Mazaapan, Yahualiuhcan, Atenco, and Tzihuinquilocan. A document of 1593, however, lists among the "patrimonial" lands of Nezahualpilli not the entire area of Calpollalpan, Mazaapan, and Yahualiuhcan, but only nine named places within their boundaries (AGN: Tierras 1740, f. 152v; cf. Ixtlilxóchitl 1952[2]: 209). Atenco, which appears on this list, also appears on another list of six regions obligated to provide food for the palace (Ixtlilxóchitl 1952[2]: 169). A document of 1574 indicates that in actuality the macehualtin of eight small communities in Atenco were obliged to cultivate one or more specific fields for food for the palace (AGN: Vínculos 234, Exp. 1; Hicks 1978).

As a general rule in Central Mexico, when the landholdings of a tlatohuani or other important noble are listed, the list takes the form of a large number of named places, not of towns, and the amount of land in each place may have been relatively small (e.g., Nazareo 1940; Munch 1976: 45–46; AGN: Tierras 1735, Exp. 2, f. 426v; AGN: Tierras 1740, ff. 154v–155r). The Códice Kingsborough (1912) depicts more than sixty named places and the number (usually between five and twenty) of macehualtin in each who were obligated to serve one or another of the nobles of Tepetlaoztoc. Acolhuacan contained, in addition to major town centers, hundreds of small named communities, each one with a specific set of tequitl obligations.[5] Many of them must have served local lords (and some may have served the king of Tenochtitlan), while others had obligations to the palace in Tetzcoco. For administrative and record-keeping purposes, the appropriate official in Tetzcoco grouped together those communities in a given region that had similar obligations, and local officials, probably *calpixque,* distributed the tasks among and within these communities (for a partial description of such record-keeping methods, see AGN: Vínculos 234, Exp. 1, ff. 258r–263v). What the tribute lists provided by Ixtlilxóchitl, Torquemada, Motolinía, and other sources give us, probably, are regions within which there were communities having the obligations specified.

Lands or communities which served in one way or another for the support of the city are listed in the sources as follows:

(1) Lands in various parts of central and northern Acolhuacan which Nezahualcoyotl took for himself shortly after taking control of the kingdom (table 7.1, Col. 2). These were distinguished from lands restored to the dependent *tlatoque* (Col. 1) and those distributed to other nobles (Ixtlilxóchitl 1952[2]: 167–68).

(2) Lands remaining after the aforementioned allocations, and which were distributed in eight regions, each of which was placed under a *calpixqui,* who saw to it that the macehualtin fulfilled their obligations (table 7.1, Col. 3). Six of these regions were obligated to provide food for the palace for a certain number of days each year: three regions for seventy days, one for sixty, and two for forty-five days each year (Ixtlilxóchitl 1952[2]: 168–69). The remaining two regions (Tetitlan and Tecpilpan) apparently did not give food, but Tecpilpan provided obsidian blades (Relación de Zempoala 1952). I have elsewhere suggested that these administrative entities, or calpixcazgos, may have been regions kept in reserve by the king for possible future allocations (Hicks 1978: 131).

(3) Ten towns "and many others" that Nezahualcoyotl kept for his household after restoring the dependent *tlatoque* (table 7.1, Col. 4). He also assigned calpixque to oversee the tribute from them (Ixtlilxóchitl 1952[1]: 234). The context would suggest that this refers to the same distributions described in (1) and (2) above, but only six of the ten named towns are the same as those on the first two lists.

(4) Thirty towns, listed by Ixtlilxóchitl (1952[2]: 210) and Torquemada (1975[1]: 167), were required to provide for the service,

adornment, and maintenance of the palace of the king; fifteen for the first half of each year and fifteen for the second half (table 7.1, Cols. 5 and 6).According to Torquemada this obligation was met principally in labor. They swept floors, hauled water, provided firewood, charcoal, and mats, and performed any other service required of them. He also states that they provided maize from fields that they cultivated, and they probably also supplied maguey-fiber garments (Castañeda 1905: 213, 221). The places carrying this obligation for the first half of each year were all relatively close to Tetzcoco (the most distant was Chiucnautlan), while those carrying it for the second half were more distant (the nearest was Oztoticpac, in the Teotihuacan Valley).[6] Most of these places also appear on other lists: five as calpixcazgos, three are among the ten towns Nezahualcoyotl took for himself, and eleven of them were seats of dependent tlatoque. Torquemada mentions elsewhere (1975[2]: 164) that thirty towns, which he does not name, supplied the temples with firewood, charcoal, and oak bark (for braziers), fifteen for one half of the year and fifteen for the other. This probably refers to the same thirty towns. Motolinía (1971: 394–95) lists sixteen towns that provided firewood service for the temples; they are the same towns, minus Chalco, Tetliztacan, Tetzcoco, and all of the seats of dependent tlatoque. Motolinía's list is very similar to one in the Anales de Cuauhtitlan (1975, Par. 1346) which is headed "nican hualtequitia" ("they come here [to Tetzcoco] to do service"), although the Anales list adds many conquered regions outside of Acolhuacan.[7]

(5) In addition to the thirty towns on the above list, there were five towns, or at least certain fields in them, that were assigned to the king's household (Ixtlilxóchitl 1952[2]: 209, 210; see table 7.1, Col. 7).

These lists are incomplete and oversimplified, as the basic sources themselves sometimes indicate. In colonial documents of the later sixteenth century one can find mention of additional tribute lands or estates of the lords of Tetzcoco, but it is difficult to tell where they fit in this five-fold classification. In particular, one cannot be sure whether they are additional places, or whether they were included within one of the places already listed. After the Spanish conquest, moreover, there were changes in the functions of land-holdings and the roles of the macehualtin who worked them, as the Indian nobles sought to convert the remaining vestiges of their political power into economic power. Ixtlilxóchitl and the other sources cited were attempting to describe the system as it functioned and was administered in pre-Spanish times; if we restrict our consideration to places mentioned by them, we can get a better idea of the relative numbers of places having different kinds of tribute obligations.

Labor is specifically mentioned as an obligation only of the thirty localities listed in Columns 5 and 6 of table 7.1. Actually there are only seven places listed that do not also appear among the thirty that gave labor. These include all five of the towns in Col. 7, and three of the calpixcazgos (Atenco appears in both categories). We have supplemental data on some of these localities, which may clarify the situation.

Of the calpixcazgos, Tecpilpan, in the Cempohuallan region, included a major source of obsidian (Spence and Parsons 1972), and labor there was perhaps more usefully employed in extracting this material. Tetitlan is mentioned by one source as a "cabecera" in 1579 (Salazar 1905: 49), but in pre-Spanish times it may have been simply the name of the calpixcazgo or its headquarters community. Ixtlilxóchitl (1952[2]: 169) explains it as a region "en que entran los pueblos de Coatepec, Itztapalocan, Tlapechhuacan y sus aldeas," and two of those places did give labor. There are legal proceedings from the early colonial period in which the nobles of Tetzcoco presented their claims to tribute from the Atenco region (AGN: Vínculos 234, Exp. 1), and although these proceedings are quite extensive, Tetzcoco claimed only food, not labor.

Of the five towns in Col. 7, there is a sketchy account of claims to tribute from Calpollalpan (AGN: Tierras 3594, Exp. 2), and again labor is not mentioned. Calpollalpan and Tzihuinquilocan were settled, at least in part, by colonists from Tetzcoco sent there originally by Nezahualcoyotl to raise food for the city (Ixtlilxóchitl 1952[2]: 199; Pomar 1941: 7; AGN: Tierras 3594, Exp. 2, f.2v), and this, rather than palace labor, may have been their tequitl. The Atenco region included the sites of Nezahualpilli's recreational palaces of Acatetelco and Tepetzinco, and along with Calpollalpan,

Mazaapan, and Yahualiuhcan, it contained fields of the king "en donde por gusto y entretenimiento le hacían sementeras, hallándose al beneficio de ellas personalmente" (Ixtlilxóchitl 1952[2]: 209).

The fact that labor does not figure in the early colonial claims is not entirely conclusive, partly because Spanish authorities apparently discouraged claims by Indian nobles to unpaid labor, but also because after the Spanish conquest of the kingdom, with the destruction of the temples, the elimination of most Indian political duties, and the labor demands of the *encomiendas,* it would have been both pointless and impossible for macehualtin to continue to give labor to Indian lords on a scale anywhere near that of preconquest times. It seems plausible to infer, nevertheless, that within the eight regions listed in Col. 3, those communities that were administered through the calpixcazgos did not provide labor for the palace, and that what are listed in Col. 7 are certain lands or other establishments with which the royal lineage had a special close relationship. Atenco is on both lists because it contained lands or communities of both kinds.[8] There were probably other communities, or barrios, in most of these regions which did give labor, and they would be included in the places listed in Columns 5 and 6. Tetzcoco, for example, appears both as a calpixcazgo and as a labor-giving region. As the latter, it probably included those barrios of Atenco (which was within the boundaries of the city) that were not included in the calpixcazgo. Missing from all these lists are the three most distant tlatohuani seats: Tollantzinco, Cuauhchinanco, and Xicotepec. Apparently they were too far away to serve as a regular source of either food or labor. Ixtlilxóchitl (1952[2]: 210) states that Nezahualcoyotl assigned these places, along with several in Morelos, "para los bosques y jardines."

We have no explicit data from Acolhuacan on how the rotational labor was mobilized in the distant community and organized in Tetzcoco, except that calpixque were involved. When we cast about in the ethnohistorical sources for an institution through which it might have been done, the one that seems most likely is the system of so-called "work squads" (*cuadrillas*), under a graded hierarchy of calpixque. This system has been described for various parts of Central Mexico (e.g., Anguiano and Chapa 1976; Relación anónima 1940; Carrasco and Monjarás-Ruiz 1976; Durán 1967[2], Ch. 41; Prem

1974; Reyes 1972; Rojas 1977); although it has not been reported from Acolhuacan specifically, it would be odd if it should prove to be absent there. At the lowest level was a calpixqui (often called a *tepixqui* or *tequitlato* in these accounts), who had charge of a small number of households (the unit was always a household, not an individual).[9] A superior calpixqui was responsible for several minor calpixque and their charges, and there might be still higher levels before reaching the head calpixqui, who was responsible to the king directly. The Spanish adapted this system to their own purposes, and most accounts describe it in a Spanish colonial context; Durán's account, however, is in the context of the election of a successor to the emperor Tizoc, who died in 1486. In some areas, particularly in the Valley of Puebla-Tlaxcala, quasi-numerical terms denoted positions in this hierarchy. At the lowest level was a *cetecpanpixqui,* "guardian of one score of people," and above him a *macuiltecpanpixqui,* "guardian of five score of people," but such quasi-numerical terms do not seem to have been in general use everywhere.

A group of families under the direction of a calpixqui thus formed a work squad, or at least could be mobilized as such at the proper time. One early source (Relación anónima 1940) remarks that through this system the labor force of an entire town could be mobilized on very short notice. It is often described in connection with the *cohuatequitl,* but it was almost certainly not limited to that. Such a work squad formed, or was formed of, a local community or neighborhood, usually called *tlaxilacalli* in Nahuatl, although sometimes called calpullli.[10] That is, a tlaxilacalli or calpulli was a group of households forming a small barrio and having common tributary obligations. It included people of all ages and both sexes, although men and women worked at different tasks, and youths and the elderly were exempt from labor service. Not only did the people of many tlaxilacalli make seasonal moves in the performance of their rotational labor duties, but the tlaxilacalli could be moved from one region to another, permanently or for an extended period, if the need arose. Chimalpahin, for example, tells us (1963, 7th Rel., 4 calli 1509) that when Moteuczoma gave his daughter in marriage to the ruler of Tlalmanalco, in Chalco, he also gave "ome tlaxil-lacaltin in Otomi quinhualhuicac cihualpilli ("two tlaxilacalli of Otomíes to accompany the princess").

The supervisors of these work squads, who in Acolhuacan were apparently called simply calpixque (Hicks 1978), received formal training for their duties in establishments that Ixtlilxóchitl (1952[a]: 235) called *órdenes*—apparently a specialized kind of youths' house. The man appointed by Nezahualcoyotl as the first head calpixqui of Atenco was a commoner who had earlier earned distinction for his military accomplishments, and the position was held by his descendants in later generations (Hicks 1978).

We can infer, therefore, that when the time came for the macehualtin to fulfill their labor obligations in Tetzcoco, the head calpixqui of a region contacted his subordinates, who most likely had charge of individual barrios (tlaxilacalli or calpulli); they in turn mobilized the families in their charge, and all went to the politico-religious center to perform the work that was required of them there. Contingents from nearby places may have returned home each evening, but those from more distant areas must have been housed in the city, probably in clusters of dwelling places near the politico-religious center that would have been called "barrios" in Spanish. When their period of duty was up, they would return to their home areas where, probably under the supervision of the same calpixque, they tended their subsistence plots, performed any other duties that might have been assigned them, and awaited any call that might come for extraordinary duty or for war. Not all calpulli in Acolhuacan were subject to regular rotational labor service in the politico-religious center each year, but those that were, were distributed throughout all parts of the kingdom except, apparently, the far northeast.

PERMANENT LABOR

Many of the people who were obligated to give rotational labor service in the palace lived in Tetzcoco, and thus were permanent residents of the city, at least in its extended sense, although not part of the permanent palace staff. There were surely many commoners working full time in the city for one or another agency of the state, but data concerning them are far from clear. One group of people that needs to be considered are those called *tecpanpouhque* by Torquemada (1975[2]: 546) and Ixtlilxóchitl (1952[2]: 170).

It is hard to be sure from the brief accounts in these two sources whether the tecpanpouhque were nobles or commoners. When Torquemada (1975[2]: 546) tells us that they were "la gente más estimada, y más arrimada y conjunta a las casas del rey, y a quien más respetaba el común," and that "no pagaban ningún género de tributo, si no eran ramilletes y pájaros de todo género, con que saludaban al rey," it sounds like they were nobles; an apparently similar group was called "nobles y caballeros" in a 1554 account dealing with Central Mexico generally (Carrasco 1967: 122). His description of their housing provisions could apply to those of don Carlos Chichimecatl, mentioned above (cf. Ixtlilxóchitl 1952[2]: 187), although it might possibly apply to commoners as well. On the other hand, Torquemada tells us that they cultivated lands and were obliged to clean the gardens and repair the houses, duties often associated with commoners. Perhaps the solution is to take the word at its face value. *Tecpanpouhque* means simply "[people] affiliated with the palace," and incorporates the same verb (*pohui*) that is normally used to indicate affiliation or attachment to a place, institution, or other person; its synonym *tecpantlaca* means quite literally "palace people." It seems most likely that these words simply referred to all of the people who regularly lived, worked, or hung about the palace, regardless of their social class or estate. They formed the king's retinue and generally made themselves as useful as possible at various tasks befitting their status and training. Torquemada indicates that there were lands, called *tecpantlalli,* that were cultivated by tecpanpouhque. If this refers to lands in the immediate vicinity of the royal palace in Tetzcoco (any major noble's palace was a *tecpan,* and tecpantlalli was the land on which it stood), it could indicate subsistence plots to support commoners working at the palace year-round (cf. Corona S. 1976: 93), but it could also refer to "kitchen gardens" of noble houses.

The literature on Central Mexico in general indicates that there were some people who lacked use-rights to land, and it is likely that many such people served in the politico-religious center on a permanent basis. They might be pawns, purchased slaves, or "orphans" (i.e., people without kin) (Hicks 1975: 255–59). Generally such people were attached to individual households and thus did not constitute an easily visible social group, but the extensive royal household may have been able to accommodate quite a few of them. The occasional mention of "criados" in Tetzcoco may refer to them. Some work may also have been done by boys in the telpochcalli or by women who served in the temple area (Pomar 1941: 26–29; Ixtlilxóchitl 1952[2]: 185). Some craftsmen may have been permanently attached to the palace, but many doubltess served in a rotational capacity.

Ixtlilxóchitl (1952[2]: 266) gives us figures for the amount of food disbursed from the royal stores each year to feed the people residing or working in the palace. It amounts to 31,600 *fanegas* of corn, 243 loads of cacao, 8,000 turkeys, 5,000 fanegas of *chile ancho, delgado,* and *pepitas,* and 2,000 measures of salt. It is tempting to try to use these figures as a basis for estimating the size of the labor force or the proportion of it that was made up of rotational labor, but it is impossible to do so. In the first place, the list is clearly incomplete, since it omits many fruits, grains, meats, vegetables, and aquatic fauna known to have been important in the Aztec diet (Dávalos Hurtado 1955; Ivanhoe 1978: 138). In the second place, we do not know precisely who this was intended to feed, except that it included people in a variety of social positions, nor what proportion of their food supply it constituted. For whatever it may be worth, I will offer the suggestion that if we accept Molins Fábrega's (1955: 310; cf. Castillo F. 1972: 205–6) metric equivalents, meaning that the amount of corn distributed annually was 1,753,800 liters, and estimate the per capita corn consumption in prehispanic times as about one liter daily of shelled corn, one could conclude that this could have provided the entire food supply for somewhat less than five thousand people, or less than the entire food supply for a larger number. The only thing this enables us to infer is that there were a minimum of five thousand people living or working in or for the palace. There were doubtless more than that, but we do not know how many more. My hunch is that rotational laborers working under the auspices of the palace outnumbered permanent laborers there, because they came from so many places throughout the kingdom, and the institutionalized means for mobilizing them were so widespread. The various noble households in the urban nucleus probably had their own service staffs, however, so rotational workers may have been a minority of the total macehualli population of the urban center.

IMPLICATIONS

Economically it should have been quite possible for the outlying communities of Acolhuacan to have provided tribute, in food and raw materials alone, to support a full-time urban labor force in the service of the government and its various agencies. We cannot explain why this was not done to a greater extent than it was, but we can consider some of the possible implications of this extensive use of rotational labor.

First, it can be seen as a means of uniting the kingdom, impressing forcefully upon the commoners of most parts of it their obligations to the king of Tetzcoco, and his power over them. Through this system, many macehualtin, from virtually all parts of the kingdom, were brought into the politico-religious center where, in addition to performing service, they would be impressed by its magnificence and awed by the pageantry of the periodic religious ceremonies, which represented, above all else, the power of the state and its ruler (Broda 1978). Not only macehualtin, but nobles as well, if they were from outlying regions, were required to spend some time in the politico-religious center. A ruler must have some way to maintain regular contact with his people and subordinate regional officials, at least for surveillance purposes. In many early states he periodically toured his domain (Claessen 1978: 584–85), but in Mesoamerica, ever since the Late Preclassic period, lavish politico-religious, or ceremonial, centers were built, and efforts were directed instead to getting the people to come to them.

Second, one can speculate that the system also allowed for a desirable degree of flexibility. The need for labor, particularly unskilled labor, was probably not constant, nor was there always the same amount of food in the storehouses to feed them. Hard data on this are apparently lacking, but one would expect that if there was relatively little work to be done, or if the food supplies were running low, some work groups could be sent back to their home communities ahead of time, rather than remain in the city center as an idle and discontented mass.

Third, the system must have hindered the development of a clear distinction between rural and urban, or between peasant and proletarian. The same people who for one part of the year cultivated the land and lived a rural existence, at other times worked at urban occupations, mostly service of some sort, in the city center. They remained, however, subjects of the same lords and supervised by the same calpixque, as they moved from one activity to the other in a predictable fashion each year. There was indeed a city as distinct from the rural settlements around it, but only a weak development, at best, of an urban proletariat. Olivera (1978: 100) has made a similar point with respect to the Cuauhtinchan-Tecali region, but for a different reason: that no settlement derived its livelihood primarily from artesanry. Actually, when we consider that urban centers in so much of the world arose primarily as centers of government (Wheatley 1971), one would expect that service activities would typify early urban occupations to a greater extent than artesanry. Rojas R. (1977) has noted that this use of rotational labor in Mesoamerica may require some modification in the way the division of labor is usually conceptualized. "Instead of creating permanent full-time specialized groups," she observes, "there were created specialized functions, in which the majority of the population participated, seasonally and part-time" (Rojas R. 1977: 21). To an extraordinary extent, given the degree of urban development, cultivation of the land remained the basic means of livelihood, at least for the macehualtin. Occasional services were recompensed in goods, but a system of wage labor never developed. There was, of course, a class distinction, which was accompanied by the development of an elaborate status culture (Fallers 1959), and because the upper class was associated with the higher levels of government, the status culture reached its apogee in the politico-religious centers. But it remained fundamentally a class distinction, not a rural-urban one.

Finally, it follows from all this that Tetzcoco did not develop into a large, compact, tightly nucleated area of homes and workshops, such as characterized the early cities of Europe and the Near East. The palaces were indeed very extensive, and there were a number of them fairly close to each other, along with a market plaza and a temple precinct where many people often gathered.

There must also have been some housing facilities for rotational workers. But what the Acolhua regarded as their city proper consisted for the most part of a large region of dispersed settlement in which agriculture was a major activity. This is not really unusual in early cities, as Trigger (1972) has pointed out. I am sure, however, that if we could see the whole of Tetzcoco mapped as an archaeological site, we would be reminded much more of Tikal than of Teotihuacan.

NOTES

1. Research in Mexican archives was made possible in part by a grant (No. 79-9) from the College of Arts and Sciences, University of Louisville.

2. The relevant passage is not entirely unambiguous. It was written in Tetzcoco and reads, "Juan de la cruz + huexotzincatl pinlli chane ȳ nican nipā ciudad sant pedro, yxayoc calpulpan pohuia." The comma is in the manuscript. I read it as "Juan de la Cruz Huexotzincatl pilli (noble), resident of San Pedro here in this city, belonging to the *calpulli* of Ixayoc." (The insertion of *n* before *ll* occurs frequently; cf. Karttunen and Lockhart 1976: 11.) I think that "San Pedro" refers not to Ixayoc but to the *parcialidad* of Colhuacan, called San Pedro Colhuacan in early colonial times (see below). In other documents of this series a person is usually identified first as to his parcialidad, then his *calpulli*. If this is the same Ixayoc, however, and if Juan de la Cruz was descended from a royal prince, it is curious that his calpulli should belong to Colhuacan, rather than to the royal palace directly. But the document dates from 1577, and it may be that by that time San Pedro had become merely a part of the city in which he happened to have acquired a house.

3. They are: San Sebastián Chimalpan, Santa María Tlailotlacan, San Juan Mexicapan, San Pedro Colhuacan, San Lorenzo Tecpan, and San Pablo Huitznáhuac. They are referred to in this way in numerous early colonial documents. San Sebastián, San Juan, San Pedro, and San Lorenzo are barrios of modern Texcoco, centered on churches. Parsons (1971: 120) has suggested that six mound groups in and around the modern city could represent the centers of the six parcialidades. His "tlateles" 17 and the 89-90-91 group ("los Melones") are more likely to represent the central administrative area, but his suggestion seems plausible with regard to the other four, even though it is not possible to match them with specific parcialidades (with the possible exception of "tlatel" 95, which is near the center of present-day San Juan). Dr. Parsons kindly made available to me his field map of sites in Texcoco.

4. An awareness of this distinction is important for evaluating Spanish sources on the subject. The Spanish commonly rendered both words as "tributo," but they were not consistent; sometimes only tlacalaquilli was so glossed. Statements in Spanish sources to the effect that one or another group did or did not "tributar" are therefore not necessarily clear or conclusive.

5. In various documentary sources I have found, so far, references to at least twenty, and possibly over thirty such small, named communities within the limits of Tetzcoco alone. The exact number is uncertain because it is not always clear whether what is named is a community, a land-holding, or just a portion of the countryside. A fuller account of Tetzcoco's internal structure is in preparation.

6. We have previously mentioned a barrio of Tetzcoco that was also called Oztoticpac; it was a different place altogether.

7. Some of these places (Axapochco, Coyohuac[?], Cuauhtlatzinco, Itztapalocan, Tepechpan, and Tlallanapan), plus some that were not among the thirty towns listed, figure in a document of 1531 which I discovered in Seville after this paper was written (AGI: México, 203, No. 15). The document involves doña Ana, a daughter of Nezahualpilli. Several witnesses, including nobles of Tetzcoco, affirmed that these places or parts of them, and their inhabitants, had been assigned by Nezahualpilli to doña Ana at the time of her birth, as dowry lands. She married a Spaniard, and under the direction of her calpixque in these towns, in accordance with pre-Spanish custom, the people gave personal service to her and her husband in their house in México and elsewhere, as well as tribute of an unspecified nature.

8. There may be some significance to the fact that the noble "descendants of Nezahualpilli" managed to hold onto the lands listed in Col. 7, as entailed estates, for nearly a century or more after the Spanish conquest, while losing control of most other regions. They apparently held onto a large part of the Atenco region also, by successfully blurring the distinction between the calpixcazgo and the royal household lands, and claiming it all as their patrimony. The nobles, in a court case of the 1570s, claimed a certain landholding as Acatetelco and the macehualtin who worked it as their tenants. These macehualtin claimed that the landholding in question was called Quetzalxalotitlan, that they worked it for the community, and that the king's lands were elsewhere. It seems clear to me now (as it was not when I discussed this case in Hicks 1978) that in pre-Spanish times, the duties of the macehualtin assigned to the calpixcazgo were to cultivate Quetzalxalotitlan to provide food for the palace, while Acatetelco was serviced under a different system.

9. Durán (1967[1], Ch. 20) lists *tepixqui* and *calpuleque* as regional variants of calpixqui. Zorita (1941: 86) used the term *calpuleque* to refer to the leader of a calpulli, which he equated with a barrio. Zorita's calpulli were probably units with common tributary obligations, and his calpuleque a regional variant of calpixqui.

10. There has been some uncertainty as to the difference between a calpulli and a tlaxilacalli. On the basis of a passage in Torquemada (1975[2]: 545), in which he compared tlaxilacalli to "streets," some have concluded that a tlaxilacalli was a subdivision of a calpulli (e.g., Caso 1956), but one can find passages and even pairs of minimal contrasts which clearly demonstrate that the two terms could be synonymous (e.g., Anderson, Berdan, and Lockhart 1976: 94; Chimalpahin 1958: 20 [2nd Rel., 1 tecpatl 1064]; AGN: Tierras 1520, Exp. 6, ff. 8r, 11r), and one can also find the compound term *calpoltlaxilacalli* (Chimalpahin 1963, 8th Rel., Pt. 1). My impression is that a given group is more likely to be called a tlaxilacalli when the focus is on its function as a tribute-giving or work group, and calpulli when the focus is on nationality, community, kinship, or religion. In a collection of late sixteenth-century land-sales documents from Tetzcoco, written in Nahuatl (INAH-AH, PEA: Ser. 3, Leg. 30), "calpulli" is the only word used, always to indicate the place of residence of a person or the location of a piece of land. The word seems to apply to a noble establishment as well as to a small community of macehualtin.

REFERENCES

AGN (Archivo General de la Nación, México)
		Documents cited by Ramo, Volumen, Expediente, and in some cases Folio.

Aguilar, Francisco de
1977		Relación breve de la conquista de la Nueva España. México: Universidad Nacional, Instituto de Investigaciones Históricas.

Anales de Cuauhtitlan
1975		Die Geschichte der Königreiche von Colhuacan und México. Walter Lehmann, ed. and trans. Stuttgart: Verlag W. Kohlhammer.

Anderson, Arthur J. O., Frances Berdan, and James Lockhart
1976		Beyond the Codices: The Nahua View of Colonial Mexico. Berkeley and Los Angeles: University of California Press.

Anguiano, Marina, and Matilde Chapa
1976		Estratificación social en Tlaxcala durante el siglo XVI. *In*

Estratificación social en la Mesoamérica prehispánica. Pedro Carrasco and Johanna Broda, eds. pp. 118–56. México: SEP-INAH.

Berdan, Frances F.
1977   Distributive Mechanisms in the Aztec Economy. *In* Peasant Livelihood: Studies in Economic Anthropology and Cultural Ecology. Rhoda Halperin and James Dow, eds. pp. 91–101. New York: St. Martins.

Borah, Woodrow, and Sherburne F. Cook
1963   The Aboriginal Population of Central Mexico on the Eve of the Spanish Conquest. Ibero-Americana 45. Berkeley and Los Angeles: University of California Press.

Broda, Johanna
1978   Relaciones políticas ritualizadas: El ritual como expresión de una ideología. *In* Economía política e ideología en el México prehispánico. Pedro Carrasco and Johanna Broda, eds. pp. 221–55. México: Nueva Imagen.

Carrasco, Pedro
1967   Relaciones sobre la organización social indígena en el siglo XVI. Estudios de Cultura Náhuatl 7: 119–54.

1978   La economía del México prehispánico. *In* Economía política e ideología en el México prehispánico. Pedro Carrasco and Johanna Broda, eds. pp. 15–76. México: Nueva Imagen.

Carrasco, Pedro, and Jesús Monjarás-Ruiz
1976   Colección de documentos sobre Coyoacán: Visita del oidor Gómez de Santillán al pueblo de Coyoacán y su sujeto Tacubaya en el año de 1553. México: Instituto Nacional de Antropología e Historia, Centro de Investigaciones Superiores, Colección Científica, 39.

Caso, Alfonso
1956   Los barrios antiguos de Tenochtitlan y Tlatelolco. Memorias de la Academia Mexicana de la Historia 15(1): 7–63.

Castañeda, Francisco de
1905   Relación de Tecciztlán y su partido. *In* Papeles de Nueva España. Vol. 6. Francisco del Paso y Troncoso, ed. pp. 209–36. Madrid: Sucesores de Rivadeneyra.

Castillo F., Víctor M.
1972   Unidades nahuas de medida. Estudios de Cultura Náhuatl 10: 195–223.

Chimalpahin Quauhtlehuanitzin, Domingo Francisco de San Antón Muñón
1958   Das Memorial: Breve acerca de la fundación de la ciudad de

Culhuacan. Walter Lehmann and G. Kutscher, ed. and trans. Stuttgart: Verlag W. Kohlhammer.

1963   Die Relationen Chimalpahin's zur Geschichte Mexico's, Teil 1: Die Zeit bis zur Conquista 1521. Günter Zimmerman, ed. Hamburg: Universität Hamburg, Abhandlungen aus dem Gebiet der Auslandskunde, Band 68—Reihe B, Band 38.

Claessen, Henri J. M.

1978   The Early State: A Structural Approach. *In* The Early State. Henri J. M. Claessen and Peter Skalnik, eds. pp. 532–96. The Hague: Mouton.

Cline, Howard F.

1972   The Oztoticpac Lands Map of Texcoco, 1540. *In* A la Carte: Selected Papers on Maps and Atlases. Walter W. Ristow, comp. pp. 5–33. Washington, D.C.: Library of Congress.

Códice Kingsborough

1912   Memorial de los indios de Tepetlaoztoc al monarca español contra los encomenderos del pueblo. Francisco del Paso y Troncoso, ed. Madrid: Fototipia de Hauser y Menet.

Corona Sánchez, Eduardo

1976   La estratificación social en el Acolhuacan. *In* Estratificación social en la Mesoamérica prehispánica. Pedro Carrasco and Johanna Broda, eds. pp. 88–101. México: SEP-INAH.

Dávalos Hurtado, E.

1955   La alimentación entre los mexicas. Revista Mexicana de Estudios Antropológicos 14(1): 103–18.

Durán, Diego

1967   Historia de las Indias de Nueva España e islas de la tierra firme. 2 vols. México: Purrúa Hnos.

Fallers, L. A.

1959   Despotism, Status Culture, and Social Mobility in an African Kingdom. Comparative Studies in Society and History 2: 11–32.

Gibson, Charles

1956   Llamamiento General, Repartimiento, and the Empire of Acolhuacan. Hispanic American Historical Review 36: 1–27.

Hicks, Frederic

1975   Dependent Labor in Prehispanic Mexico. Estudios de Cultura Náhuatl 11: 243–66.

1978   Los calpixque de Nezahualcóyotl. Estudios de Cultura Náhuatl 13: 129–52.

INAH-AH, PEA: Instituto Nacional de Antropología e Historia (México),
          Archivo Histórico, Papeles de la Embajada Americana. Doc-
          uments cited by Serie, Legajo, Documento, and in some cases
          Folio.
Ivanhoe, Francis
1978   Diet and Demography in Texcoco on the Eve of the Spanish
          Conquest: A Semiquantitative Reconstruction from Selected
          Ethnohistorical Texts. Revista Mexicana de Estudios Antropo-
          lógicos 24: 137–46.
Ixtlilxóchitl, Fernando de Alva
1952   *Obras históricas* (2 vols.). México: Editora Nacional.
Karttunen, Frances, and James Lockhart
1976   Nahuatl in the Middle Years: Language Contact Phenomena
          in Texts of the Colonial Period. University of California Pub-
          lications in Linguistics, 85.
Molins Fábrega, N.
1955   El Códice Mendocino y la economía de Tenochtitlan. Revista
          Mexicana de Estudios Antropológicos 14(1): 303–35.
Motolinía, Toribio de Benavente
1971   Memoriales, o libro de las cosas de la Nueva España y de los
          naturales de ella. México: Universidad Nacional, Instituto de
          Investigaciones Históricas.
Munch G., Guido
1976   El cacicazgo de San Juan Teotihuacán durante la colonia (1521–
          1821). Instituto Nacional de Antropología e Historia, Centro
          de Investigationes Superiores, Colección Científica, 32.
Nazareo, Pablo
1940   Carta al rey don Felipe II, de don Pablo Nazareo de Xaltocan
          . . . México, 17 mar 1566. *In* Epistolario de Nueva España.
          Vol. 10. Francisco del Paso y Troncoso, ed. pp. 109–29.
          México: Porrúa.
Olivera, Mercedes
1978   Pillis y macehuales: Las formaciones sociales y los modos de
          producción de Tecali del siglo XII al XVI. México: Instituto
          Nacional de Antropología e Historia, Centro de Investiga-
          ciones Superiores, Ediciones de la Casa Chata, 6.
Parsons, Jeffrey R.
1971   Prehistoric Settlement Patterns in the Texcoco Region, Mex-
          ico. Ann Arbor: University of Michigan, Memoirs of the Mu-
          seum of Anthropology, 3.

Pomar, Juan Bautista
1941   Relación de Texcoco. *In* Nueva colección de documentos para la historia de México. Vol. 2. Joaquín García Icazbalceta, ed. pp. 3–64. México: Salvador Chávez Hayhoe.

Prem, Hanns J., ed.
1974   Matrícula de Huexotzinco (Ms. Mex. 387 der Bibliothèque Nationale, Paris). Graz, Austria: Akademische Druck- und Verlagsanstalt.

Relación anónima
1940   Relación anónima, describiendo la división que tenían los indios en sus tierras en tiempo de Moctezuma y el orden que tenían en la sucesión de las mismas. *In* Epistolario de Nueva España. Vol. 14. Francisco del Paso y Troncoso, ed. pp. 145–48. México: Porrúa.

Relación de Zempoala
1952   Relación de Zempoala y su partido, 1580. Tlalocan 3: 29–41.

Reyes García, Luís
1972   Ordenanzas para el gobierno de Cuauhtinchan, Año 1559. Estudios de Cultura Náhuatl 10: 245–313.

Robertson, Donald
1959   Mexican Manuscript Painting of the Early Colonial Period. New Haven: Yale University Press.

Rojas Rabiela, Teresa
1977   La organización del trabajo para las obras públicas: El coatequitl y las cuadrillas de trabajadores. México: Instituto Nacional de Antropología e Historia, Centro de Investigaciones Superiores, Cuadernos de la Casa Chata.

Salazar, Cristóbal de
1905   Relación de Coatepec y su partido. *In* Papeles de Nueva España. Vol. 6. Francisco del Paso y Troncoso, ed. pp. 39–86. Madrid: Sucesores de Rivadeneyra.

Sanders, William T.
1970   The Population of the Teotihuacan Valley, the Basin of Mexico, and the Central Mexican Symbiotic Region in the Sixteenth Century. *In* The Teotihuacan Valley Project, Final Report, Vol. 1: The Natural Environment, Contemporary Occupation, and 16th Century Population of the Valley. University Park: Pennsylvania State University, Department of Anthropology, Occasional Papers in Anthropology, 3.

Spence, Michael W., and Jeffrey R. Parsons
1972   Prehispanic Obsidian Exploitation in Central Mexico: A Preliminary Synthesis. *In* Miscellaneous Studies in Mexican Prehistory. pp. 1–44. Ann Arbor: University of Michigan, Museum of Anthropology, Anthropological Papers, 45.

Torquemada, Juan de
1975   Monarquía Indiana. 3 vols. México: Porrúa.

Trautmann, Wolfgang
1968   Untersuchen zur indianischen Siedlungs- und Territorialgeschichte im Becken von Mexico bis zur frühen Kolonialzeit. Hamburg: Hamburgischen Museum für Völkerkunde und Vorgeschichte, Beiträge zur Mittelamerikanischen Völkerkunde, 7.

Trigger, Bruce
1972   Determinants of Urban Growth in Pre-Industrial Societies. *In* Man, Settlement, and Urbanism. P. J. Ucko, R. Tringham, and G. W. Dimbleby, eds. pp. 575–99. Cambridge, Eng.: Schenkman.

Vetancurt, Agustín de
1971   Teatro mexicano: Crónica del Santo Evangelio. México: Porrúa.

Wheatley, Paul
1971   The Pivot of the Four Quarters: A Preliminary Enquiry into the Origins and Character of the Ancient Chinese City. Chicago: Aldine.

Zorita, Alonso de
1941   Breve y sumaria relación de los señores y maneras y diferencias que había de ellos en la Nueva España . . . *In* Nueva Colección de documentos para la historia de México. Joaquín García Icazbalceta, ed. pp. 67–205. México: Salvador Chávez Hayhoe.

8

Agricultural Implements in Mesoamerica

Teresa Rojas Rabiela

Our knowledge of the agricultural tools used by indigenous Mexicans at the time of the conquest is very poor.[1] The subject has been inexplicably ignored, perhaps due to an a priori assumption that New World technology is somehow more "simple," less varied historically and less "developed" in comparison to Old World technology. Even in the eighteenth century Clavijero complained of the "carelessness" of the ancient chroniclers in discussing this subject. After describing the *coatl* (Nahuatl: *uictli*) and the ax used by the ancient Mexicans, Clavijero (1979: 230) stated that, "They employed several other implements but the carelessness of the ancient authors with respect to this subject deprives us of more detailed knowledge about them."

There is a definite lack of adequate studies concerning agricultural implements at the time of the conquest, both with respect to their function as well as with respect to the tools and techniques used

Fig. 8.1.   Instruments and other objects of obsidian (*iztetl*). An obsidian core, two blades (the one on the left with a type of cover), a bark beater (to make paper), and a hammerstone (the instrument for making obsidian objects) can be identified. The latter is included in other codices, such as the Matrícula de Huexotzingo (Prem 1974), and the Códice de Santa Maria Asunción, for example. (Códice Florentino, lib. 2, cap. 8, f. 208v)

in their manufacture (Boserup 1965: 27) (figure 8.1). The lack of adequate description has contributed to a further confusion of names used to designate the different tools. The greatest difficulty is presented by hand tools used in the actual cultivation of the soil, which appear to be the ones which have undergone the greatest transformation and substitution since 1519.

This essay is a first attempt to glean from pictorial and written records information on cultivation tools as well as axes, hoes, and other tools used for irrigation, harvest, etc. At present the evidence indicates that hand tools predominated over tools also powered with the feet. While I have distinguished three types of hand tools, I found but one foot tool, called the uictli, or *coa de pie.* The first type of hand tool is the planting stick, or *uitzoctli* (*palo,* or *baston plantador*), the second is a kind of wooden spade, the uictli, or *coa de hoja,* and the third is the *uictli axoguen,* or coa with zoomorphic handle. This set of implements, along with others used for weeding and harvesting, was of course closely shaped by the characteristic style of agriculture in Mesoamerica and in the New World generally, in which plants are sown and treated as individual units, rather than broadcast, as in the cereal cultivation systems of the Old World.

At the beginning of the seventeenth century Fray Juan de Torquemada called this entire set of tools by the generic name of uictli, noting that regional differences existed at the time and that some were hand and others hand and foot tools; other evidence suggests

that uictli was in fact a generic name. According to Torquemada
(1969[2]: 481; lib. 13, cap. XXXI):

> [After the conquest] they also continued their rustic mode of
> cultivating the earth with wooden shovels called Huictli, made of
> oak wood and very strong; and the form of these instruments
> varies with the Province, some being used only with the hands
> while squatting or standing on their feet while others are used
> with both feet and hands, driving them into the earth.

What usually occurs now is that all uictlis are grouped under
the name of coa, or "digging stick," or "planting stick," partly
because of the confusion among the different types and partly because
they are considered variants of a single type of tool. For example,
Katz (1966: 24) states that the Aztecs used "a kind of stick to dig
called a huictli or coa with a fire-hardened point. . . ." Similarly,
Kirchoff (1967: 8) listed "digging stick of a certain form (coa)"
among the cultural elements he used to define the Mesoamerican
Culture Area.

The term "coa" has been applied in the same way to practically
all cultivation tools of pre-Columbian America; in this sense it is
a generic term, just as the Nahua term "uictli" is. The origin of
the word seems to have been settled now, after several years of
controversy in which different authors attributed either a Nahuatl
or an Antillean etymology to the term. The Nahua interpretation
(such as Clavijero's) would have it derive from the word *coatl,*
"serpent," or (according to others) from *cuauitl,* meaning "stick."
But the Antillean interpretation has proved to be correct, as Santamaría (1974: 254) and others have shown; he finds the term already
in use in las Casas's *Memorial* (1516). The word came to Mexico
during the sixteenth century, along with others such as *canoa* ("canoe"),
maíz ("maize"), *maguey* ("century plant"), and others.

The European implements with which the chroniclers and historians of the colonial period compared the uictlis were the hoe and
the shovel, and these names have been revived in modern studies:
the "aboriginal hoe" or "aboriginal shovel." We note, for example,
that Molina (1970) registered the verb *uictica* in his *Vocabulario* as
meaning to employ "the *coa* or oak stick to work the soil," as well
as enumerating a number of other related terms which he translated

from Spanish to Nahua. He translated *azada* or *azadón*, for example, as: (1) "Hoe or coa of oak for working the soil. *uictli;*" (2) "Hoe (*açada*). *tlatepuztli.*" He translates the Spanish for "work the soil with *uictli* or *pala*" as *nitla uicuia.* Torquemada (1969[2]: 55; lib. 6, cap. XXI) refers to "the *coas* and shovels with which they dig the soils and cultivate them."

However, Clavijero (1826[1]: 340; lib. 7) clearly saw a difference between the *coa* of the Ancient Mexicans and the Spanish hoe: "To dig or stir the soil they employ the *coatl* or *coa*, an instrument of copper with a wooden handle but very different from the hoe (*de la azada y del azadón*)."

Whether one chooses to consider here a single type of implement with several variants, or three or more different types, it seems desirable to describe the principal characteristics of these tools and bring some order to the confusion of terminology. Donkin (1970), Santamaría (1974), and Palerm (1967), in particular, have attempted to clarify these issues. In the following discussion I treat each of what I consider distinct cultivation tool types and I explore the hypothesis that each type corresponds to a particular agricultural system.

UITZOCTLI

The uitzoctli is the simple digging stick which Torquemada (1969[2]: 481; lib. 13, cap. XXXI) called a *"palo tostado,"* whose point is sharpened and hardened in the fire or covered with a piece of metal (figure 8.2). Carl O. Sauer (1969) considered it to derive from a tool used by gatherers to unearth roots and tear up plants.

The sixteenth-century Nahuatl term is still used in some regions of Mexico today. According to Molina's *Vocabulario* (1970) "uitzoctli" was a "sharpened oak staff used to uproot sod and open the soil"; *uitzoctica* meant "with a round oak stick." Documents written in Spanish during the same century also make a clear distinction between "sticks for breaking the ground" and two other types, called coas and *palas* ("shovels") (Tepeaca, Puebla, 1571, in Martínez 1977: 148). Sahagún (1975: 476) in his list of objects sold in the market of Tenochtitlan, mentioned the following agricultural implements: coas, staffs (*palancas*), and palas; or uicti, uitzoctli, and *tlateconi,* in

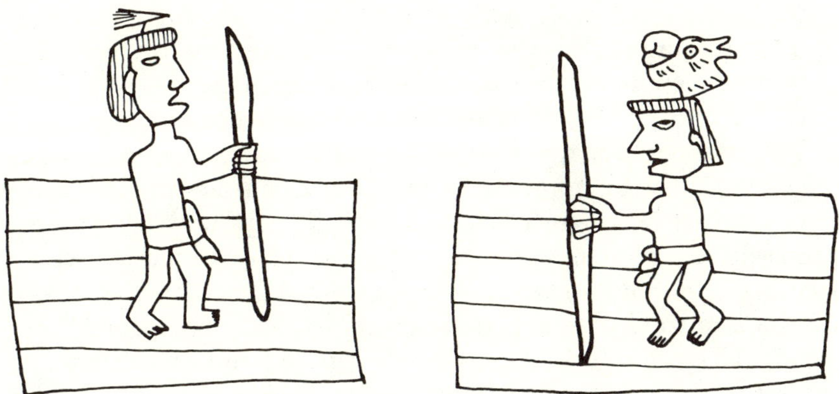

Fig. 8.2.   Uitzoctli, digging, or planting, stick being used by two workers from Huamantla, Tlaxcala. (*Huamantla Codex,* sixteenth century)

the corresponding Nahuatl version (Códice Florentino: lib. 8, cap. 19). While describing the "Repose of the Useful Instruments" ceremony in *Etzacualistli,* Durán (1967[1]: 260; cap. IX, 6) recorded the same three types, even in the same order: "the *coas* and the sharp sticks with which they plant and the shovels with which they dig the earth. . . ."

The uitzoctli of that era, as it is today, was made in different sizes and of varying materials, chosen from among the most resistant hardwoods. Oaks are mentioned under various names: *roble,* or *carrasco* (Sahagún 1975: 661), and *encino* (Torquemada 1969[2]: 481; lib. 13, cap. XXXI). Among the species used today are the *otate* (West 1948: 37–38), the mesquite (Donkin 1970: 509), the *ocotillo,* the *parotillo,* the *diente de molino,* and the *quebracho,* or *tepuzcuauil* (Hendrichs 1945[1]: 77). Palerm (1967: 46) refers to the use of sticks, left over from the burning of brush during the preparation of the fields, which were made even stronger by the fire. The length of these digging sticks varies between 1.5 and 3.0 meters, according to desired weight and the age and sex of the user.

Documents of the sixteenth century indicate that the uitzoctli was made entirely of wood in prehispanic Mesoamerica, but Donkin (1970: 507) has found evidence for the use of stone and metal tips in other parts of America. Then as now the digging stick was used primarily in swidden systems for digging holes to receive seed or seedlings, and for replanting. Burgoa (in Dahlgren 1954: 94), with reference to the Mixteca Alta region, describes a "sharpened, hard-wood staff with which they open the ground and there they bury the seed. . . ." But the possibility that the uitzoctli was used in systems where the soil was tilled must be considered (Turner 1978: 14–15).

The digging stick most likely was used as a lever to lift the ground, to cultivate the roots of plants, and to uproot tubers (Palerm 1967: 46), uses clearly suggested by the translation of Fray Molina (1970): "*Uitzoctli*—sharpened oak staff for uprooting sod and open-ing the soil," as well as by Sahagún's (1975) list: "*coas* and staffs and shovels." In his study of pre-Columbian agricultural imple-ments, Donkin (1970: 507), apparently unaware of these references, also observed that sticks of greater weight could be used as levers; he classes them more closely with the wooden spade, or *coa de hoja,* than with the true digging stick.

The distribution of the uitzoctli extended far beyond the bound-aries of Mesoamerica: Peru, Colombia, Venezuela, the Antilles and Central American (Donkin 1970: 507). In other words the digging stick as described here cannot be considered as a diagnostic trait of the Mesoamerican area.

The uitzoctli, with or without a metal tip and of varying forms, is frequently used in many regions of Mexico today. Since the con-quest the metal used has been iron. According to representations in the codices from the sixteenth century, together with observation of current practices, the staff is held with both hands close together, with the body straight and parallel to the stick, if it is being used to perforate holes, or leaning backwards to function as a lever, if it is a matter of lifting soil. Among the names this instrument has received in Spanish are: *bastón* (alone or with modifiers such as *puntiagudo* [sharp], *plantador* [planting], *sembrador* [sowing], etc.), *palo* (alone or with modifiers), *espeque, macana, barra, barreta, palanca, estaca, cavador, chuzo*. The terms most frequently used in Mexico are *macana* (Campeche, Yucatán, Tabasco, and Chiapas) and *espeque* (Veracruz). The term macana was used by Fernández de Oviedo (1851–53[1]: 226; cap. 1) in his description of swidden agriculture on the island of Hispaniola. I consider it unlikely that the *macauitl,* a wooden sword with a double row of embedded flint chips along the edge, ever saw the agricultural use suggested by Palerm (1967: 47). According to him the macana (which is what he calls the macauitl) was used as a weapon and as a tool, being replaced by the steel machete after the conquest. It is a fact that wooden clubs, which are now called macanas, were used as weapons during the prehispanic period, but they were simple clubs, not macauitl. It is also possible that clubs and sticks were used to break up dirt clods, as is the case with the *couitectle* of present-day Acatlán, Guerrero.

UICTLI, OR COA DE HOJA

In the prehispanic and sixteenth-century codices from Central Mexico the *uictli de hoja* (literally "stick with blade") appears as a symbol of both the worker (the tributary peasant) and tributary work itself, the *tequitl* in Nahuatl (figures 8.3–8.5). What I call uictli de hoja is, just as in the case of the digging stick, an ideal type with respect to form and design, but differs from the latter in being a nonspecialized, multiple-use tool. It was used in agricultural systems which involved turning the soil. Since the term coa has been applied not only to the uictli de hoja but to the digging stick, as well as to other tools mentioned below, I propose to reserve the term coa, or uictli de hoja, spade, for that implement considered by Kirchhoff (1967) to be a specific Mesoamerican element and which he described as similar to a spatula or a baker's pallet. I have found more representations of this implement in the pictographic sources than of any other agricultural tool, perhaps due to its use at the time of the conquest or when the sources were compiled.

Coas are made from the same resistant hardwoods as the digging stick, that is, of oak—*roble* (Molina 1970, 2a: 157v) or *encino* (Torquemada 1969[1]: 612; lib. 5, cap. XII; [2]: 481; lib. 13, cap.

Fig. 8.3.   Uictli, or coa de hoja, wooden spade, being used for planting corn. (Códice Florentino, lib. 4, f. 72r)

XXXI; Molina 1970, 1a: 2v), as well as of mesquite and others. They were made either of one solid piece of wood or of two pieces, the blade being made of hardened copper, as Clavijero (1979) and some codices seem to indicate. In both cases the blade was flat and was wider near the point; then it tapered off to form a more or less triangular figure, straight on one side and curved on the other.

Important examples of the two-piece spade with metal blade are some from the Purépecha area (*Lienzo de Jucutácato,* cited by West 1948: 38) and those from the Mixteca (Codex Féjérváry-Mayer). According to these and other naturalistic pictorial examples the coa was used, according to the task, while standing, or down on one knee, or sitting, with the handle in both hands, slightly separated, the left below and the right above. When digging or turning the soil the tool moved parallel to the body; and when lifting to remove the soil the body was inclined forward, forming an acute angle with

Fig. 8.4.   Uictli, or coa de hoja, used in weeding a hill of corn. (Codex Féjérváry-Mayer)

the horizon. The uictli de hoja was also used to break up clods by holding the top end in both hands placed together (Códice Florentino: lib. 11, cap. 12, párr. 3).

Although the coa de hoja of solid wood still exists in Mexico—it was observed, for example, among the Otomís by Manrique (1969: 689, Fig. 8)—it has practically disappeared and very little is known of its history. The implement observed today with the name of uictli, which is similar in appearance to the pre-Columbian variety, has an iron blade and is used, just as are the wooden ones of the Otomís, to plant, weed, and to hill up corn (Donkin 1970: 514; Kelly and Palerm 1952: 108–9; Manrique 1969: 689–90). Other modern implements receive the name of coa, such as those used in the region of Cuauhtinchan, Puebla, and in Huixquilucan, México, to "castrate" the maguey plant in pulque making (L. Reyes and H. Harvey, personal communication) or in Yucatan, where it is used

184

Fig. 8.5   Uictli, or coa de hoja, as a symbol of the tributary worker obliged to clean the canals in the city of Mexico. (Códice de 1576)

for weeding the cornfield (*loob* in Yucatec, *Enciclopedia Yucatanense* [6]: 43).

After 1519 the uictli of wood or metal gave way to or coexisted with the plow, hoe, and iron shovel introduced by the Spanish for the agricultural tasks mentioned above (figure 8.6).

The uictli, or spade, was a standardized, "multiple-use" implement (as Castillo [1972: 265] astutely observed), which was employed widely in agricultural as well as in many other tasks, such as construction and repair of buildings, houses, and hydraulic works (cleaning canals, for example), and by artesans who worked stone, feathers, etc. (figure 8.7). (See the Códice Osuna; Códice de 1576, or Códice Aubin; and Códice Florentino, lib. 10 and 11, especially.)

In agriculture this tool was used in practically every task; in this regard we may recall Sahagún's informants' list of activities carried out by a good gardener: breaking ground, digging, hoeing, making holes and beds for planting, weeding, hilling up, watering, making seedbeds, pulling grass, etc. In other words the wooden spade was not only used for making holes for seed, but was rather a tool used in a great variety of ways. Torquemada (1969[1]: 612, lib. 5, cap. XII) also mentions "coas of oak (which they call huictli) with which they clean and cultivate their cornfields."

There were variants of the uictli de hoja with special names, associated with particular tasks of the production cycle, such as weeding and hilling up. From Molina's vocabulary (1970) I have

Fig. 8.6.   Indian tributaries of Mexico City working in the garden of a Spaniard in the vicinity of the city (ca. 1565). This fragment shows the varieties of new plants as well as the use of the wooden spade, uictli, or coa de hoja de madera, of prehispanic origin, simultaneous with the Spanish hoe (azadón), introduced by the colonizers. (Códice Osuna, f. 38v)

Fig. 8.7.   Artisans who make mirrors, utilizing the digging spade (uictli, or coa de hoja) and a mallet. (Códice Florentino, lib. 2, cap. 8, f. 210r)

been able so far to identify the following tools for those tasks: *tlaxiuhcuicuiuani,* "a cultivator or coa called uictli for cleaning or weeding something"; and five more terms similarly translated: *tlaxippopoaloni, tlaxiuhochpanoni, tlaxiuhpopoaloni, tlaxiuhtopeualoni* and *tlatlamoleuililoni.*

These terms are translated *sacho* or *escardillo* in Spanish. Works from the early eighteenth century as well as Herrera (1819 [1513]) and his later commentaries lead us to suspect that these terms referred to a tool different from the indigenous wooden spade, more similar to the Spanish spud (*almocafre*), or weeding hoe. Perhaps one of the various axes pictured in the codices is referred to by these terms (see especially those which appear in the *Matrícula de Huexotzinco* [Prem 1974]). Another possibility is that they were straight or curved blades of obsidian, flint, or metal, with wooden handles— a kind of sickle. We know so little about the actual use of many archaeological artifacts that it is likely that many a museum piece labeled "ax" was in reality used in agriculture or in the exploitation of maguey, such as those from southwestern Tlaxcala, beginning in the Texoloc phase (800–300 B.C.; Tesch and Abascal 1974). We are also reminded of reliefs in ruins such as the *castillo* of Teayo, in the Huastec region, where we observe representations of tools similar to those used in the region today (*uingaros*) for weeding swidden cornfields.

The sacho, according to the *Diccionario de autoridades* (1976; originally published in Spain, in 1726) was a metal blade and a handle "small and manageable" in the form of a hoe used for weeding (*sachar,* defined as "digging the planted ground so that the seed will grow more and they take out any weeds there may be.") Similar to it was the escardillo, "a curved wooden-handled iron tool for weeding the earth, also called *almocafre.*" In *Agricultura general* (Herrera 1819 [1513]) we find such instructions as "take a *sacho* and make holes deeper than five fingers." This all seems to deal with cultivating, digging the earth, and removing weeds.

UICTLI AXOQUEN

The representation of this tool in the *Historia Tolteca Chichimeca* (Kirchhoff, Odena, and Reyes 1976, f. 39r, Ms. 46–50, p. 35) was brought to my attention by L. Reyes; I was later able to find several others in the *Matrícula de Huexotzinco* (Prem 1974, ff. 535v, 544v, and 592v), in which its name is written in Latin characters as axoquen and *uiuic*.

The uictli axoquen has a handle which is less than the height of a person (about two-thirds, according to the *Historia*) and is composed of two pieces tied together with fiber, leather, or vine. It is not possible to ascertain whether the flat blade is of wood or metal, but it is a different color of ochre from the handle, in the pictographic representation, and is drawn at a right angle to it. At the end of the handle is a curved animal head very similar to those on canes manufactured in México. Axoquen is defined by Molina as "a bird with white plumage," but I have found no representations of the use of this tool. In the *Historia* cited above, the man has it in his left hand; in the other he carries a short club, while on his back he wears a *cacaxtle,* a pannier for transporting cargo. A woman carrying a basket accompanies him (figure 8.8). Both are peasants migrating from Cholula to Cuauhtinchan, in what is now the State of Puebla (Kirchhoff, Odena, and Reyes 1976: 209).

In the following commentary, after describing the ceremony of the "Repose of the Useful Instrument," Durán (1967[1]: 260, cap. XI, 7) is probably referring to this type of uictli, although with an iron blade, and gives us some information about its area of distribution and about the adoption of iron by the colonized population:

> Oh the strange bestiality of these people! In many things they have good discipline and government and understanding and capacity and polish but in others strange bestiality and blindness. . . . What more can be said? I have observed that nowadays there are hoes of iron which they use to work the soil which have handles with the butts shaped into monkeys, dogs or devils. And it does not seem good to me and it is so general that there is not a single Indian without one, especially in Chalco and in the mountainous part of the region.

UICTLI, OR COA DE PIE

The tool represented in the Códice Florentino (lib. 10, cap. 12, f. 28v) is probably the same type as Torquemada (1969[2]: 481; lib. 13, cap. XXXI) affirmed as driven into the earth "by force of foot and hand," or as that registered in the Spanish-Otomí Dic-

Fig. 8.8.   Uictli axoquen, or hoe with zoomorphic handle. Also shown is the cacaxtle, a pannier with basket, worn on the back. (Historia Tolteca-Chichimeca [Kirchhoff, Odena, and Reyes 1976], f. 39r, Ms. 46–50, p. 35, 519v)

tionary as "a great coa which they work with the foot, *nottaathi* (1640, in the National Library of Mexico, cited in Carrasco 1950: 49). This is possibly the tool referred to by Durán and Sahagún as a pala (*tlateconi* in the Nahuatl version of the latter; this same term is also found in a document from Colhuacan, from around 1577, in León Portilla 1976: 30). However, the definition given by Molina (1970) for this term corresponds to a different tool: "ax for cutting something or other similar instrument." Undoubtedly more information will have to be uncovered in order to resolve the contradiction; for the moment I suggest we associate the Nahuatl tlateconi with the shovel-like uictli or with another, described at the end of this section, which is pictured in the *Descripción* (Muñoz Camargo 1981) and the *Lienzo de Tlaxcala* (1979).

The uictli shovel appears in the Códice Florentino as a flat shovel with a single triangular blade, made of a single piece of wood (figure 8.9). One could describe it as a kind of magnified uictli de hoja, or a development of this latter tool for achieving greater application of force with the foot. It is held in the hands in a similar way, left above and right below, with the foot on the curve of the blade.

Based on Torquemada's comments on the whole set of uictlis, one may postulate that the uictli de pie was used in agricultural systems involving turning the soil. It seems unlikely that this tool is a postconquest development, as Donkin (1970: 509) believes, although the question is still open to future investigation.

IMPLEMENTS FOR CULTIVATION, HARVEST, IRRIGATION, AND OTHER PURPOSES

Modern methods for opening land and clearing vegetation for swidden or for permanent cultivation involve cutting the larger trees with an ax and the smaller ones, including brush, vines, etc., with a machete, curved or straight, or with some other steel tool, such as the *tarpala,* from Chinantla, Oaxaca, or the "coa" or *loob,* from Yucatán. A forked stick is also used to pull and bend the vegetation while cutting. The dried refuse is then burned, or left to rot into the soil. The *Vocabulario* of Molina (1970) gives two definitions for the verb *rozar* ("to prepare a swidden plot"): "Roçar. *nitla chichiqui, nitla momotzoa";* or "Roçar yerva. *ni cacapi."* This

Fig. 8.9. Uictli, or coa de pie, shovel. Shown is the method of harvesting corn. (Códice Florentino, lib. 10, cap. 12, f. 29r)

latter term derives from the transitive verb *pi* (*nitla*) which means "collect herbs without pulling their roots" (Molina 1970).

During the prehispanic era axes were undoubtedly not the only tools used for swidden; there were other tools and alternative methods to that of felling the vegetation.

The earliest reference to the use of axes is in the *Historia de las Indias,* by Fray Bartolomé de las Casas (1951). Describing the trip of Francisco Hernández to the coast of Campeche, in 1517, he wrote (1951[3]: 163; lib. 3, cap. XCVIII) that "[In Champotón] Captain Francisco Hernández went ashore with all his men and many Indians came at them with their arms and a certain kind of metal hatchet with which they must do their swiddens and household jobs." Landa, in the *Relación de las cosas de Yucatán* (1978: 52; XXIX) described axes: "They had hatchets of a certain metal such as in the drawing which were fitted into a wooden handle and served as weapons and to work wood. They sharpened them by giving blows with a stone since the metal is soft." Clavijero (1979: 230; lib. VII, 28) referred to the agricultural use of axes: "They used axes of copper for swidden and for other functions in agriculture; their axes do not differ from ours except that in ours the handle enters through the ring of the ax while in theirs, on the contrary, the ax enters through the handle in the manner represented in the illustration of the costumes." (This illustration was not found in the editions of this work which I consulted.)

There is abundant evidence concerning the characteristics of the heads and handles of these axes in the codices, as well as information on the way they were held (figure 8.10). We lack information, however, which would allow us to associate the different types with particular uses. On the other hand the Nahuatl or Purépecha terms used to designate the different axes do indicate some uses or are descriptive of certain characteristics; the task of relating the terms with the pictorial representations is still to be done. Among the Nahuatl terms (Molina 1970) are: (1) "Ax for cutting firewood. *tepusquauhxexeloloni. quauhtlateconi.*" (2) Ax for working wood. *tlaximaltepuztli.*" (3) "Small ax. *tlaximaltepuztontli.*" (4) "Ax to cut in two parts. *castilan tlaximaloni necoctene.*" (5) "*Tlateconi.* ax to cut something or other similar instrument." In the Códice Florentino

Fig. 8.10.   Scene in which a man is shown felling a tree with an ax of Type 4 and another carving a wooden figure with an ax of Type 3 (?). (Códice Florentino, lib. 1, f. 26r)

(lib. 8, cap. 19) the group of "axes of copper to cut wood" are called: *"tepoztli, quauhxeloloni, tepozcoiolomitl, tlacuicuioaloni, tepoztlaquauh icuiloloni.*

Among the Purépechas (Gilberti 1975: 359–60) we find the following: (1) "Ax for cutting firewood. *tiyamu y viraqua, chaparaqua.*" (2) "Ax for working wood. *tiyamu tecaraqua.*" (3) "Small ax. *visiraqua.*" (4) "Ax to cut into two parts. *tiyamu tzimarahcanda ambaquemuri.*"

I have grouped the various pictographic examples of axes into eight types, based on the form of the head and the manner in which it is mounted onto the handle (figures 8.11–8.13). It is still not possible to distinguish which are of stone and which of metal, nor to associate a specific term with a given representation. The forms differ greatly in the way they are represented; several are probably

194

Fig. 8.11.   Axes, Types 1, 2, 3, and 4.

a. Ax as a toponym of Tepoztitla. Figure representing the tributory
    province of Tlalcoacautitlan. (Códice Mendocino f. 40r)
b. Ax used by the *tetzotzonqui* and the *texquini,* stoneworkers.
    (Matrícula de Huexotzinco [Prem 1974] f. 829v)
c. Ax used by the *quauhxinqui,* carpenter. (Matrícula de Huexotzinco
    [Prem 1974] f. 641v)
d. Ax of the carpenters (Códice Osuna, f. 15r or 477r). In the
    Matrícula de Huexotzinco (Prem 1974) the same implement is used
    to represent the *tlaxinqui,* literally the "destroyer of things," and the
    carpenter.

of European origin, as indicated by some of the terms cited above.
Others are clearly specialized artesans' tools, such as the carpenter's
hatchet or the stoneworker's mace.

In the Códice Tudela (1980) we find two figures which are important with respect to axes. The first is the representation of the
god Ometochtli (f. 31r), carrying in his right hand a Type 1 ax
with what appears to be a metal axhead, next to which we read:
"Of this form are the axes for working wood" (figure 8.14). Thus
it would seem that this kind was a woodworker's tool, while those
of the other kind are for cutting in general. The second figure of
the codex (f. 74r) refers to aspects of daily life of the Yopes and
shows the groom alongside his instruments of work: a coa with
wooden blade, a tumpline, and a metal cutting ax. The Spanish
text (f. 74v) says: "and her parents called the groom and they put
before him an ax and a coa and a tumpline and asked him if he was

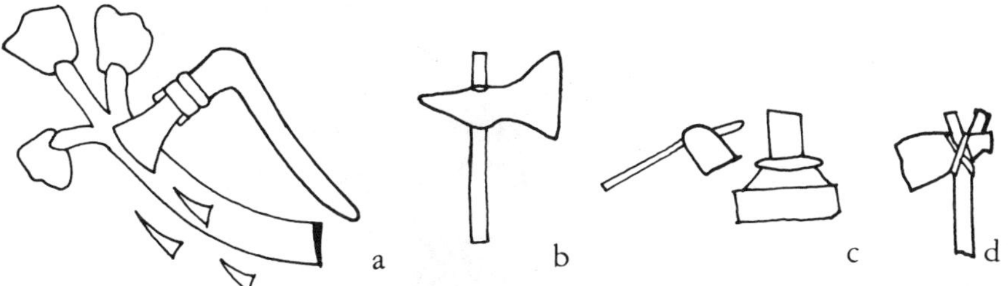

Fig. 8.12.   Axes, Types 5, 6, 7, and 8.

a. Ax as toponym for Quauhximalpan. (Códice Mendocino, Pl. V). The same kind of device is used for the *tlaxinqui* ("destroyer of things") in the Matrícula de Huexotzinco (Prem 1974), f. 769v or 770v.

b. Ax of the stoneworker, *texinqui* (Matrícula de Huexotzinco [Prem 1974], f. 519r)

c. Ax of the stoneworker, *texinqui* (Matrícula de Huexotzinco [Prem 1974], f. 484r), and of the *tlaxinqui*, "destroyer of things."

d. Ax of the stoneworker, *teztotzonqui* (Matrícula de Huexotzinco [Prem 1974], f. 770r). Similar axes are found in this same source to indicate *texinqui*.

a worker and was going to use those things, and he said yes and then they gave him the woman." (figure 8.15).

For swidden, other instruments may have been used besides axes. Palerm (1967: 47) suggested the macauitl, but did not provide his source. In the *Vocabulario* Molina (1970) describes a *"Roçador instrumento. tlachichiconi,"* as does the *Diccionario* of Purépecha (Gilberti 1975: 469) *"Roçador instrumento. varaitqua."* Some authors have proposed that methods other than felling with axes could have been employed during the prehispanic era; some of them have been observed ethnographically. They include: gradually killing large trees by removing the bark (Tabasco, West et al. 1976: 159) or by making circular incisions all or partway around, so that the tree dries up; it is then pushed over (Morley 1975: 165).

For carrying seed during planting both gourds and fiber bags have been used, hung from the shoulder or diagonally across the

Fig. 8.13. Ax, Type 1, in the hand of a Mexican merchant disguised
in the costume of the province of Tziacantla. (Códice Florentino, lib.
9, cap. 5, f. 18v)

body. These are the *talequillos* or *espuertas* of the chronicles, the
sabucanes of the Yucatec Maya, or the *morrales* of other parts of
Mexico. Also reported are shells or armadillo hides, tied to the belt
or hung from the shoulder. To gather the harvest, baskets were
employed, and nets were carried on the back over panniers, tied
with rope or suspended by a tumpline from the forehead or shoulders.

For husking the ears of corn a tool in the form of a pick, or pin,
was made of wood, deer bone, or metal. There were various methods
for shelling, including scraping the ears on the surface of an *olotera*
(a wheel made from cobs tied together) or on a stone slab, or striking
them in a net (Códice Florentino, lib. 10, f. 130v), on *petates* (grass
mats), or wooden grills (constructed on four corner stakes). Home
methods for small quantities included striking the ear on the grind-
ing stone, hitting it with an old tool, or shelling it with the hands.

Fig. 8.14.   Representation of the god Ometochtli with two axes, one of Type 1 and the other of Type 4. Next to the first we read: "of this form are the axes for cutting in this country," and next to the other: "of this form are the hatchets for working wood." (Códice Tudela f. 31r)

The problem of protecting the crops from birds at crucial periods in the agricultural cycle was addressed by building little towers, *torrecillos*. Clavijero (1826, lib. VII, 29) mentions raised *tapestles* made of wood, branches, and mats, built and manned by adults at times, but mainly by children—on whom has almost always fallen the task of living scarecrows. Techniques include making all kinds of noises and throwing rocks by hand or with slings or slingshots. Artifical scarecrows, made of different plant parts, were also used. To scare rodents away people have traditionally used bonfires and traps placed in the holes or on trails. It is possible that poisons were formerly used against rodents, such as the herb called *quimichpatli,* which Sahagún (1975: 667) says was mixed with food and used to kill rats.

Implements used for watering were all manual, apart from large

Fig. 8.15.   Instruments of work of the common man in the Yope region. A Type 1 ax; a wooden spade, or uictli de hoja; and a tumpline. (Códice Tudela f. 74r)

irrigation works, which were widespread throughout the prehispanic era. Watering was done by hand, plant by plant, from wells, ditches, ponds, etc., or by gravity, with ditches and deliberate flooding. Manual watering of plants in seedbeds or in the fields was achieved by splashing or throwing water from containers made of clay, wood, or gourds. Other tools were probably also employed, such as the wooden long-handled spoon of Pátzcuaro (*batea, pala,* or *t'aparataracua;* West 1948: 47) and the *zoquimaitl,* a pole with a bag attached to one end, from Central Mexico (Alzate 1831[2]: 390–91; West and Armillas 1950; Peña 1978: 37). Foster (1972: 51) claims, however, that the long wooden spoon is a primitive Spanish tool and not an indigenous implement.

In the illustrations of the *Descripción* of Tlaxcala, by Diego Muñoz Camargo (1981), made around 1581, we find another implement represented which was probably used in irrigation agriculture, since it is drawn crossed with a paddle inside a canoe in the figure corresponding to Tetzcoco (figure 8.16). This drawing is comparable to the better-known version in the *Lienzo de Tlaxcala* (1979, Pl. 41) made in the nineteenth century, which presents such a stylized drawing that the original instrument is hardly recognizable. This tool is similar to the ax with a curved and reinforced handle, but is longer, more like a hoe than an ax, and might well be the pala of Sahagún (1975) or the tlateconi Molina (1970) translates as an "ax to cut something or other similar instrument."

Fig. 8.16. Fragment of an illustration, showing a canoe containing a paddle and a tool of unknown origin, but which may have been used in agriculture (for pulling grass?) (Lienzo de Tlaxcala, Pl. 41, corresponding to Tetzcoco)

CONCLUSIONS

It would appear unwise to equate apparent simplicity of implements with a "simple" or technologically uniform agriculture, or with primitiveness in the organization of work. This characterization of Mesoamerican agriculture, based on a few implements in an isolated context, ignores the complex system of management of biotic resources developed by the Mesoamericans, the historical product of centuries of experimentation with agricultural systems. The known agricultural implements were adapted to the characteristics of prehispanic cultivars (the corn-beans-squash complex and amaranth, for example) and to the dominant cultivation technologies. Thus plants, technology, and implements formed a harmonious and coherent whole. To categorize the implements as poorly or highly developed is premature until more is known; the evaluation of implements must take cognizance of the technical and biotic factors in agricultural production and of the highly developed ability of native society to organize the abundant labor supply in agricultural pursuits.

Everything seems to indicate, however, that technological success came in the area of human and biotic resource management, rather than in the elaboration of agricultural tools.

NOTE

1. The author wishes to express her gratitude for information and suggestions received from Luis Reyes G., Alfredo Lopez Austin, and Constantino Medina. I also wish to thank Catalina Loza and Pilar Reyes for typing the early versions of this essay, and Ronald Nigh for translation. Thanks are also due José Luis Ramos, for producing the drawings.

REFERENCES

Alzate y Ramirez, Joseph Antonio de
1831 Cacetas de Literature de México. 4 vols. Puebla: Oficina del Hospital de S. Pedro.
Boserup, Ester
1965 The Conditions of Agricultural Growth. The Economics of Agrarian Change under Population Pressure. Chicago: Aldine.
Carrasco, Pedro
1950 Los otomíes. Cultura e historia prehispánicas de los pueblos mesoamericanos de habla otomiana. México: Universidad Nacional Autónoma de México.
Castillo, Victor M.
1972 Estructura ecónomica de la sociedad mexica según las fuentes documentales. México: Instituto de Investigaciones Históricas, Universidad Nacional Autónoma de México.
Clavijero, Francisco Javier
1826 Historia antigua de México. 2 vols. London: R. Askerman, Strand.
1979 Historia antigua de México. México: Editorial Porrúa (Sepan Cuantos, 29).
Códice de 1576
1963 Historia de la nación mexicana. Charles E. Dibble, ed. and trans. Madrid: Editorial José Porrúa Turanzas (Colección Chimalistac 16).

Codex Féjérváry-Mayer
1901–2   Codex Féjérváry-Mayer. E. Seler, ed. Berlin.
Códice Florentino
1980   Edición facsímil del manuscrito 218-20 de la Colección Pal-
           atina de la Biblioteca Mediciea Laurenziana. 3 vols. México:
           Gobierno de la República [Mexicana].
Códice Mendocino
1964   Antiguedades de México. José Corona Núñez, ed. Vol. 1: 1–
           149. México: Secretaría de Hacienda y Crédito Público).
Códice Osuna
1973   Pintura del gobernador, alcaldes y regidores de México. Mad-
           rid: Ministerio de Educación y Ciencia.
Códice Tudela
1980   José Tudela de la Orden, ed. Madrid: Ediciones Cultura His-
           pánica del Instituto de Cooperación Iberoamericana.
Dahlgren de Jordan, Barbro
1954   La Mixteca. Su cultura e historia prehispánicas. México: Im-
           prenta Universitaria (Cultura mexicana 11).
Diccionario de Autoridades
1976   Real Academia Española. Edición facsimilar (de la de 1726).
           3 vols. Madrid: Editorial Gredos (Biblioteca Románica His-
           pánica, Diccionarios 3).
Donkin, R. A.
1970   Pre-Columbian Field Implements and Their Distribution in
           the Highlands of Middle and South America. Anthropos 65:
           505–29.
Durán, Diego
1967   Historia de las Indias de Nueva España e islas de la Tierra
           Firme. Angel Ma. Garibay, intro. and notes. 3 vols. México:
           Editorial Porrúa.
Enciclopedia Yucatanense
1977   9 vols. México: Edición oficial del gobierno del Estado [de
           Yucatán].
Fernández de Oviedo, Gonzalo
1851–53   Historia general y natural de las Indias, islas y Tierra Firme
           del mar Oceáno. 4 vols. Madrid: Real Academia de la Historia.
Foster, George M.
1972   Tzintzuntzan. México: Fondo de Cultura Económica.
Gilberti, Fray Maturino
1975   Diccionario de la lengua tarasca o de Michoacán. Morelia:
           Edición facsimilar de Balsal Editores.

Hendrichs, Pedro R.
1945   Por tierras ignotas. Viajes y observaciones en la región del río
            de las Balsas. 2 vols. México: Editorial Cultura.
Herrera, Gabriel Alonso de
1819   Agricultura general. Corregida según el texto original de la
            primera edición publicada en 1513 por el mismo autor y
            adicionada por la Real Sociedad Matritense. 4 vols. Madrid:
            Imprenta Real.
Katz, Friedrich
1966   Situación social y económica de los aztecas durante los siglos
            XV y XVI. México: Universidad Nacional Autóma de México.
Kelly, Isabel, and Angel Palerm
1952   The Tajin Totonac. Part I: History, Subsistence, Shelter and
            Technology. Washington, D.C.: Smithsonian Institution of
            Washington, Institute of Social Anthropology (Publication 13).
Kirchhoff, Paul
1967   Mesoamérica. México: Escuela Nacional de Antropología e
            Historia (Suplemento de la revista Tlatoani 3).
Kirchhoff, Paul, Lina Odena Guemes,
and Luís Reyes
1976   Historia Tolteca-Chichimeca. México: Centro de Investiga-
            ciones Superiores del Instituto Nacional de Antropología e
            Historia.
Landa, Diego de
1978   Relación de las cosas de Yucatán. México: Editorial Porrúa
            (Biblioteca Porrúa 13).
Las Casas, Fray Bartolomé de
1951   Historia de las Indias. 3 vols. México: Fondo de Cultura Econ-
            ómica (Biblioteca Americana 15, 16, 17).
León Portilla, Miguel
1976   El libro inédito de los testamentos indígenas de Culhuacán.
            Su significación como testimonio histórico. Estudios de Cul-
            tura Náhuatl 12: 11–31.
Lienzo de Tlaxcala
1979   A. Chavero, orig. publ. México, 1892. México: Editorial
            Cosmos.
Manrique, Leonardo
1969   The Otomí. Handbook of Middle American Indians. Vol. 8,
            pp. 682–722. Robert Wauchope, gen. ed. Austin: University
            of Texas Press.

Martínez, Hildeberto
1977   Tepeaca en el siglo XVI: tenencia de la tierra y organización
             de un señorío. Tesis. Facultad de Antropología, Universidad
             Veracruzana.

Molina, Alonso de
1970   Vocabulario en lengua castellana y mexicana. México: Editorial
             Porrúa (Biblioteca Porrúa 44).

Morley, Sylvanus G.
1975   La civilización maya. México: Fondo de Cultura Económica.

Muñoz Camargo, Diego
1981   Descripción de la ciudad y provincia de Tlaxcala de los indios
             y del mar oceáno para el buen gobierno y ennoblecimiento
             dellos. Edición facsímil del manuscrito de Glasgow, con un
             estudio preliminar de René Acuña. México: Instituto de In-
             vestigaciones Filológicas, Universidad Nacional Autónoma de
             México.

Palerm, Angel
1967   Agricultural Systems and Food Patterns. Handbook of Middle
             American Indians. Vol. 6, pp. 26–52. Robert Wauchope, gen.
             ed. Austin: University of Texas Press.

Peña, Elsa
1978   El trabajo agrícola en un pueblo chinampero: San Luis Tlax-
             ialtemalco. Tesis. México: Escuela Nacional de Antropología
             e Historia.

Prem, Hanns J.
1974   Matrícula de Huexotzinco. Graz, Austria: Akademische Druck-
             und Verlagsanstalt.

Sahagún, Bernardino de
1975   Historia general de las cosas de Nueva España. México: Edi-
             torial Porrúa ("Sepan Cuantos . . ." 300).

Santamaría, Francisco J.
1974   Diccionario de mejicanismos. México: Editorial Porrúa.

Sauer, Carl O.
1969   Agricultural Origins and Dispersals. Cambridge, Mass.: MIT
             Press.

Tesch, Monika, and Rafael Abascal
1974   Azadas. Comunicaciones 11: 37–40.

Torquemada, Juan de
1969   Monarquía Indiana. Edición facsimilar de la de 1723. 3 vols.
             México: Editorial Porrúa.

Turner, B. L. II
1978   The Development and Demise of the Swidden Thesis of Maya
            Agriculture. *In* Pre-Hispanic Maya Agriculture. P. D. Har-
            rison and B. L. Turner II, eds. pp. 13–22. Albuquerque:
            University of New Mexico Press.
West, Robert C.
1948   Cultural Geography of the Modern Tarascan Area. Washing-
            ton, D.C.: Smithsonian Institution of Washington, Institute
            of Social Anthropology, Publication 7.
West, Robert C., and Pedro Armillas
1950   Las Chinampas de México. Poesía y realidad de los "jardines
            flotantes." Cuadernos Americanos 50: 165–82.

9

Early Spanish Colonization and Indians in the Valley of Atlixco, Puebla

Hanns J. Prem

Not all aspects of the historical events that occurred in Central Mexico during and after the conquest are equally open to scientific evaluation. Certainly the military side of the conquest and the political measures taken subsequently can be discerned most clearly; this is due both to the many contemporary observers as well as to the official documentation produced by the colonial administration. What followed immediately after the wars of conquest can be seen far less distinctly: the Indians were slowly but nevertheless effectively reduced to an inferior and dependent status in every sphere. It is clear that this gradual process escaped the attention of contemporary observers, since the change was not of a drastic and conspicuous nature. It seems that only the leading royal officials became aware of the broadening gap between the intention and the wording of the Spanish policy, on the one hand, and its execution, on the other. But the occasional reports of the viceroys and *oidores,* although they show considerable subjective insights into the prevailing problems, cannot be considered a reliable basis for detailed historical investigation.

The intention of Spanish colonial policy could not be transformed into reality because of two limiting factors: the imperturbable determination of the Spanish invaders to consider themselves noblemen, and hence to exploit the labor of the Indians; and the precariousness of the colony's economy as a result of the dwindling Indian population, i.e., labor force. This discrepancy between political intention and colonial reality is reflected also in recent historical research. If an investigation were based primarily on the official colonial documentation, the resulting picture of colonial Mexico would necessarily diverge considerably from that obtained by a study which also considers those aspects of the colonial period slighted by official records. The discrepancy becomes evident if one considers the socioeconomic side of the foundation of the town of Puebla de los Ángeles, together with the installation of European-style agriculture in the nearby Valley of Atlixco, some 100 kilometers southeast of Mexico City.

François Chevalier (1957) defends the thesis that one of the most important objectives in founding the city of Puebla was to grant arable land to the ever-increasing number of Spanish colonists who were flocking into the country, roaming about, and molesting the Indians. In this alarming situation the Spanish government's intention was to find an alternative source of income, different from the limited institution of *encomienda,* under which a Spaniard would live on the work and services of the Indians in a certain area assigned to him. Rather, it was the crown's desire to make the Spaniards themselves engage in agriculture "in the mode of Spain" (Motolinía 1971: 263). At the same time the native population was to be freed of its direct dependence upon single Spanish individuals (*encomenderos*) and thereby from abuse and oppression as well. The idea was to have an initial period of appropriation of native labor, and then allow the Indians to hire themselves out to landowners of their choice. Treating these concepts in detail, Chevalier (1957) came to the conclusion that, in spite of occasional difficulties and setbacks, the original goals for founding the city of Puebla were generally realized. Indeed, official records of the first few years (after a brief period of setbacks) appear to indicate success, both economic and social.

Chevalier, however, relied heavily on selective documentation, which biased his interpretation. Since the foundation of the town of Puebla and its later fate offer a good insight into the economic and social situation of early Mexico (on the Indian as well as on the Spanish side), it appears justifiable to contrast the picture drawn by Chevalier with a more complete one based on sources and methods he used either insufficiently or not at all. To do this it is appropriate to reassess the degree of realization of the fundamental social objectives connected with the foundation of Puebla as presented by Chevalier and widely accepted by others (Martin 1957: 41–51; Albi Romero 1970: 78:84; Castro 1977: 494–95).

Attention will be focused on the following diagnostically significant areas of Spanish policy, central to Chevalier's presentation:

(1) It was intended to create an agricultural structure based on small, independent landholdings. Originally this was achieved; but did this structure survive for some longer period of time?

(2) As a result, it was intended that the citizens of Puebla should derive their income mainly from personal agriculture enterprise. In the beginning the precondition for this was created by allotting land to all citizens; did it, however, continue to exist in later times?

(3) It was intended, furthermore, that Indian laborers should be assigned to individual Spaniards for only a short, transitional period. Was this in fact what happened?

THE STRUCTURE OF LANDOWNERSHIP IN THE AREA OF PUEBLA

The selection of the site on which Puebla was founded, in the spring of 1531, was not determined by agricultural considerations, such as the suitability of the land for growing wheat. Nevertheless, arable land was apparently distributed at once in the immediate environs of the community, which according to numerous reports was built on uninhabited terrain. The plots, called *caballerías*, were initially of no standard size (Echeverría y Veytia 1962[2]: 72–74); the units of land were standardized only in a later period. As all three objectives center on Spanish landholdings in the Valley of Atlixco, the situation of these landholdings has to be examined more closely than the few short inventories and the scanty contemporary description of landed properties allow. The necessary data have to be assembled from numerous isolated statements, deeds, and the like, since the colonial administration did not keep a fully documented register of landholdings. Nevertheless, a complete record of Spanish estates can be reconstructed with great precision (Prem 1978: 133–45). This record must not be restricted to succession of ownership, but must also include the location and size of each plot of land, as precisely as possible. The reconstruction requires two complementary procedures, described below in more detail.

The Additive Exploitation of Isolated Data

The two main sources are the registers of the colonial administration (*libros de las Reales Mercedes*) and those of the local notaries (*libros de protocolos*), in which the grants and purchases of lands were recorded. Further documents of this type can be found in the files of haciendas of the records of the probate court. According to the jurisdiction referred to in each document and the more specific place-names, these documents can be assigned to a certain region or even tract of land. However, areal toponyms, natural boundaries, and points of reference (the reconnaissance of their modern counterparts is an unavoidable prerequisite of this sort of investigation) do not designate a certain plot with the necessary precision. The toponyms, however, are a valid tool in establishing groups of neighboring properties, even though their exact spatial configuration remains undetermined. The types of documents mentioned not only contain toponyms but also state the names of the neighbors on all sides.

These references to neighbors permit the reconstruction of chains of properties and even make it possible to bridge documentary lacunae. To be sure, there is much imprecision in the documents due to incomplete statements made by solicitors for grants, vendors of land, witnesses, experts and many other involved persons. Undocumented changes of ownership in neighboring lots occurred, while others neglected to mention the previous owner (which sometimes may have been unknown) or to describe an exceptionally irregular limit. Many of these deficiencies can be remedied by means of supplementary data from other sources, even from recent information. Since most documents refer to neighbors and other relevant features in all cardinal directions, the chains of landed properties can be linked to form an extended network covering a large area. This method is the basis for the reconstruction shown in figure 9.1. In this case, however, there was a special condition: the primary source contained only short summaries of the original documents and they mention only a few topographical details without giving their names. The localization, therefore, is based on scanty indications in other documents, and proved to be the only place in the valley where this configuration of land plots fits the topographical situation. This less favorable point of departure is compensated for by the order of the summaries, which seems to reflect the path followed by the surveyor during his official registration of the properties (see sequence numbers in figure 9.1). It makes irregular loops and zigzags, which can be reconstructed by means of the neighbor references; these latter confirm the chains of properties mentioned above.

Lists of Properties with Full Coverage

The *Composición Real* (legalization of all previous land titles), decreed by the crown for the first time around 1643, produced the first nearly complete inventories of landholdings (only lands of Indians remained excluded; they can be reconstructed by determining the tracts of land not occupied by Spanish owners). The *Composición* produced documents consisting of long lists of properties, usually including detailed information on ownership, location (e.g., toponyms, neighbors, topographic features), size, and quality of the land (e.g., by amount to be paid). The sequence reflects chains of properties along such features of the landscape as rivers or mountains and follows a zigzag pattern in less definitely structured terrain. The necessary linking and localization can only be achieved, however, if the lists contain sufficient information, or if a considerable part of the listed properties can be identified with estates on which more detailed information is available in other sources. In every case the reconstruction of the pattern of landholdings is more difficult and less precise if it is based on lists, since they do not refer to single plots of land but to larger and sometimes very complex

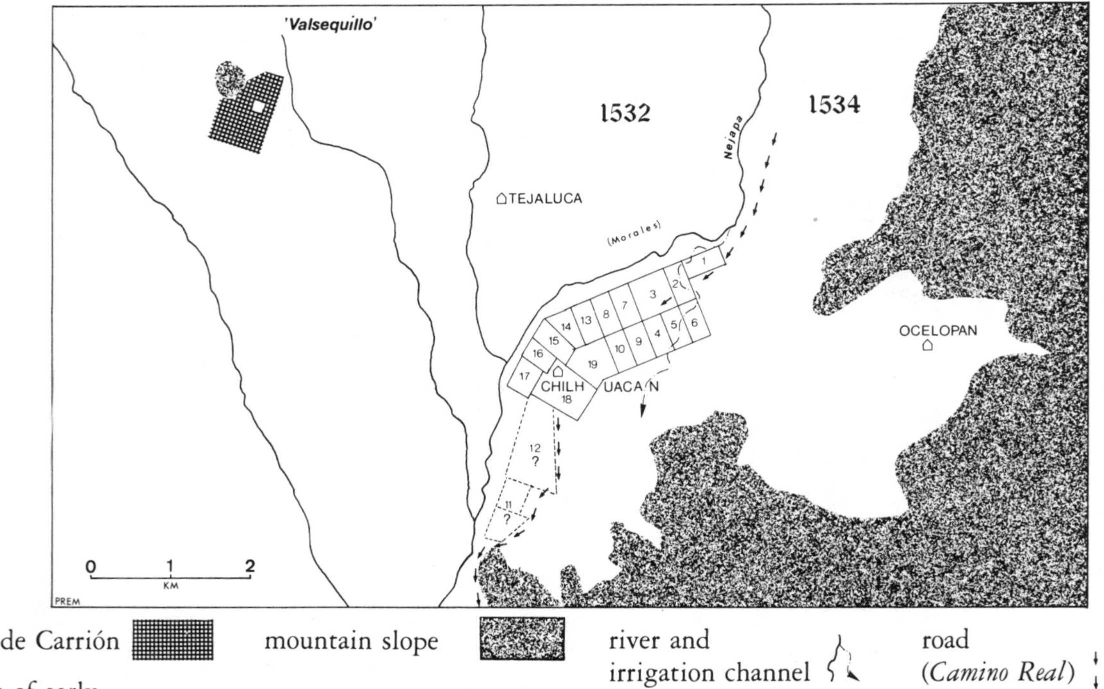

Fig. 9.1.   Land purchased between 1540 and 1550 by Diego de Ordás Villagómez in the eastern part of the Valley of Atlixco (see table 9.1 for detailed information on the former proprietors of the plots). Hacienda Chilhuacan, which certainly evolved from these transactions, can be found on figure 9.2, under number 6.

estates that were accumulated, and perhaps even broken up and rearranged, over the course of time. Figure 9.2, which shows all properties listed in the 1643 *Composición,* has been reconstructed mainly on the basis of this single source; the sequence of numbers corresponds to the order of listing there.

Besides the information necessary for the reconstruction and identification of estates, the lists in most cases also supply quantifiable data. As these data can be correlated with definite localities (soil condition, irrigation, and the like), more detailed comparisons within smaller units of area of investigation can be made. Lists compiled for different reasons or at different times enable some diachronic research, e.g., of the temporal fluctuations in the landholding structure, both for Spanish and, indirectly, for Indian properties. It will be demonstrated that these points of view are essential for challenging Chevalier's interpretation of the Puebla experiment, especially if seen from the Atlixco Valley.

The first few Spanish settlers in the newly founded city of Puebla de los Ángeles, probably still unfamiliar with local climatic conditions, came to realize within a year that their community had to be relocated to a site less susceptible to flooding. Another problem was that the surrounding land would not produce much grain except corn. Understandably disappointed with the Puebla site, they became interested in the so-called Valley of Atlixco, about 20 km to the southwest of Puebla. Compared to Puebla the Atlixco area had certain advantages: being located approximately 300 meters lower in elevation, there was no danger of frost; an abundance of water made the area suitable for irrigation; it experienced higher rainfalls due to the proximity of the volcano Popocatepetl.

The advantages of the Valley of Atlixco had been known to the Spaniards for some time; even before Hernán Cortés's expeditionary forces reached the Aztec capital of Tenochtitlan, the Valley of Atlixco had been visited by Spaniards (Vázquez de Tapia 1952: 35), and from then on until the overthrow of the Aztecs, several visits are recorded for this area (Cortés 1963: 53, 85, 106–9). Thus there is no doubt that Cortés and other members of his forces were familiar with the region and knew of its potential agricultural value and its sparse native population. Cortés petitioned the crown for possession of the province of Huejotzingo, a region which included the Valley

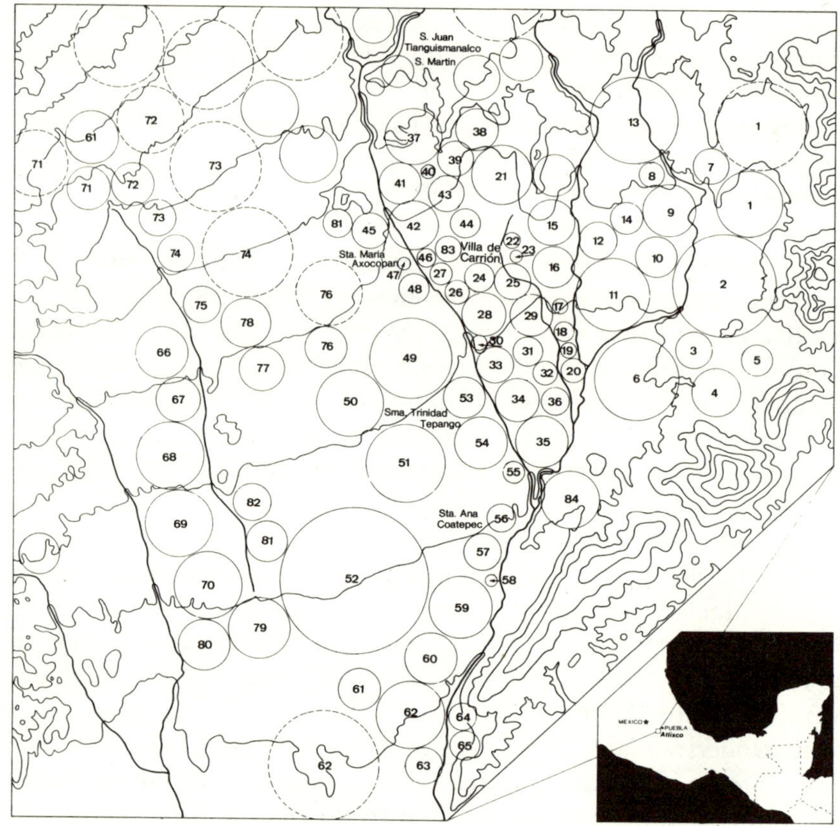

Fig. 9.2. Spanish landholdings in the Valley of Atlixco around 1643. The circles indicate the approximate location of each estate, the size of which corresponds to a square with sides equal to the diameter of the circle. The numbers refer to the list of the 1643 *Composición* (see table 9.2). The area not covered by the circles, especially in the western and northern part of the valley, was Indian land.

of Atlixco. His various requests were granted in 1528, and he was actually in possession of the area for a short time (Prem 1978: 38–39). Early in the first decade after the conquest, his successor in the *encomienda* of Huejotzingo, the conquistador Diego de Ordás, introduced cattle breeding and wheat farming to the Atlixco Valley (Prem 1978: 146); this enterprise probably occupied the site of some dispossessed Indian owners. Presumably the success of the Ordás *estancia* influenced the choice of the people of Puebla: their petitions to the Audiencia of Mexico requested land in the valley where not only wheat but also orchards and vineyards could be planted (Echeverría y Veytia 1962[1]: 111–12).

The importance the Audiencia placed on this land distribution becomes evident from the fact that in 1532 one of its members, the *licenciado* Salmerón, was personally charged with the supervision of it (ENE 2: 222–25; a different version is found in AAP-SI-1-1). In close cooperation with the Franciscans, who at that time were the most influential non-Indian group in the region, he managed to persuade the Indians of both Huejotzingo and Calpan to cede substantial areas of land to the settlers of Puebla. Immediately afterward, in the final days of 1532, the survey and distribution of the plots began, an operation which lasted several months (Echeverría y Veytia 1962[1]: 72–74). In a first step the thirty-three *vecinos* of Puebla were each allotted one small tract of land (6–9 ha). Although this land distribution is mentioned in numerous documents, references are so vague that it is no longer possible to determine where exactly in the Valley of Atlixco the first plots of land were granted. In all probability it was in a tract of land approximately 3 km wide and 4 km long, between the Río Nejapa and another river farther to the west, with the modern name Río de la Leona, and beginning in the north along the course of a (prehispanic?) irrigation channel (Echevarría y Veytia 1962[1]: 110–17; López de Villaseñor 1961: 38; AAP-SI-1-2/3). Soon, in 1534, the council of Puebla demanded an increase in the Atlixco lands (López de Villaseñor 1961: 65); it was granted by the Audiencia a few weeks later (AAP-SI-1-13). New lots were staked out by Spanish officials of the neighboring Indian community of Huejotzingo and also of Puebla (AAP-SI-1-13).

Because all the available land was apportioned in a very short time, new acquisitions became imperative if colonization was to continue (AAP-SI-1-187). Answering a request by the city of Puebla, the king authorized Viceroy Mendoza to distribute more land in the Atlixco Valley. In 1551 his successor, Viceroy Velasco, forced the Indians of Huejotzingo to cede land to Puebla once again. In accordance with the original idea, this land, comprising some twenty-eight lots, or *suertes,* was distributed in small units to several individuals (various documents in INAH-FM-Misc-194, NLC-A-1195, and AGN-M-3-291). It seems that this additional land was completely distributed within less than three years. Among the recipients were persons who had already received land in Atlixco. Thus the accusation of the Audiencia that members of the council of Puebla and their friends had enriched themselves by unlawfully acquiring land is quite convincing. Be that as it may, in 1557 a new survey of the land was ordered, for which Puebla had pleaded for many years (AAP-SI-1-91, 95; Cervantes 1927: 316–24).

In the following period more and more land was acquired by Spaniards in the Atlixco Valley, in part by viceregal grants of allegedly hitherto uncultivated land (*baldíos*), in part by means of leases from Indians, which soon led to sale by the Indian owners (Torquemada 1723[1]: 321). As the number of land grants by the Audiencia in the Valley of Atlixco gained importance from mid-century on, the size of the allotments also changed. They adapted to dimensions of units customary in the neighboring districts: lots of two or three *caballerías* were granted, measuring, in accordance with official specifications, ca. 86 or 128 ha, respectively. The tendency in neighboring areas toward larger units can also be observed in the Atlixco Valley around the end of the century. This increase in the size of land grants suggests that after 1555 the Audiencia itself moved away from its former policy of small subdivisions and thus initiated a structural change in the pattern of land tenure in the Valley of Atlixco. Such a conclusion is not necessarily accurate, however. As far as can be determined the more generous land grants did not apply to that central part of the valley originally parcelled out to settlers of Puebla. Those tracts were favorably located in terms of water supply, and although small, nevertheless produced an adequate yield. The records show, however, that even before the size of the grants was increased by the

Audiencia, the settlers of Puebla had already abandoned the objectives which the Audiencia was attempting to realize in the founding of this community. Albi Romero (1970: 90) stresses the buying up of land by a few rich landholders. Clear evidence is indicated by the purchase of a larger number of adjacent units of land by the nephew of the former encomendero of Calpan, Diego de Ordás Villagómez, who was one of the most important and wealthy citizens of Puebla (see table 9.1 and figure 9.1). At first he purchased eighteen subdivisions, which had been allotted to several individuals by the council of Puebla between 1536 and 1540, and which bordered on the unit he himself had received or, more precisely, the possession of which had been officially approved in 1540. A second parcel of land acquired at the same time had been given to a certain Pedro Ladrón de Guevara only days before. This Pedro Ladrón later became a landed proprietor and *corregidor* of several communities in the area. In a second land transaction before 1550, Ordás purchased an additional six neighboring units. Apparently this purchase constituted the basis for the later Hacienda Chilhuacan of the Ordás family (AGN-M-3). Was the Ordás purchase an isolated case or was it typical? To answer this question it is not necessary to make a detailed inquiry into the rather inadequate contemporary documentation. An evaluation of the first compilation of all Spanish-owned property in the Atlixco Valley for the *Composición* in 1643 provides a clear picture (see table 9.2 for a detailed list, and figure 9.2 for the location of the estates).

In 1643 the whole valley region records eighty-four subdivisions, with a total of 443 *caballerías* (18,915 ha). Of these, 44 percent (195 caballerías) were irrigated, but the percentage of potentially irrigable land was much higher. The average unit measured 5.26 caballerías, with units varying between 46 caballerías and 40 *fanegas* (*de sembradura,* a little less than ¹/₂ caballería). On the average subdivisions comprising irrigated land contained 2.35 caballerías, whereas nonirrigated units contained 2.94 caballerías. However, in comparison, the standard deviation in the case of irrigated land (2.26 caballerías) is only half what it was with nonirrigated land (4.8 caballerías), since the largest land parcels were situated on the periphery of the irrigated part of the valley (see figure 9.3). On the other hand, the smaller subdivisions existed in the part between

Table 9.1. Lots (*suertes*) Purchased by Diego de Ordás Villagómez

No.	Previous possessor	Size	Date of grant
1	Sancho Ordóñez	1 suerte	13 iii 1538
2	Rodrigo de Mendoza	1 suerte	16 vi 1536
3	Alvaro López	2 suertes	10 iii 1536
4	Hernando de la Cadena	1 suerte	2 iv 1546
5	Hernando de Robledo	1 suerte	9 viii 1536
6	Francisco Hernández	1 suerte	6 vi 1536
7	Alonso de Salzedo	1 suerte	10 iii 1536
8	Gonzalo Rodríguez	1 suerte	20 iv 1540
9	Andrés de Herrera	1 suerte	29 x 1540
10	Gonzalo Gutiérrez	1 suerte	7 iv 1536
11	Francisco de Vallejo	2 suertes	8 x 1540
12	Hernando Marín Cortés	4 suertes	27 ix 1540
13	Francisco Rubio/Ruiz	1 suerte	3 ix 1540
14	Hernando Robledo	1 suerte	3 ix 1540
15	Pedro López de Alcantara	1 suerte	n.d.
16	Gutierre Maldonado	3/4 suerte	18 v 1537
17	Juan López de la Rosa	1 suerte	9 viii 1537
18	Diego de Ordás	2 suertes	27 viii 1540
19	Francisco Figueroa	2 suertes	3 ix 1540
20	Pedro Ladrón de Guevara	1 suerte	9 v 1547
21	María Rodríguez	1 suerte	18 ii 1541
22	Martín Gutiérrez de Saavedra	1 suerte	21 ii 1541
23	Indians of Calpan	2 suertes	4 xi 1541
24	Francisco Alvarez	1 suerte	6 x 1547
25	Gonzalo Hidalgo de Montemayor	1 suerte	27 v 1547
26	Francisco de Reynoso	1 suerte	4 iv 1547

Plot numbers refer to figure 9.1. Plots 20 to 26 have not been located. Source: AGN-M-3-34ff.

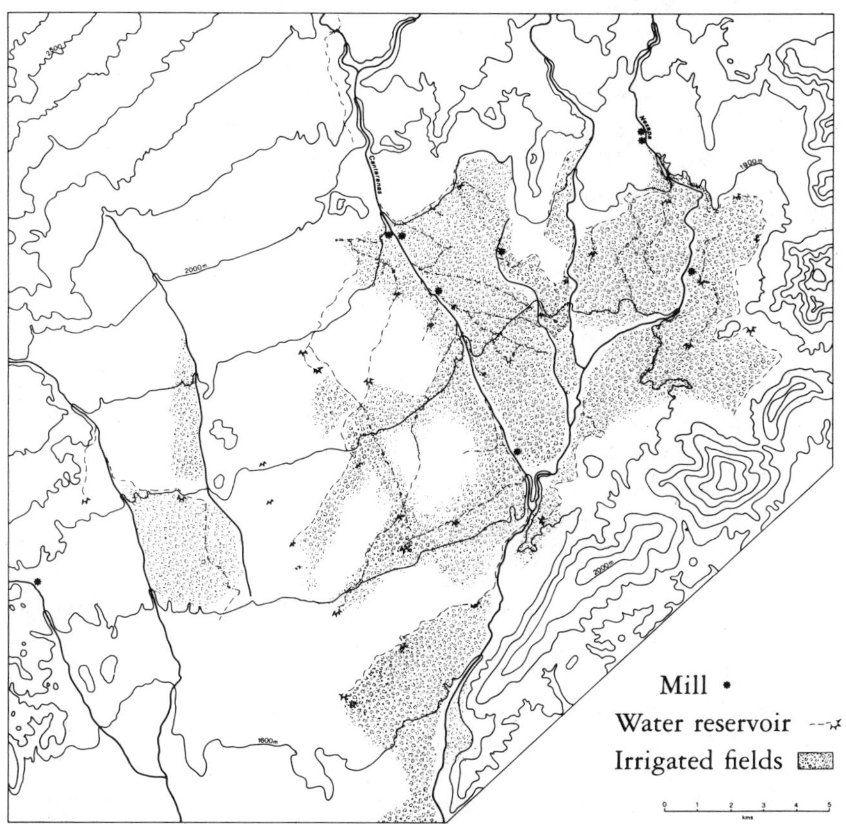

Fig. 9.3.   Irrigation in the Valley of Atlixco during colonial times (courses of channels according to colonial documents and maps, recent air photographs, and ground verification).

Table 9.2. Spanish-Owned Property in the Atlixco Valley, 1643

No.	Proprietor (Hacienda)	Land irr.	n-irr.	Additional features	Payment
1	Juan de Paez (Portezuelo)	8	9	estancia	500 poc
2	Juan Juárez Rallón [ex *suertes*]	8	15	molino	560
3	Juan de Paez (Ocelopa) [ex *suertes*]	3	5.5	jaguey	300
4	Juan de Paez ex Benito Bautista [ex *suertes*]	2	3	jaguey	200
5	Convento Sto. Domingo in Izúcar [ex *suertes*]	2.5	4		200
6	Antonio de Ordás (Chilhuacan)	8	8	jaguey	500
7	Alonso Cano de Villegas	2	1		100
8	Alonso Benítez Quintanilla	1	.5		80
9	Diego Delgado ex B. García, Diego de Meneses	4.5			300
10	Miguel de Salas ex Pedro de los Tíos	4			250
11	Hernando Larios (Tejaluca)	5	7		180
12	Blas de Burgos Cortés	3			200
13	Convento S. Agustín in Puebla	5	12	jaguey	200
14	Pedro Ladrón de Guevara	2.5			150
15	Antonio de Arellano (Tesayuca)	1.5	3	jaguey	140
16	Francisco de la Llosa	2.5	2		200
17	E. Cr. Benítez Quintanilla ex P. de la Sierra	35f			60
18	Canónigos de Puebla	10f	40f		70
19	Rodríguez de S. Miguel	40f			70
20	Diego de Balparda	1.5			85
21	Juan Rodríguez Crespo	.5	7		100
22	(La Tabla)	45f		molino	60
23	Beatriz Zambrano (La Tabla)	30f			50
24	Fernando Altamirano	2			170
25	Juan Larios Jiménez	3			150
26	Isabel del Castillo	1.5			110

Table 9.2. (continued)

No.	Proprietor (Hacienda)	Land irr.	Land n-irr.	Additional features	Payment
27	Mayorazgo Francisco de Sarrandón	1.5		molino	250
28	Companía de Jesús	4			350
29	Juan de la Rosa	3.5			120
30	Tomás Delgado	30f		jaguey	60
31	Diego López Grajales	2			200
32	Francisco Hernández Lucas	1.5			150
33	Gerónimo Martín de Arévalo	2.5			160
34	Antonio Rodríguez Yáñez	4			260
35	Mayorazgo Juan Ramírez de Arellano	6		{ molino jaguey	500
36	Teresa de Guzmán	2	2	estancia	300
37	Juan García Serrano ex Frailes del Carmen	40f	6	{ calera jaguey	190
38	Isabel de Ayala	?	4		50
39	Pedro Macis ex Gonzalo García	3.5	1.5		90
40	Gonzalo García	2f	30f		20
41	Juan Rodríguez Marqués		3.5		100
42	Juan Andrés de Acevedo	1	4	molino	300
43	Rodrigo Hidalgo ex M. Ramírez (Hacico)	3 + ?	1.5		400
44	Diego López de la Torre ex Cabrera	2			120
45	Isabel de Acevedo	1.5		molino	280
46	Monjas de Sta. Clara	45f			50
47	Gerónimo Carabantes	30f			35
48	Francisco de Vivaldo (Techochalpa)	2			80
49	Alvaro de Vivaldo	3	12	jaguey	380
50	Antonio de Olivares (Tenextepec)	10		jaguey	500
51	Antonio de Ordás	5	3	jaguey	400
52	Convento de Sto. Domingo ex Deán de Tlaxcala	9	37	jaguey	900

Table 9.2. (continued)

No.	Proprietor (Hacienda)	Land irr.	Land n-irr.	Additional features	Pay-ment
53	Ana de Villegas ex Alonso Vázquez Rubio	2	2	jaguey	100
54	herederos de Sebastián Vázquez	2	4		120
55	Agustín Meléndez	1			80
56	Juan Gallardo	1	1		90
57	Miguel de Cavallero ex Pedro de Nava	1	2	jaguey	100
58	Miguel Cavallero ex Diego Pérez de los Ríos	.5			20
59	herederos de Pedro Núñez de Guzmán	6	2	jaguey	390
60	Miguel de Toro	2	4		230
62	Francisco de Jaem	5	5	$^1/_2$ estancia	450
63	Alonso Marín	1.5	1.5		120
64	Diego de Loaiza (Tlaxco)	1.5			150
65	García de Orta ex Marina de Orta	?			160
66	Juan del Castillo (Coyula)	1.5	4.5		200
67	Ascensio del Castillo ex Diego López de N.	.5	4		120
68	Ascensio del Castillo ex Agustín López	2	8	jaguey	280
69	Bartolomé Castilla et al. (Agueguete)	5	5		300
70	Juan Benítez Quintanilla ex G. Meléndez	5	5	2 estancias	460
71	Bartolomé de León		4	$^1/_2$ estancia	100
72	Pascual Pérez and Juan Saénz		4	$^1/_2$ estancia	100
73	Cristóbal de Burgos		3	estancia	100
74	Basco Luis		3	$^1/_2$ estancia	100
75	Alonso Hernández		3	"agua"	80
76	Andrés de Bivaldo (Sta. Teresa)		4	$^1/_2$ estancia	100
77	Juan Núñez ex Carlos de Carranza		4		100

Table 9.2. (continued)

No.	Proprietor (Hacienda)	Land irr.	n-irr.	Additional features	Pay-ment
78	Cristóbal de la Torre (Coyula)		5		120
79	José Domínguez		4		100
80	José Nava ex Juan Rodríguez Muñoz		6		160
81	Francisco de Herrera Arteaga	2.5	1.5		190
82	Alonso Jiménez		3		60
83	Convento S. Agustín in Atlixco	1.5			90
84	Diego Zapata ex Marcos Rodríguez Zapata	4.5	3	jaguey	500

Property numbers refer to figure 9.2. Land units: caballerías (42.8 hectares) or (f) *fanegas de sembradura de trigo* (.62 hectares, approx.); units of payment: (poc) *pesos de oro común*. The amount of each payment provides some indication of extension and quality of the respective property. Source: Composición de tierra y aguas de la jurisdicción de Atlixco (1906: SRH-CN).

the rivers, where the percentage of irrigated land (even including less-favored areas on the fringes) was especially high (59 percent), or where for vast stretches nothing but irrigated land existed. Between the rivers the average size of the units was 3.3 caballerías. This area was subdivided by smaller waterways into three parts and here (in an east-west direction) the units had the average dimensions of 2.99, 1.68, and 6.36 caballerías, respectively. The standard deviation in each case is relatively high (1.95, 1.65, and 5.4 caballerías), pointing to a very inconsistent distribution.

Based on these data, conclusions may be drawn as to the differences in the historical development of these estates. A distribution of landed properties like the one described above follows almost necessarily if an original structure of properties, equal in size, is altered by a small number of landowners buying out their neighbors. How strongly these purchases influenced the structure of the region can be understood by a comparison of records. Comparing the data of the early land division with those of the *Composición*, in 1532 only units measuring from 10 to 15 fanegas (.14 to .21 caballerías) were distributed, whereas in 1643 there are no single pieces of property of this size anywhere in the Atlixco Valley, but rather only multiples thereof. Ten properties were between 30 and 50 fanegas, certainly composed of several lots of 10 or 15 fanegas each. Thus the property size originally deemed sufficient for the subsistence of a Spanish family did not survive into the seventeenth century anywhere in the valley. Individual lots which a citizen of Puebla could have worked alone with some Indian help were regularly transformed into much larger units that required the assignment of great numbers of Indian farmhands. The Ordás case is but one example of this process.

The documentation for the Atlixco Valley refers almost exclusively to tracts of land that were already in Spanish possession when they became incorporated into larger units, but it can be assumed that this process affected land held by Indians to an even greater degree. The examination of the 1643 *Composición* shows convincingly that in the central portion of the valley there was barely any space left for Indian settlements and cornfields; they were confined to the marginal zones. Thus the Indians who remained in the central valley became available as farmhands for the increasing Spanish estates.

PUEBLA—A SETTLEMENT OF *LABRADORES*

Puebla, as one of the most important towns of New Spain, was undoubtedly rather attractive to newcomers. It is therefore not surprising that a small number of encomenderos, whose encomiendas were situated not too far from the community, came to live in Puebla. But the underlying concept of the Audiencia's settlement plan for Puebla was to provide all other citizens with their own small plot of crop land. The land grants of the first decades more or less kept pace with the growing number of the town's inhabitants.

(1) The first land distribution apparently provided every citizen of Puebla with land close to the town, and later also in the Atlixco Valley.

(2) During the period from the founding of the town until 15 October 1543, 177 citizens of Puebla were allocated land (Echevarría y Veytia 1962[1]: 74, n).

(3) Around 1550 a new acquisition of land from the Indians of

Huejotzingo enabled the Audiencia to hand out land to additional residents of Puebla. Between October 1551 and May 1553, alone, twenty land grants are documented (INAH-FM-Misc-194; NLC-A-1195).

Thus, up to the middle of the century, more than two hundred individuals received land grants in the Valley of Atlixco. By 1643, however, the number of independent properties decreased to a mere eighty-one units in an area larger than the originally allocated region (see table 9.2). Due to rental agreements, the number of landowners was even smaller. Since the number of citizens in Puebla had considerably increased in this one-hundred-year period, the percentage of individuals owning land must also have declined steadily. Another important factor was undoubtedly the founding of the Villa de Carrión (today, Atlixco de Mugica y Osorio) which, after an earlier unsuccessful attempt at settlement in a place called Valsequillo (see figure 9.1), appears to have become the residence for the majority of landowners in the Valley of Atlixco in the last decades of the sixteenth century.

Only a few decades after the first land grants in the Atlixco Valley, Spaniards also acquired property in the more distant environs of Puebla, i.e., in the Valley of Texmelucan, in the vicinity of Cholula and Huejotzingo (Prem 1978), and in the area of Tepeaca, Tecamachalco, and the nearby Valley of San Pablo. These lands were less desirable climatically and topographically. After an initial phase in which smaller land parcels were purchased from the Indians, these land acquisitions were based on *reales mercedes,* viceregal grants rarely above 2 to 6 caballerías in size, and these were soon combined into larger estates. Thus the economic structure of Spanish landholdings in the present state of Puebla underwent a marked change; individual, small-scale agriculture did not survive, and only a fast-dwindling minority of Puebla's citizens continued to possess land in the Valley of Atlixco.

SPANISH AGRICULTURE WITHOUT APPROPRIATION OF NATIVE LABOR

The goals of the Spanish authorities, when they permitted the foundation of the city of Puebla, required that enough arable lands be available in the vicinity of the settlement, lands uninhabited and uncultivated by Indians. All written sources concur that this was the case with Cuetlaxcoapan, the location selected, a situation seldom found in the heavily populated Mexican highlands. Evidently impressed by the experiences of the first settlers, some contemporary authors felt that its susceptibility to frost was responsible for this condition (Zarate 1544, in ENE 4: 137). In reality, however, the site of Cuetlaxcoapan seems to have been in a sort of limbo between the prehispanic territories of Tlaxcala, Cholula, and Totimehuacan (Castro 1977: 494), and it also separated the independent and the Aztec-dominated political entities in the Valley of Puebla. This explanation is corroborated by the total absence of late post-Classic archaeological material in and near Puebla (Castro 1977: 494), constituting a marked contrast to the large settlements and ceremonial constructions of earlier times slightly east of the city (Tschohl and Nickel 1972: 205, 1977: 436–42).

From its very beginning the city of Puebla depended upon Indian laborers for the construction of public buildings and houses for the Spanish settlers. These Indians had to be recruited from a wide area, as there was no local Indian population. The same was true for the agricultural enterprises of the settlers, especially after some tracts in the thinly inhabited parts of the Valley of Atlixco had been assigned to them.

The land where these allotments were located was also uninhabited by Indians (López de Villaseñor 1961: 65); it was the southern continuation of the geopolitical limbo. No Indian settlement seems to have existed in the northeastern and eastern parts of the Valley of Atlixco, according to both documentary and archaeological evidence. But there is yet another reason for only a small population in this region. In the middle of the fifteenth century the then-dominant people of Huejotzingo had expelled the Cuauhquecholteca from their former place in the Valley of Atlixco (Dyckerhoff, in Prem 1978: 20–21). The few remaining Indians were subjugated by Huejotzingo and its ally Calpan. Even in early colonial times only some twelve hundred Indian families lived in the Huejotzingo portion of the valley, mostly in its western part (Prem 1974: 486). The remaining part of the valley, therefore, was virtually uninhabited when the first allotments were made, thus forcing the Spaniards to bring their farmhands from more distant places.

In 1531, the *oidor* Salmerón was of the opinion that after a transitional period of from six to ten years the forced appropriation of Indian labor could be abolished and the natives would voluntarily work the fields of the Spaniards (Salmerón, in ENE 16: 11). This optimistic expectation, however, did not materialize. It has been conclusively documented that since the beginning of land distribution, the success of agriculture was dependent on Indian labor for the first fifteen years (Hirschberg 1979). For example, from five hundred to six hundred Indians were at work in Atlixco in 1551 (AGN-M-3-632), and almost eight hundred from many places in the vicinity in 1552 (NLC-A-1121-174). In the early seventeenth century the use of *indios de repartimiento* for the construction of the drainage system in the Basin of Mexico apparently considerably decreased the number of Indian farmhands in the Atlixco Valley. These circumstances were the cause of repeated petitions by the Atlixco landowners, pleading that without these contigents of Indians only one-third of the harvest of former years could be obtained. As a result, some one hundred and fifty Indians were released from their work on the *desagüe* for a month and a half, and were sent to work on the Atlixco fields (INAH-TP-3-21 {1630}; Zavala and Castelo 1945{6}: 547, 568).

During the first century after the conquest, as the Indian population of Mexico severely declined, a more or less constant number of Indian laborers was assigned to Atlixco landowners. Thus the labor demands on the Indian population proportionately increased. The sociopolitical concept involved in the founding of Puebla, therefore, was not fully successful either for the Indians or for the Spaniards (Hirschberg 1979: 164).

CONCLUSION

For all three objectives in founding the city of Puebla, it is possible to demonstrate that the intentions of the Audiencia did not or could not permanently materialize, at least as they were advocated and practiced by Salmerón. One of the most important reasons for this failure can be seen in the general sociopolitical situation during the time of the conquest and initial colonization of New Spain. However, of greater importance is the fact that the Puebla concept was an isolated case, with no consequence for later policies concerning Spanish settlers. The immense land grants given to Spaniards in all parts of New Spain, and particularly those in the immediate vicinity of Puebla, worked at cross-purposes to those originally conceived for that community.

No citizen of Puebla could be expected to be satisfied with a few hectares, however fertile, working them at a scale not very different from Indian agriculture, when other, nearby Spaniards were able to acquire ten times the amount of land, of equal quality, and with little difficulty or cost, often establishing the nuclei for large enterprises.

In view of this situation it seems that Salmerón's intentions were never seriously supported by either the Audiencia or the crown. On the contrary, they were undermined by the overall land policy. The Indians of the neighboring regions, who made the Puebla agricultural experiment possible by giving away part of their land, derived no advantage whatsoever from their cooperation.

REFERENCES

Albi Romero, Guadalupe
1970   La sociedad de Puebla de los Angeles en el siglo XVI. Jahrbuch
            für Geschichte von Staat, Wirtschaft und Gesellschaft Latein-
            amerikas 7: 76–145.
Castro Morales, Efraín
1977   Puebla de Zaragoza. Enciclopedia de México 10: 493–511.
            México: Enciclopedia de México.
Cervantes, Enrique A.
1927   Documentos para la historia de Puebla. Memorias de la So-
            ciedad Científica Antonio Alzat, 48.
Chevalier, François
1957   Significación social de la fundación de la Puebla de los Angeles.
            Publicaciones del Centro de Estudios Históricos (Puebla). (first
            published Paris, 1947).
Cortés, Hernán
1963   Cartas y Documentos. Biblioteca Porrúa 2. México: Porrúa.

Echeverría y Veytia, Mariano Fernández
1962   Historia de la fundación de la Ciudad de los Angeles en la Nueva España, su descripción y presente estado. Puebla: Ediciones Altiplano. (first ed. 1780).

ENE (Epistolario de Nueva España 1505–1818)
1939–43 Francisco del Paso y Troncoso, ed. México: Robredo.

Hirschberg, Julia
1979   An Alternative to Encomienda: Puebla's Indios de Servicio, 1531–45. Journal of Latin American Studies 11: 241–64.

López de Villaseñor, Pedro
1961   Cartilla vieja de la nobilísima Ciudad de Puebla. México: Imprenta Universitaria. (first ed. 1781).

Motolinía, Toribio de Benavente
1971   Memoriales o libro de las cosas de la Nueva España y de los naturales dello. México: Universidad Nacional, Instituto de Investigaciones Históricas.

Martin, Norman F.
1957   Los vagabundos en la Nueva España, siglo XVI. México: Edit. Jus.

Prem, Hanns J.
1974   Matrícula de Huexotzinco (Ms. Mex. 387 der Bibliothèque Nationale, Paris). Graz, Austria: Akademische Druck- und Verlagsanstalt.
1978   Milpa y hacienda; tenencia de la tierra indígena y española en la cuenca del Alto Atoyac, Puebla, México (1520–1650). Wiesbaden: Steiner-Verlag.

Torquemada, Juan de
1723   Monarquía indiana. Madrid: Nicolás Rodríguez Franco.

Tschohl, Peter, and Herbert J. Nickel
1972,   Catalogo arqueológico y etnohistórico de Puebla-Tlaxcala,
1977   México. 2 vols. Cologne: Privately printed.

Vázquez de Tapia, Bernardino
1953   Relación de méritos y servicios . . . Jorge Gurría Lacroix, ed. México: Universidad Nacional Autónoma de México.

Zavala, Silvio, and Maria Castelo
1945   Fuentes para la historia del trabajo en Nueva España. Vol. 6. México: Fondo de Cultura Económica.

Documentary sources

AAP-S- . . .   Archivo del Ayuntamiento de Puebla, Suplemento al libro . . .

AAP-SI- . . .	Archivo del Ayuntamiento de Puebla, Suplemento al libro . . . (Indice).
AGN-M- . . .	Archivo General de la Nación, México, Ramo de Mercedes, vol. . . .
INAH-FM-Misc . . .	Instituto Nacional de Antropología e Historia, México, Fondo de Micropelículas, Miscelanéa, rollo . . .
INAH-TP- . . .	Instituto Nacional de Antropología e Historia, México, Fondo de Micropelículas, Tierras de Puebla, rollo . . .
NLC-A- . . .	Newberry Library of Chicago, Ayer Collection, vol. . . .
SRH-CN	Archivo de la Secretaría de Recursos Hidráulicos, Cuenca del Río Nexapa, Edo. de Puebla.

10

Mexican Toponyms as a Source
in Regional Ethnohistory

Ursula Dyckerhoff

The study of local toponymy has a long tradition in Mexico, but until recently its main aim has been the translation and semantic analysis of the names of towns and villages. This has been due not only to the public interest in understanding the meaning and correct orthography of indigenous place names, but also to the more academic interest in deciphering the central Mexican hieroglyphic system, in which the semantic and phonetic properties of the names are of primary importance. Toponyms constitute one of the largest categories of hieroglyphs.

METHOD AND SCOPE OF INVESTIGATION

The research on Mexican toponyms (that is, names used in designating all the geographical features of an environment; "place-name" refers to settlements only) to be presented in this essay takes a different approach.[1] Method and procedure were influenced by the historical-linguistic studies of toponyms in European countries. These

have achieved important and interesting results over the past century—besides clarifying the etymologies of toponyms, they have
shed light on regional, rural, and settlement history.[2]

Many years ago, Paul Kirchhoff and Anton Nowotny (1960),
among others, recommended the historical investigation of toponyms. They felt that this approach could yield important ethnohistorical insights into those regions or periods of Mexican history
where written sources were deficient or lacking altogether, or into
themes not treated by the sources.[3] However, neither of them explained in any detail the procedures warranted. They also did not
question the applicability of European research principles to the
Mexican situation. One objective of my program of toponymic
research was, therefore, to test to what extent specific principles
and particular hypotheses were applicable to the analysis of toponyms in Mexico, if indeed they were applicable at all.

The basic premises of these historical-linguistic investigations are
derived from diachronic research on Indo-European languages.[4] First,
sites are named according to the speech norms of their time. These
norms provide a set of grammatical devices for the formation of
toponyms. They are used selectively according to general fashion
or preferences, which change in the course of time. Thus, toponyms
at different times may obey different rules of grammatical construction, or different locative forms may be preferred, which later on
fall into disuse. This implies that the various locative devices of a
language with more or less the same meaning (for example, "place
where," "home of") were never used simultaneously in the formation
of toponyms, but rather in some temporal sequence.[5]

Second, toponyms often persist for a very long time; once formed
they do not change in step with the general historical modifications
of language. They continue to exist even in cases where the dominant
language of a region is replaced by another. Toponyms from a
replaced language or from obsolete speech forms still occur in every-
day usage or in written texts of much later times as so-called "fossil
names." Although they are still used as names, they cannot really
be understood by speakers, because their structure and/or semantic
content is no longer in accord with current speech norms.[6] But
despite their conservatism, toponyms do not remain unaltered for
all time and they, too, reflect the general changes of the language,

although with considerable delay.[7] Besides those slow "natural changes," which follow the general linguistic and cultural modifications, there are others caused by more violent circumstances, such as the consequences of war or political and religious upheavals, that may even lead to deliberate renaming.[8]

Given these principles, it is feasible and expedient to classify toponyms in a historical study according to formal properties, without necessarily taking into account their individual semantic content. The result is the identification of one or more types of construction which are representative of the toponymy of a given time. Such characteristic traits are called "diagnostic." Nevertheless, it must be remembered that even diagnostic traits were not exclusive in their own time.[9]

Therefore, this type of investigation requires a careful recording of the toponymy of the region under investigation, including both historical and contemporary names. Depending on the quality and extent of historical documentation, it is usually possible to establish chronological sequences of the various diagnostic traits. In the more favorable instances it is possible to trace back certain classes of toponyms to their origin and to understand the meaning of their components.

The questions as to what extent geographical names in Mexico may be systematically explained and used as a source for ethnohistory, and where the problems in such a procedure may lie, have to be answered by the study of the toponyms of a historically determined and delimited region. The region of Huejotzingo in the central Mexican highlands, in the state of Puebla, was chosen for this purpose. During the prehispanic period Huejotzingo was for several centuries the leading power in the region east of the Valley of Mexico. It came under the influence of the Aztec Empire only during the very last years before the European conquest. Nahuatl was spoken in the region, and to a certain extent has survived to the present.

The linguistic analysis of the Huejotzingo toponyms was preceded by a compilation of all the rules governing the generation of toponyms and gentilic names, both of which are intimately related in Nahuatl ("gentilic names" denote national, tribal, or civic affiliation). This "toponymy grammar," derived from the grammar of classical Nahuatl (relying most heavily on Andrews 1975), served as the necessary frame of reference against which the individual toponyms were checked, in order to determine whether they were in accordance with grammatical rules valid in sixteenth-century Nahuatl.

The poor quality of many etymologies offered in works on Mexican toponyms shows the necessity of a more rigorous approach such as this. The following example of an unacceptable etymology illustrates the point: "Aztama, (del náh. *Aztamatl*) de *aztatl,* garza, *ma,* tomar, coger algo, a *c,* final de lugar. En donde se cazan garzas" (Anaya Montoy 1965: 49). But a combination of the noun *aztatl* and the verb *ma* would be verbal (*aztama*), and then the nominalization *aztamatl* is impossible, according to Aztec nominalization rules. On the other hand, the proposed original locative suffix, *-c,* never combines with verbal forms. A locative derivation of the verb *ma* would have produced *aztamacan.* A grammatically acceptable etymology for Aztama should read either *"aztatl,* 'heron,'" with the locative suffix *-man* apocopated to *-ma,* as in many other cases; or—if one wants to trace back Aztama to Aztamac—a lexicographically independent noun, **aztamatl* or **aztamaitl,* has to be postulated, from which a locative Aztamac could be derived.[10] The deficiency of most etymological studies lies in their restriction to the use of Nahuatl dictionaries, which encompass only a small fraction of all Aztec words (cf. Garibay 1961: 318), and to the folk etymologies of today, as well as in their almost total neglect of Aztec grammar, which is so famous for the logic of its structure.[11]

A somewhat critical point with respect to the validity for the Puebla region of Molina's dictionary and the old and new grammars of classical Nahuatl, which are mainly based on the Nahuatl of the Valley of Mexico, is the nearly total absence of works treating regional differences. These differences are generally supposed to have been of little importance, although a frequent sixteenth-century comment was that the Nahuatl spoken outside the Valley of Mexico was less refined (Garibay 1961: 314ff.; Sahagún 1961: 175). Referring to modern local differences within the Puebla area, Hertle (1972: 85) denies different dialects within the western part of the valley and admits only phonetic variations. On the other hand, a recent study by Knab (1979) finds concrete evidence of dialect differentiation of a prosodic, phonetic, morphemic, and semantic nature within the Cholula, Tlaxcala, and Huejotzingo regions. Since some of these differences can be traced back to the sixteenth century, a comparative study of local native documents from early colonial times may be promising in the attempt to establish firmer knowledge of classical Nahuatl regional variation. In the present study of toponyms, which covers a more restricted area than Knab's research, most of these differences can be ignored. However, in the semantic field, cases of differences in comparison with the Valley of Mexico were indeed found.[12]

THE TOPONYMY OF HUEJOTZINGO: 1560–1972

Following the European tradition, the present study is not only concerned with the names of the settlements, but also with those of farm tracts and topographic features. The contemporary names were collected during fieldwork between 1971 and 1973. The historical names were extracted from the very rich store of colonial documents pertaining to this region, especially those dating from the sixteenth and seventeenth centuries.

From this corpus of historical toponyms, the toponymy of the Huejotzingo region had to be reconstructed; that is, the location and extent of each area designated had to be determined. This was achieved by comparing historical toponyms with the contemporary names and by considering the topographic situation to which they apply, as well as by employing additional procedures developed in another research project, whose purpose was to reconstruct rural landholdings around 1600 (Prem 1978; see especially pp. 133–42). On the one hand the reconstructed toponymy is a historical source in its own right; on the other, it can serve as a very useful tool for the interpretation of ethnohistorical data and can enable the researcher to cope more adequately with special themes. For example, locating settlements that have disappeared since the sixteenth century provides a spatial framework for the sociopolitical data found in early colonial documents from Huejotzingo (Dyckerhoff 1973, 1976; Prem 1978: 73–113). In turn, knowing the exact location of sites where historic events took place makes the general history more meaningful and geographically precise (Dyckerhoff 1978: 30,

32). The toponymy in general also conveys information helpful for assessing the extent of prehispanic and early colonial irrigation in Huejotzingo (Dyckerhoff 1982).

A comparison between historical and contemporary toponymy constitutes the frame for observing the modifications which have taken place during the last four centuries. The present comparison is limited spatially to the area of Huejotzingo proper and the Valley of Texmelucan.[13] Some of the principal findings are discussed below.

The indigenous toponymy of the sixteenth century outside the settlements used proper names for two territorial levels. The upper level corresponded more or less to the so-called *"pago"* of Spanish land grants, and denoted a considerable piece of land, such as an entire hill or a large stretch situated between two rivers or ravines.[14] The flatter the area was, the more extensive the territory referred to by a single name. In the Nahuatl documents these names are mostly introduced by the term *itocayocan*. The lower level consisted of the names which designated points and sites of lesser extent, frequently pinpointing them within the larger territorial unit. Names of the latter type are frequently encountered in the wills of the Indian nobility and in Spanish land-purchase documents. Because of their small size, they can be extremely difficult to locate. The toponyms of both levels show no difference in their linguistic structure or semantic content. Other designations used in environmental descriptions cannot be classified as toponyms proper, because they were applied to extremely small localities and seem to have been known or used only by a small number of people, perhaps the owner of the field and his family, as also occurs today.[15] Although by 1600 Spanish landholdings in the Huejotzingo region were considerable (Prem 1978: 164, 165), this was not reflected in the toponymy. Spanish influences occurred only in a very few hybrid names formed with Christian concepts, or in the names of Christian saints which were the patrons of the villages and haciendas.

Today the pattern of toponyms is completely different. In wide areas names with Spanish or hybrid origin have replaced the Indian ones. This is a continuous process which began after the introduction of European agricultural practices and the formation of the haciendas. It has been accelerated recently by the establishment of industrial plants in the region. Generally speaking, the present occurrence of Nahuatl toponyms is correlated with the continuing use of Nahuatl as a spoken language, although the language is disappearing more rapidly than the toponyms. It should be noted, however, that the great majority of Nahuatl toponyms which now exist are not survivals from the sixteenth century, but are more recent innovations. The sixteenth-century toponyms still used today, on the other hand, are distributed more or less regularly over the whole region, without any discernible correspondence with the general distribution of Nahuatl toponyms or Nahuatl speakers. This implies that the sixteenth-century toponyms have been retained independently of Nahuatl as a spoken language.

Several factors may account for this phenomenon. First, some of the settlements continued from the sixteenth century to the present with little or no interruption, and thus their original Nahuatl names were conserved, even in those environments where names were gradually influenced by Europeans. Second, where a large tract of Indian land was subdivided among several Spanish individuals the tract name tended to survive in individual parcel names. In a tract subdivided by a hacienda into various fields, each subdivision was apt to have received a new name.

It is commonly thought that rivers and other bodies of water retain their names for extremely long periods of time. However, in the Huejotzingo region a number of rivers acquired Spanish names by early colonial times, or else received new Nahuatl names in the centuries following the conquest. Those rivers which did preserve their old names are no longer designated by original names with the absolute noun ending *-atl,* "water," but with the locative ending *-ac,* "in the water," or *-apan,* "place of the water." This holds true for the neighboring parts of Mexico as well. The change from *-atl* to *-ac* or *-apan* is related to the present custom of using the names of fields, which usually end with a locative suffix, to designate the adjacent segments of ravines, creeks, and rivers. In the sixteenth century, names of sites were more often derived from those of the rivers flowing along them. For example, the creek formerly called Temizatl once gave its name to the ground and rancho Temizac, but now the creek itself is called Temizac. Likewise, the former

river Zahuatl in Tlaxcala, which was mentioned in this form as late
as 1645 by the grammarian Carochi (1904: 531), is known today
as Zahuapan.

TEMPORAL ASPECTS OF SOME TOPONYM CLASSES

Since most Nahuatl toponyms are marked by their locative endings, they are easily classified according to the different suffixes or
locative morphemes.[16] With this classification, it is possible to
establish a certain, although not always absolute, chronological
order between classes or subclasses of toponyms.

-man

The earliest toponyms in the region seem to be those with the
locative morpheme *-man,* with their gentilic equivalent *-mecatl* (for
example, Olman, Olmecatl).[17] The greater antiquity of this class
of toponyms compared to the others is clear because the suffix *-man*
was no longer productive in classical Nahuatl at the time of the
conquest; that is, *-man* was no longer used in general speech nor
in the formation of new toponyms. Names of this class are extremely
rare in the region under investigation, and the only positive case
is the old barrio Chalma(n) in the Atlixco Valley, a name associated
with the pre-Toltec population living south and east of Popocatepetl.

External Subject Locative

The toponyms of another old class usually consist of the two
components of a possessive construction. In a vast majority of cases,
a verbal locative expression (B) is linked by the possessive to a
preceding substantive (A). These toponyms have a high narrative
content, denoting "the place where A did B." A well-known example
is Cuextecatl ichocayan ("Where the Huaxtec weeps"), which represents the formal characteristics of its class. In the Mexican version
of the migration legend, toponyms of this class abound in the
itineraries of the wandering groups after the fall of Tollan and among
the sacred-place toponyms or metaphors of their final settlements
(for example, Chalco, Cholula, Tenochtitlan). It was probably these
"narrative" names which Muñoz Camargo had in mind when he
wrote (1892: 52, my translation), "places which they settled and

named in conformity with the events which happened to them during their journey." These narrative names apparently did not persist very long and were seldom found at the time of the conquest. With respect to their origin the following question arises: Were there really sites named in this way, or are their names at least partly due to a misreading of hieroglyphs? Perhaps the real meaning of the glyphs was unknown because they were based originally on names in a foreign language. The two names of this class in the Huejotzingo region, where they are documented since the sixteenth century—Atlimeyayan and Atlicholoayan—both contain the noun *atl,* "water," and are in fact related to the presence of water. Unfortunately no documents are extant which might prove their origin in the migration period.

-hua'can

Related to tribal or other groupings of people is the class of toponyms ending in *-hua'can; -hua'* expresses possession, and the complete name indicates the idea of "place where owners of X are" or, in a more figurative sense, "place where many X are," "X" indicating the possessed noun root.[18] Structurally these toponyms are derived from the names of ethnic groups.[19] As is known from general anthropology, such tribal names were coined by other ethnic groups to refer to characteristic traits which they themselves did not possess. The best known Mexican examples of this class are Michhua'que' (pl.) and Michhua'can (locative) and Mazahua'que' (pl.) and Mazahua'can (locative), by which the Nahua of the Valley of Mexico referred to their western neighbors. In Huejotzingo and in the adjacent region, toponyms of this class refer especially to settlements, mainly those of secondary rank—the *barrios, calpulli,* and *estancias.* In the rare cases where the names pertain to uninhabited lands, a now-deserted settlement with the corresponding name may be assumed. Moreover, comparison with contiguous regions shows that these names are quite frequently repeated. Tribal groups with names ending in *-hua-que* were among the first immigrants to the region around the volcanoes after the fall of Tula, as was the case with the Tolteca-Chichimeca of Cholollan with, among others, their subgroups called Quetzalhua'que' and Calmecahua'que', and the Acxoteca of Chalco, with the Mihua'que', Tlapechhua'que', etc. It can be assumed, therefore, that the corresponding place-names (e.g., Mihua'can, Tlapechhua'can, Quetzalhua'can) originated here in early post-Toltec times, with various immigrant groups of more or less the same ethnic stock who spread over a relatively large area.

-c, -co

The great majority of toponyms mentioned in the historical documents from Huejotzingo consists of names ending in *-c* or *-co* (*-co* is attached to a noun stem ending in a consonant or glottal stop, while *-c* is added to stems ending in a vowel). This is the locative suffix par excellence for the formation of place names, with the implicit meaning of "in X." Among these place names, the class ending in *-tzinco* stands out, in which two structurally, and probably also temporally different subclasses have to be distinguished.

(*1*) Primary derived names in *-tzinco*. In this subclass *-tzin* (mostly interpreted as reverential) is added to a noun stem and the locative is formed by suffixing *-co.* The nouns with which these toponyms are formed designate animals, plants, and natural phenomena. They appear also with other locative suffixes, although rarely with the simple *-c/-co* locative. Compare such parallel forms as Huexotzinco, Huexotitlan, Huexotla, but apparently not Huexoc; Chiauhtzinco, Chiauhtla, but not Chiauhco; Teotlaltzinco, Teotlalpan, but seldom Teotlalco. On the other hand, Tepetzinco is found beside Tepec, and Quauhtzinco beside Quauhco. No semantic or structural criterion common to all the nouns that have formed toponyms with the primary derived *-tzinco* locative, and which thus might define them as a definite group, seems to exist. Toponyms with primary derived *-tzinco* locatives are quite frequent in Huejotzingo and Tlaxcala, perhaps more so than in other regions. They are associated chiefly with settlements founded before the Spanish conquest, especially with those of *cabecera* or *pueblo* rank in Huejotzingo. These place-names are seldom found more than once. It may be assumed, therefore, that their creation was due to a temporary custom, restricted locally and perhaps ethnically, which tended to designate the settlements with an honorific term.[20] It seems not unreasonable to suggest the period of Chichimec settlement as the time of their origin.

(2) Secondary derived names in *-tzinco*. These locatives are constructed by adding *-tzinco* (with diminutive connotations) to the locative suffix of an already existing place name: Contlan, Contlantzinco; Xaltocan, Xaltocantzinco; Tochpan, Tochpantzinco. In the case of a preceding locative ending in *-c/-co,* this suffix is deleted and thus the visual distinction between primary and secondary derived *-tzinco* locatives is lost (Texpolco, Texpoltzinco; Tenanco, Tenantzinco). In the case of Tlaxcallantzinco, the founders of the village were emigrants from Tlaxcala (Olivera de Vázquez 1967: 10); Quauhtlantzinco, near Cholula, was founded by emigrants from that city, where a cabecera or barrio of Quauhtlan existed (Seler 1902: 352; Carrasco 1971: 27ff.). These two cases imply the process of "hiving." This process is also suggested by the fact that in Tlaxcala a considerable number of secondary *-tzinco* names occurred parallel to villages with the corresponding simple name (*Padrones de Tlaxcala*). Further research must determine whether the formation of secondary *-tzinco* names was perhaps restricted to new settlements of early colonial times, as the above-mentioned cases of Tlaxcallantzinco and Quauthlantzinco suggest, when the "Pax Hispanica" was conducive to them.

Another possible interpretation seems to be less likely. The secondary derived *-tzinco* may have served as a general differentiator, indicating the "smallness" or "unimportance" of one village in comparison to another with the same name. In this case the name with *-tzinco* would not express any real relationship, and such a settlement might even be older than the one without this suffix. In any event, secondary *-tzinco* names are extremely rare in Huejotzingo, and do not occur in circumstances where either hypothesis may be proved.

-tlan

The locative suffix *-tlan,* "near," "among," "beneath," is attached to noun stems, either directly or by means of the ligature *-ti-,* which is generally considered of only euphonic value. Since there is no apparent reason for the choice of one or another suffix (both exist side by side, e.g., Ocotlan, Ocotitlan; Tepetlan, Tepetitlan) most authors writing on Mexican toponyms have either offered some kind of explanation or different translations (see Dávila Garibi 1942: 53ff. for a summary). However, none are very convincing, in light

of the fact that the old grammarians did not distinguish between
-tlan and *-ti-tlan*. Also, the connecting *-ti-* is not considered se-
mantically relevant in any other context. Thus, other reasons must
account for their varying use.

Both forms of the suffix have produced numerous toponyms since
early times. Apparently names formed with *-tlan* continued to increase in number after the conquest, when it also became the preferred suffix for forming hybrid names with Spanish nouns. Here
-ti-tlan was also preferred in forming toponyms derived from plants
of European origin (while also predominating in toponyms derived
from native plants), as well as from loanwords in general—not only
from Spanish, but also form the language of the Caribbean Islands
by way of Spanish (e.g., Nopaltitlan, Perastitlan, Cruztitlan, Can-
oatitlan). The simple suffix *-tlan,* on the other hand, was employed
in the formation of toponyms derived from Spanish family names.
Apocopated today to *-tla,* these names are frequently found among
the haciendas around Cholula and Atlixco (Castillotla, Serranotla),
while in Tlaxcala and Huejotzingo they occur as the names of small
plots within the villages. In the Atlixco area these hybrid hacienda
names are first documented in the middle of the seventeenth century.
However, the general pattern of attaching *-tlan* to the proper name
of a group of persons is documented in a pure Nahuatl context
nearly one century earlier (1556; "Padrones de Tlaxcala," f. 35:
Contecatlan, Teohuacatlan). There are apparently no recently formed
names of this type in the Huejotzingo region. On the other hand,
place-names from all over Mexico originating in the Republican
era, after 1821, show that in those cases *-ti-tlan* was used in the
derivation of toponyms from personal names (Hidalgotitlan, Mina-
titlan). More extensive research along this line may show further
examples of the temporally or contextually distinct employment of
-tlan and *-ti-tlan.*

DISTRIBUTIONAL ASPECTS OF TOPONYMS

The general importance for ethnohistory of the possibility of
ascribing different time depths and ethnic affiliations to various
classes of toponyms is especially evident in a historical setting where
multiethnicity seems to have been the rule, but where written

sources are scarce. The spatial distribution of toponyms is especially significant in this respect. In favorable instances, the correspondence between ethnic groups and certain toponyms is already well documented, as is the case with the names Tepetenchi and Panchimalco, characteristic of the Xochimila-Tlalhuica. In other cases only analogies between the place-names of several regions can be detected, where the differing intensity of the analogy reflects different historical relations. Without additional sources coming to light, it will not be possible to say anything very precise about the nature of these relations.

A good illustration for this is offered by the toponym Tlama(y)oco, to which the title "Tlamaocatl tecutli" was related; this is one of the most characteristic titles in Huejotzingo, Calpan, and Chalco. In Chalco the title belonged to the cabecera of Panohuayan Amaquemecan, which was founded by the very latest of the many immigrant groups to settle in this region (Chimalpahin 1963: 57). In Chalco, as well as in Huejotzingo and Tlaxcala, there existed various settlements named Tlamaoco. From other sources it is known that people called Tlamayoca left Huejotzingo and emigrated to the south, by way of Tlaxcala, and finally settled in Tepeaca (Reyes 1977: 53). The numerous Tlamaoco toponyms indicate that these Tlamayoca were not an isolated or insignificant group, but rather that they lived in an extensive territory, from which some emigrated. No conclusion, however, can be drawn about the settlement process itself.

The wide regional distribution of another ethnic group is indicated by the toponym of Chimalpan, associated with the Tlayllotlaque-Chimalpaneca, of Mixtec origin. They are reported to have migrated to Cuauhtinchan, in southern Puebla, from the Mixteca, and spread north as far as the Valley of Mexico where, entering from Chalco, they were reputed to have acted as a kind of civilizing agent in fourteenth-century Texcoco (Chimalpahin 1963: 30; Ixtlilxóchitl 1975: 315, 402; Reyes García 1977: 62). According to the toponyms, they must have settled in Huejotzingo and Tlaxcala as well.

Toponymy also reflects the close historical relations prevalent during long periods between Huejotzingo and the Acolhua state of Coatlichan, both of which traced their origins back to Tzontecomatl as their leader during the migration and settlement period (Bitman

1968: 41, no. 61; Ixtlilxóchitl 1975: 306, 411, 1977: 17; Kirch-hoff, Odena Güemes, and Reyes G. 1976, par. 219ff.). A series of names corresponding in Huejotzingo to settlements of the secondary rank (barrios, calpulli) are repeated in Coatlichan as the names of barrios or cabeceras. Since they also have parallels in Cholula, Chalco, and/or Tlaxcala, they reflect the many Tolteca-Chichimeca popu-lation groups that settled in those regions (among others the Quetz-alhuaque and Tlaltecahuaque). It is also noteworthy that among the six cabeceras of Coatlichan, Tlacochcalco, and Tlalnahuac are those which show the highest incidence of repeated Huejotzingo names, while in the two cabeceras of Culhuacan and Mexicapan, no repe-tition occurs (see table 10.1). This distribution seems to anticipate the infrequency of shared place-names between Huejotzingo and the central Valley of Mexico, and gives strong hints concerning the ethnic composition of Coatlichan, about which little is known from other sources. The name Coatlichan itself is repeated in Huejotzingo as that of a barrio of Tetzmollocan; this can be interpreted as a confirmation for its founding in Tetzmollocan by people coming in late preconquest times from Coatlichan to this northern part of Huejotzingo, a fact which the native chronicles mention in con-nection with various historical events (Ixtlilxóchitl 1975: 342, 379, 1977: 89; Chimalpahin 1963: 95). Unfortunately it is impossible to specify which of these events gave rise to the settlement.

CONCLUSION

The Huejotzingo material demonstrates that principles of his-torical toponymic research can be used effectively as a tool for reconstructing Mexican culture history.

Comparisons between modern and sixteenth-century toponyms reveal changes which do not always correspond to the expected pattern. For example, the names of rivers and other bodies of water tend to persist over long periods of time, but in the Huejotzingo area they changed during the colonial period. New toponyms were generated in both Spanish and Nahuatl, corresponding to the changed situation under the Spaniards. Nahuatl toponyms present in the sixteenth century persist today, independent of Nahuatl as a spoken language.

Table 10.1. Comparison of Cognate Settlement Names Indicating Ethnic Differences

Coatlichan[a]	Huejotzingo	Calpan
Coatlichan		
Ahuachtlan		
Xacopan		
Xomolcingo		
Avau . . .		
Tlalchiantlan		
Tleculhuacan	Tlecuilhuacan (Acxotla)	
Tepetitlan*[b]	*Tepetitlan (Tlanicontlan)	
Tlalnahuac	Tlalnahuac (Tetzmollocan)	*Tlalnahuac*
Chimalpan	Chimalpan (Xaltepetlapan, Ocotepec)	Chimalpan
Yxtlahuacan*	*	
Tecpan[c]	Tecpan (Huexotzinco)	
Quezalhuacan	Quetzalhuacan (Acxotla)	
. . . iaco		
Ahuehuetitlan		
Tlilhuacan	[Tlilhuacan (Atenco)]	
Tlaxisco	Tlaxisco (Xaltepetlapan, Ocotepec)	*Tlaxichco*
Mihuacan	Miyoacan (Xaltepetlapan)	Mihuacan-Chalcapan
Tlilhuacan	[Tlilhuacan (Atenco)]	
Tepepan*-Ayapango	*	[*Ayapanco*]
Mexicapan		
Tlacateco		
Nonohualco		
Cihuac Tecpan		
Ocotitlan*	*Ocotitlan (Cecalacoayan)	
Tlatzalan		
Tepuzahuatla		
Mexicalcingo		
Tepantitlan		
Ahuehuetitlan		
Culhuacan		

Table 10.1. (continued)

Coatlichan[a]	Huejotzingo	Calpan
Atliacan		
Xicolan Culhuacan		
Tlato . . .		
Tecpancingan		
Tapalcapan		
Chimalhuacapan		
Ahuehuetitlan		
Couatlalpan		
Mototepe(c)		
Tepaneca		
Çacualcingo		
Oztolitiqui		
Tenango	Tenanco (Tlanicontlan, Tepetzinco)	Tenanco
Tlal . . . lantla		
Ciua . . . pan		
Chalca Puchtlan	Pochtla(n) (Huexotzinco, Ocotepec, Tlanicontlan)	
Tlama . . .		
Totola	Totolla(c) (Huexotzinco, Cecalacoayan)	
. . . tepec		
Mi . . .		
Tecalco		
Tla . . . tlan		
Tlaiçayanca		
Tlacuchcalco	Tlacochcalco (Huexotzinco, Xaltepetlapan, Atenco, Tepetzinco, Cecalacoayan)	
Tlacuchcalco		
Tlalquican[d]	Tlatquican (Tepetzinco)	
Calico		
Ayapango		[*Ayapanco*]
Tlilhuacan	[Tlilhuacan (Atenco)]	
Tlilmatlan		

Table 10.1. (continued)

Coatlichan[a]	Huejotzingo	Calpan
Tlaltecaua	Tlaltecauacan (Xaltepetlapan)	
Tecpantlacal		
Tecalco		
Tepuzahua(tla)		
Techachalco		
Chiconquiauco	Chiconquiauhco (Cecalacoayan)	
Tlacat . . .		
Tlilhuacancingo		
Tlaixpan[e]		

[a]Coatlichan: Names from the "Mapa de Coatlichan," sixteenth century (complete list). The names of the "cabeceras" are italicized. The distinction made in the map between "barrios" and "estancias" is not rendered in the list, because they are not reflected in differences in the names. A complete reading of the names was impossible in some cases.

Huejotzingo: Names from the "Matrícula de Huexotzinco," 1560 (Prem 1974). The list is incomplete since only names equivalent to those in Coatlichan are given here. The name of a "barrio" is followed in parentheses by the name of the pueblo to which it belongs. More than one pueblo name in parentheses indicates that each pueblo had a barrio with the preceding name.

Calpan: Names from "Elecciones de Calpan," 1578. This list is incomplete since only names equivalent to those in Coatlichan are given here. Names of "cabeceras" are italicized; other names are "tecpan" designations (see Note c, below).

Due to the nature of the comparative listing, repetitions of settlements in Calpan and/ or Huejotzingo are inevitable; they are indicated by square brackets.

[b]An asterisk designates names which refer to natural phenomena or plants characteristic of the mountainous region of the Sierra Neovolcánica; their occurrence in various places does not indicate more than the known fact of geographic similarities. If no equivalent place-name from Huejotzingo or Calpan is given but an asterisk is present, the name is documented as a toponym, but not as a settlement name.

[c]Tecpan is the general Nahuatl designation for the house and landed property of a noble lineage; it is therefore not to be scored as a name occurring twice.

[d]The name in the Coatlichan map is clearly written as Tlalquican, while in Huejotzingo and other regions the place-name Tlatquican existed, associated with the title "Tlatquic tecutli." As no clear etymology for Tlalquican is possible, this spelling most likely is a writer's mistake or deformation of an original "Tlatquican."

[e]It is not clear from the map whether the "estancia" Tlaixpan belongs to Tlacuchcalco or to Culhuacan.

Toponyms may be segregated into classes according to formal structural criteria. An analysis of the classes and their occurrences reveal a partial chronological sequence, which, at least in one case, predates the Tolteca-Chichimeca immigration. However, it has not been possible to establish an ethinic correspondence or a fixed temporal correlation for all toponym classes. As near as can be determined, no toponymic vestiges of non-Nahuatl aboriginal languages have penetrated the Nahuatl substratum.

The interregional comparison of the distribution of selected toponyms, such as Tlamaoco and Chimalpan, demonstrates ethnic relations between adjacent areas not otherwise mentioned. On the other hand, various place-names confirm migrations to Huejotzingo mentioned in chronicles from outside the region under study.

The topics covered in this paper only briefly explore the field of systematic ethnohistorical investigation of toponyms, but the discussion should have been sufficient to show the potential worth as well as the inherent limitations in this approach. Further independent linguistic and philological research may help to surmount one obstacle to the investigation of Nahuatl toponymy, namely, the fundamental problem of language regionalism in classical Nahuatl.

Since Huejotzingo is apparently the first region of Mexico where the toponymy has been systematically studied using the historical-linguistic approach, most of these results must be considered valid for Huejotzingo only. They require corroboration from similar studies in other areas with different historical and ethnic backgrounds.

NOTES

1. Research in the Mexican archives and in the field was carried out primarily under two grants from the Deutsche Forschungsgemeinschaft (German Research Foundation), to which I extend my gratitude. I wish to thank H. J. Prem for critical comments on a first version of this paper and W. Trautmann for providing a microfilm copy of the "Padrones de Tlaxcala."

2. Jakob Grimm (1785–1863) is considered to have initiated this type of linguistic study, which touches upon a broad range of different topics. For actual trends and theoretical considerations see the two miscellaneous volumes, *Der Name in Sprache und Gesellschaft* (1973) and Debus and Puchner (1978).

3. Moreno Toscana (1969) presented a review illustrating some of the possibilities of historical interpretation applied to Mexican place names. Earlier, Anaya Monroy (1965) tried, not always satisfactorily, to relate the place-names of Tlaxcala to the culture and history of that state.

4. The linguistic principles can be treated here only in an extremely general and summary form. The same also applies to the German examples presented in the following notes. For a fuller summary and some examples in English see Bynon 1977: 273–77.

5. For instance, a certain category of German place-names is formed with the endings *-ing* (Bavarian), *-ingen* (Swabian), *-ungen* (Thuringian), which indicate "where the followers of X are" or "where the settlement of X is." The preceding, determinant part of the name expresses (at present in a very contracted form) a personal name, the name of "X"; e.g., Sigimaringen (eleventh century), "place of the followers of Sigimar," now Sigmaringen (Baden-Württemberg). This widespread type of name comes from the period of Germanic settlement of these regions and is found in written sources from the seventh and eighth centuries on. Only a short time later, and partly still contemporaneous with them, place-names ending with *-heim* ("home of X") were created, resulting in occasional rivalry, as when Sigmaringen is also documented as Sigmarsheim.

Another and somewhat later type of place-name ending with *-heim* (in Bavaria also *-ham, -cham,* or *-kam;* in England *-ham*) is distinguished from the older group by its determinant, which here is not a personal name but a geographical concept; e.g., Nordheim (Lower Saxony), Weidenham, Heigenkam (Bavaria), Leadenham (Suffolk). Parallel to them and in analogy to the old names with *-ing, -ingen,* but with a geographical determinant, are newly formed names with these endings, such as Groningen (Netherlands), from *grün,* "green," meaning "clearing in the woods." Places with those names are later settlements on royal lands.

Place-names ending in *-hausen* (western and southern Germany) and *-husen* (northern Germany), i.e., "house," correspond to a still later period of settlement expansion, promoted by the territorial lords; e.g., Holzhausen (Bavaria), Kellinghusen (Holstein).

6. Instructive examples for obsolete speech forms in German place-names and toponyms are *lützel-* and *michel-*, as in Lützenburg (the old German name of Luxembourg), Michelstadt, and others. *Lützel-* ("small") and *michel-* ("big, great") were current dimensional adjectives in Old High German (ca. A.D. 750–1100), but which were gradually supplanted by other words before the development of Modern High German, i.e., before 1500 (see Fritz 1974: 98–106 for details of the process of semantic change). The original significance of the present place-names formed with

lützel- and *michel-* is today generally unknown to the unsophisticated German speaker.

Slavic place-names in eastern and northern Germany, ending in *-ow* (Pankow, Gatow) or *-itz* (Steglitz, Lankwitz), as well as Leipzig and many others, are the most evident remnants of the Slavic tribes which dominated these regions in the Middle Ages and which later mixed peacefully with the more recent, German-speaking population.

7. In Germany, neighboring villages with homonymous names are often differentiated by adding *nieder-* or *unter-*, "low(er)" contrasting with *ober-*, "high(er)," "upper." This process of differentiation first appears in documents about the middle of the thirteenth century, with the addition of Latin *superior* and *inferior;* after 1400 these are no longer used. The first use of *nieder-* is documented in 1252. Between 1450 and 1550 there is abundant proof of place naming with *nieder-*. In 1483, *unter-* is documented for the first time in connection with a name, and after 1500 its incidence increases considerably. While the *nieder-* form persisted until 1700, both forms may even be found together in one document, applied to the same village. After 1700 names ending in *nieder-* become rare and are found mostly in documents based on older deeds, while continuing as a petrified form in the names of some villages. Various settlements were renamed at that time using *unter-* instead of *nieder-*. From then on *unter-* was added in all pertinent cases of new name differentiation (Koss, in Debus and Puchner 1978: 227–39). The foregoing description refers to Coburger Land in Northern Bavaria, but the same process also took place, although with temporal differences, in other parts of Germany, parallel to changes in the semantic content of the specific words involved (Christmann 1935). The importance of archival research is clearly demonstrated by these examples.

8. This was the case, for example, in postrevolutionary Russia and in the German Democratic Republic where, among others, St. Petersburg became Leningrad and Chemnitz is now Karl-Marx-Stadt.

9. See examples in Notes 5 and 7.

10. In this and similar cases, a definite etymology will be established only if written sources which conserve older versions of the name can be consulted.

11. Folk etymologies are the popular interpretations and new spellings of obsolete names, by which they recover a generally understandable meaning.

12. Since 1974, Lastra de Suárez has published a series of studies on Nahuatl dialectology in which considerable lexical variations between the

modern dialects within the Valley of Mexico become apparent (see, e.g., Lastra de Suárez and Horcasitas 1976).

13. For the internal politico-geographical division of the Huejotzingo region see Dyckerhoff 1973: 93.

14. According to the *Diccionario de Autoridades* (1969[3]: 79), "Pago. Significa también el distrito determinado de tierras o heredades, especialmente de viñas. En este sentido viene del Latino Pagus. . . ."

15. "nombres especiales que pondrían los indios a cada uno de los pedazos de tierra que vendieron" (1690; Archivo General de la Nación, Ramo de Tierras, vol. 149, Exp. 3, f. 36; see also Prem 1978: 139).

A comparable three-level stratification of proper names was proposed for the German Democratic Republic, correlated with three different "spheres of communication"; that is, social groupings of three different sizes, where the respective names are known and used regularly (Walther, in *Der Name in Sprache und Gesellschaft* [1973]: 24, 25).

16. Although these so-called locative morphemes or suffixes are in reality mostly morpheme clusters of which only the last morpheme constitutes the locative proper, the expressions used above are preferred for the sake of convenience.

17. This was also observed by the late Paul Kirchhoff in a manuscript preserved now in the CES-INAH, México.

18. Other toponyms with an "orthographically homonymous" suffix (without the glottal stop, which in most texts is not written) are derived from pure (noun-)verb compounds (e.g., Almoyahuacan from *moyaua,* "water is disturbed") or have been formed in exceptional cases by analogy (e.g., Ixtlahuacan, synonym to Ixtlahuac, from *ixtlahuatl,* "plain"). These are not considered here.

19. By this statement I do not mean to exclude real or legendary places of origin with the same or a *teo-* prefixed name.

20. Lastra de Suárez and Horcasitas (1976: 122) refer to cases of modern Nahuatl where a class of nouns (plants and natural phenomena) is preferentially used in the reverential form, with *-tzin.*

REFERENCES

Anaya Monroy, Fernando
1965   La toponimia indígena en la historia y la cultura de Tlaxcala.
            México: Universidad Nacional, Instituto de Investigaciones
            Históricas.

Andrews, J. Richard
1975   Introduction to Classical Nahuatl. Austin: University of Texas
            Press.
Bitman Simons, Bente
1968   Los mapas de Cuauhtinchan y la historia tolteca-chichimeca.
            México: Instituto Nacional de Antropología e Historia, Serie
            Investigación, 15.
Bynon, Theodora
1977   Historical Linguistics. Cambridge, Eng.: Cambridge Univer-
            sity Press.
Carochi, Horacio
1904   Arte de la lengua méxicana con declaración de los adverbios
            della. México: Colección de Gramáticas de la lengua Mexicana,
            1.
Carrasco, Pedro
1971   Los barrios antiguos de Cholula. Estudios y Documentos de
            la Región de Puebla-Tlaxcala 3: 9–88.
Chimalpahin Quauhtlehuanitzin, Domingo de
San Antón Muñon
1963   Die Relationen Chimalpahin's zur Geschichte México's. Teil
            1: Die Zeit bis zur Conquista 1521. Günter Zimmermann,
            ed. Hamburg: Abhandlungen aus dem Gebiet der Auslands-
            kunde, 68.
Christmann, Ernst
1935   Die Verdrängung von "nieder" durch "unter" in Siedlungs-
            namen. Zeitschrift für Mundartforschung 11: 131–46.
Dávila Garibi, José Ignacio
1942   Toponimias nahuas. México: Instituto Panamericano de Geo-
            grafía e Historia, Publicación 63.
Debus, F., and Karl Puchner, eds.
1978   Name und Geschichte: Henning Kaufmann zum 80. Geburts-
            tag. München: Wilhelm Fink Verlag.
Diccionario de Autoridades
1969   Edición facsímil. 3 vols. Madrid: Biblioteca Románica Hispánica.
Dyckerhoff, Ursula
1973   Patrones de asentamiento en la región de Huejotzingo. Co-
            municaciones Proyecto Puebla-Tlaxcala 7: 93–97.
1976   La estratificación social en Huexotzinco: Aspectos generales y
            regionales de la estratificación social. *In* Estratificación social
            en la Mesoamérica prehispánica. Pedro Carrasco et al. pp. 157–
            77. México: SEP-INAH.

1978   La región del Alto Atoyac en la historia: La epoca prehispánica. *In* Hanns J. Prem, Milpa y hacienda. Das Mexiko-Projekt der Deutschen Forschungsgemeinschaft (Wiesbaden) 13: 18–34.

1982   Wasserkontrollmassnahmen im Vorspanischen Huejotzingo, Puebla, Mexico. Indiana 8 (in press).

Fritz, Gerd
1974   Bedeutungswandel im Deutschen: Neuere Methoden der diachronen Semantik. Tübingen: Germanistische Arbeitschefte.

Garibay K., Angel María
1961   Llave del Náhuatl. México: Porrúa.

Glass, John B.
1964   Catálogo de la Colección de Códices. México: Instituto Nacional de Antropología e Historia.

Hertle, Gisela
1972   Nahua Dialekte in Puebla-Tlaxcala. Das Mexiko-Projekt der Deutschen Forschungsgemeinschaft (Wiesbaden) 4: 75–111.

Ixtlilxóchitl, Fernando de Alva
1975,   Obras históricas. 2 vols. Edmundo O'Gorman, ed. México:
1977   Universidad Nacional, Instituto de Investigaciones Históricas.

Kirchhoff, Paul, Lina Odena Güemes, and Luís Reyes G., eds.
1976   Historia Tolteca Chichimeca. México: CIS-INAH-SEP.

Knab, Tim
1979   Linguistics and Ethnolinguistics in the Valley of Puebla. Paper presented at the 43rd International Congress of Americanists, Vancouver, B.C.

Lastra de Suárez, Yolanda, and Fernando Horcasitas
1976   El Náhuatl en el Distrito Federal, México. Anales de Antropología 13: 103–36.

Moreno Toscana, Alejandra
1969   Toponimia y análisis histórico. Historia Mexicana 19: 1–10.

Muñoz Camargo, Diego
1892   Historia de Tlaxcala. Alfredo Chavero, ed. México: Oficina Tip. de la Secretaría de Fomento.

(Der) Name in Sprache und Geschichte: Beiträge zur Theorie der Onomastik
1973   Deutsch-Slawische Forschungen zur Namenkunde und Siedlungsgeschichte, 27. Sächsische Akademie der Wissenschaften zu Leipzig.

Nowotny, Karl Anton
1960   Über Aufgaben der Mexikanistik: Erschliessung neuer Ge-

schichtesquellen, religionswissenschaftliche Probleme. Archiv
für Völkerkunde 14: 119–31.
Olivera de Vázquez, Mercedes
1967   Tlaxcalancingo. México: Instituto Nacional de Antropología
            e Historia, Publicaciones 18.
Prem, Hanns J.
1974   Matrícula de Huexotzinco. (Ms. Mex. 387 der Bibliothèque
            Nationale, Paris). Graz, Austria: Akademische Druck- und
            Verlagsanstalt.
1978   Milpa y hacienda: Tenencia de la tierra indígena y española
            en la cuenca del alto Atoyac, Puebla, México (1520–1650).
            Das Mexiko-Projekt der Deutschen Forschungsgemeinschaft
            (Wiesbaden), 13.
Reyes García, Luis
1977   Cuauhtinchan del siglo XII al XVI: Formación y desarrollo
            histórico de un señorío prehispánico. Das Mexiko-Projekt der
            Deutschen Forschungsgemeinschaft (Wiesbaden), 10.
Sahagún, Bernardino de
1961   Florentine Codex: General History of the Things of New Spain,
            Book 10. Charles E. Dibble and Arthur J. O. Anderson, trans.
            Santa Fe: School of American Research and University of Utah.
Seler, Eduard
1902   Gesammelte Abhandlungen zur Amerikanischen Sprach- und
            Altertumskunde, 1. Berlin: Verlag A. Asher and Co.

Documentary Sources

The principal archives consulted in this research project on toponyms
are the Archivo General de la Nación, México (Ramo de Tierras, de Mercedes),
the Archivo General de Notarías, Puebla ("Protocolos de Atlixco," "de Tepeaca"), the Archivo Histórico and the Microfilm Collection, both in the
Biblioteca del Museo Nacional de Antropología, México, and a series of
local archives in the Huejotzingo area. The following unpublished documents deserve special mention:

"Elecciones de Calpan"
            Bibliothèque Nationale, Paris, Ms. Mex. 73.
"Mapa de Coatlichan"
            Museo Nacional de Antropología, México, Salon de Códices
            35-16. (See Glass 1964: 57).
Padrones de Tlaxcala
            Biblioteca del Museo Nacional de Antropología, México, Mi-
            crofilm Collection.

11

The Impact of Spanish Conquest on the Development of the Cultural Landscape in Tlaxcala, Mexico: A Reconstruction Using Models

Wolfgang Trautmann

The conquest of Mexico by Hernán Cortés in 1519 produced profound changes in the indigenous cultural landscape, including the transformation of Indian communities (*pueblos*), the rise of large Spanish landed estates (*haciendas*), the construction of roads, and the channeling of watercourses. These interrelated developments have been reconstructed for the ancient territory of Tlaxcala by combining the principal methods of historical geography: the critical analysis of documents and extensive archaeological and geographical surface surveys, supported by maps, aerial photos, and interviews.[1] The initial steps consisted of analyzing the spatial formation, modification, reconstruction, or decay of settlements from 1519 to 1810. The steps summarized below covered the individuals, social groups, and institutions involved, as well as their respective influence on the processes which affected the indigenous cultural landscape of Tlaxcala during the colonial period.[2] In accordance

253

with the aims of modern social geography, the investigations not only concentrated on the conditions and causes of changing settlement patterns, but also on the spatial behavior of individuals and groups; the latter can be derived from the characteristics of location as well as from the intensity and radius of actions in space (Maier et al. 1977). In this respect special attention was directed to the spatial mobility of the population, because it reflects the gravitational fields of social and economic relationships during colonial times.

Analysis of the material compiled revealed that the changing cultural landscape of Tlaxcala was a highly complex and dynamic system. However, it should be reducible to various descriptive models showing the most important and representable features (see Wirth 1979: 101ff.). Although the building of models helps to understand complicated historic processes, it is rarely used in the ethnohistory or historical geography of Mexico. This is especially true of spatial models as they are applied in modern geography.

With the diversity of the dimensions considered, both time and space as well as state and society, problems of adequate presentation arose. I therefore decided to construct models on two levels. The lower one contains models which describe the development of spatial processes, while the upper level contains a model which represents the interdependence of factors determining these processes. Possible redundancies were accepted in favor of clarity.

SUCCESSION AND DIRECTIONS OF SPATIAL PROCESSES

The development of spatial processes in Tlaxcala can be demonstrated by using a center-periphery model, which takes the shape of concentric rings. The exterior circle represents the boundaries of the ancient Indian territory and the later colonial province. The interior circles mark the limits between different settlement areas. At the time of Spanish conquest these divided the zones occupied by Nahua and Otomí from the uninhabited borderlands. During the colonial period the interior circle represents the limit between the zones dominated by pueblos and haciendas, respectively (see figures 11.1 to 11.4).

Center-periphery movements are reported initially in the colonization of the preconquest and contact period. In the late fourteenth century the Nahuatl-speaking Tlaxcalteca entered the region and defeated the Olmeca-Xicalanca. Their rulers founded the four capitals (*cabeceras*) of Tepeticpac, Ocotelulco, Tizatlan, and Quiahuixtlan in the central region, at the northern outskirts of the later town of Tlaxcala. Starting from these nuclei other noble families established filial settlements (*sujetos*) (Muñoz Camargo 1947: 115ff.). Since the end of the fourteenth century, Otomí and other foreign groups, expelled from their territories by the Aztec confederacy, had settled in the peripheral zones. This initial occupation of Tlaxcaltecan and Otomí colonists constitutes Phase 1 on figure 11.1, where it is shown by a solid arrow.

The result of this colonization before the Spanish conquest was a differentiation of the populated space between the Tlaxcalteca in the center (first circle) and the Otomí in the periphery (second circle). According to Motolinía (1967), the Tlaxcalteca mainly inhabited the central region, radially extending one to four leagues from the town of Tlaxcala. On the other hand, the Otomí settled in the peripheral zones, four to seven leagues from the town of Tlaxcala (Motolinía 1967: 191). Beyond this, there existed vacant borderlands between Tlaxcala and its neighbors, which were dedicated to war (*tierras de guerra*). The width of this zone varied between a half and three leagues, depending on the terrain (third circle) (AGN: México, Tierras, Vol. 3060, Exp. 2, fols. 22r–26r).

Apparently these marginal borderlands were colonized by Tlaxcalan Indians after the Spanish conquest. According to the dates derived from the documents, these activities started about 1523 and terminated in 1545, when the boundaries of the colonial province were delimited.[3] It is not possible to decide, however, whether this colonization was initiated by the cabeceras or their sujetos, although a few documentry references support the second possibility. This final occupation of Tlaxcalan colonists constitutes Phase 2 on figure 11.2, where it is shown by a dashed arrow.

The Indian settlements which were founded after the conquest have some characteristics in common. The related archaeological sites lack potsherds from the post-Classic period. They are primarily located on plains or plateaus, but a few occupy the tops of hills or terraces to avoid floods, for example, Santa Justina Epatepec or San

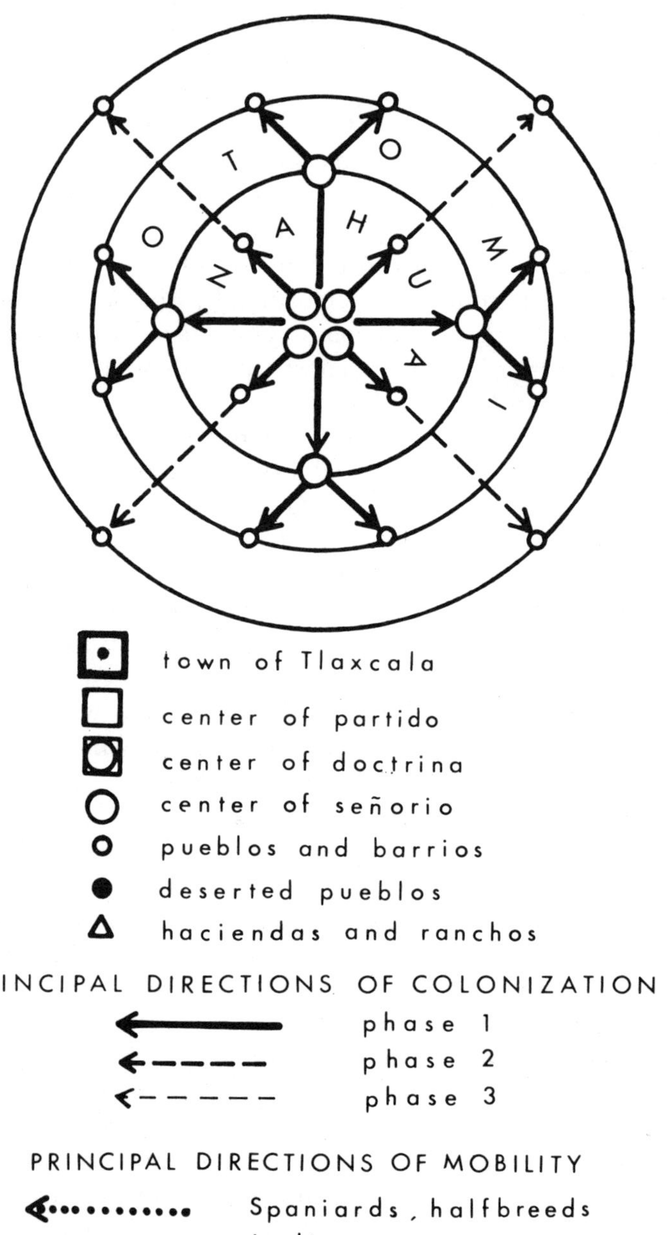

town of Tlaxcala
center of partido
center of doctrina
center of señorio
pueblos and barrios
deserted pueblos
haciendas and ranchos

PRINCIPAL DIRECTIONS OF COLONIZATION
phase 1
phase 2
phase 3

PRINCIPAL DIRECTIONS OF MOBILITY
Spaniards, halfbreeds
Indians

Fig. 11.1.   Occupation of land

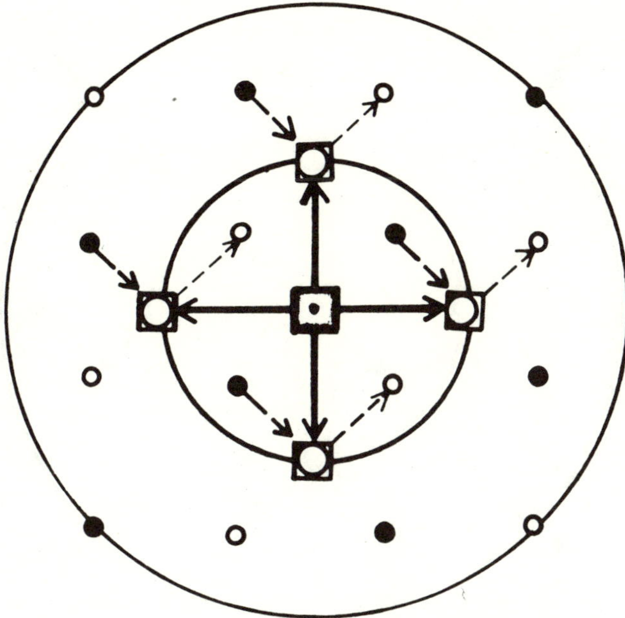

Fig. 11.2.   Foundation of monasteries and abandonment of pueblos

Miguel Xochitecatitlan. The pueblos in the northeast of Tlaxcala were not divided into barrios and possessed a distinct vigesimal structure with regard to the organization of public works (*tequitl*). A good example is provided by San Luis Huamantla, first mentioned in 1534.[4] Documentary evidence from other regions of Mexico suggests that this scheme was applied to colonization enterprises from prehispanic times (Durán 1967[1]: 363ff.; Alvarado Tezozomoc 1944: 350ff.).

According to the different phases of colonization, a settlement pattern was created which varied from the center to the periphery of Tlaxcala. The pueblos in the central region were clustered along the course of the Zahuapan River, whereas in the northwest, north, and northeast they were dispersed across the high plains, which lack perennial watercourses. This contrast in the geographical distribution of villages is supported by their ancient structure, which

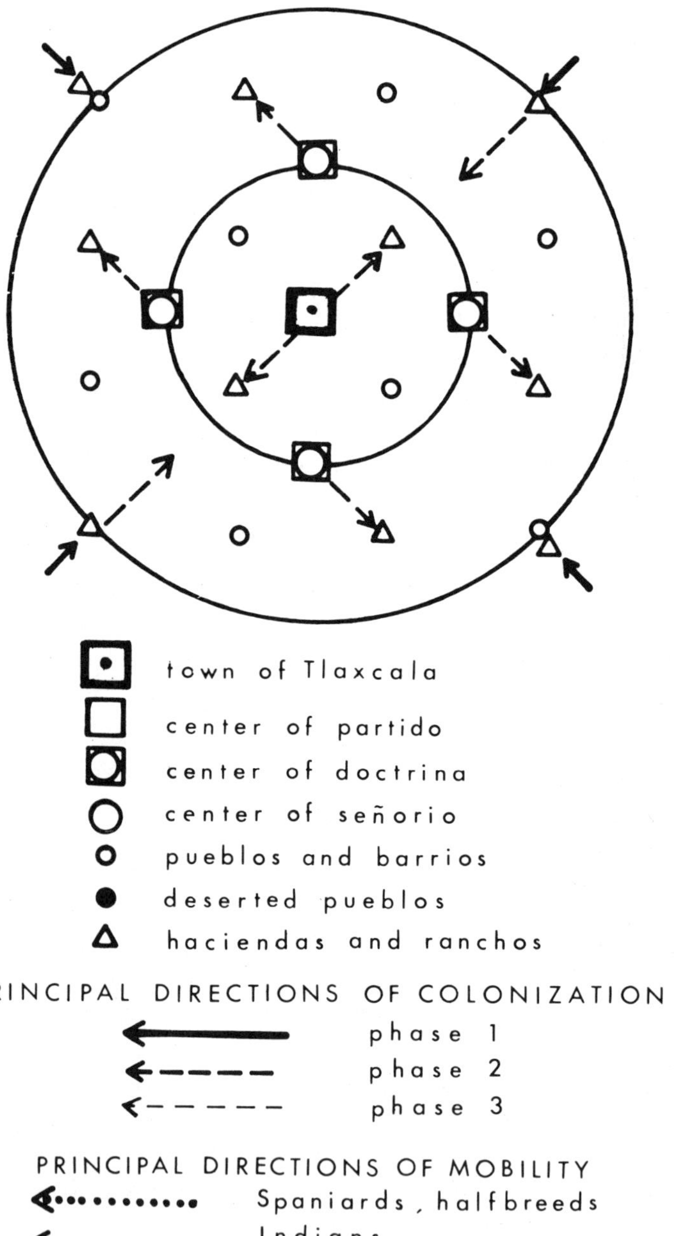

Fig. 11.3.   Genesis of the haciendas

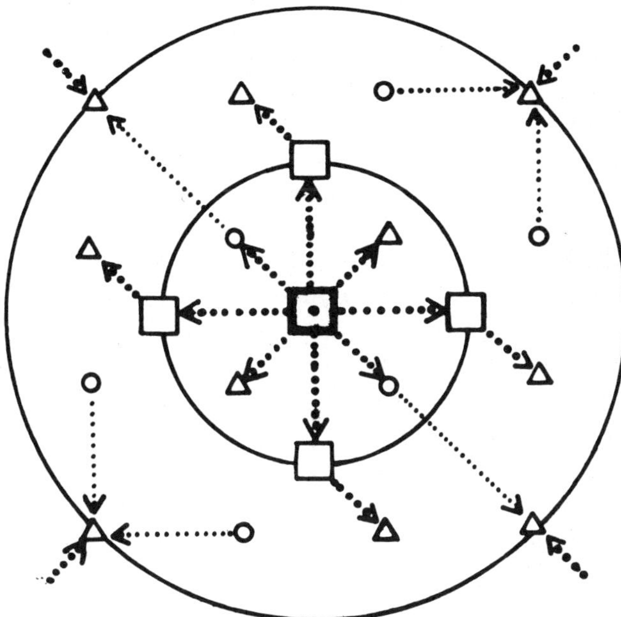

Fig. 11.4.   Movements of population

can be derived from early population statistics and the physiognomy of the related archaeological sites.[5] In the central region pueblos with more than three hundred households predominated; they were often subdivided into numerous barrios and their nuclei were strongly built up. In the peripheral zones, on the other hand, smaller settlements prevailed, often without subdivision; barrios and housesites were scattered across the terrain. Whether these distinct settlement patterns can be attributed to different areas colonized by Nahua or Otomí still remains unsolved, however.

The spatial configuration of functional relationships between the central places and the dependent villages should also be mentioned, because it shows a strong center-periphery orientation. From the analysis of the "Padrones de Tlaxcala" it emerged that the tributes and services of the Indian population were directed to their cabeceras, clustered around the later town of Tlaxcala. From there the

 Wolfgang Trautmann

connecting lines between cabeceras and sujetos, which can be reconstructed for each ancient principality (*señorío*), ran in a fan-shaped pattern to the periphery. This scheme reflects the directions of colonization described by Muñoz Camargo (1947: 116).

In 1528 the Spanish conquerors founded the town of Tlaxcala, which replaced the nearby indigenous cabeceras as a political and administrative center. After the foundation of San Francisco Tlaxcala in 1538, the Franciscans built nine other monasteries between 1554 and 1585 (Gibson 1967: 51), sometimes selecting sites within the ancient cabeceras de señorío. These monasteries served as bases not only for christianizing the Indian population, but also for spreading the innovations imported from Europe, e.g., horticulture and fruit growing, or the installation of aqueducts (Ricard 1933; "Actas de cabildo del ayuntamiento de Tlaxcala [1548]," Ms. 340, Archivo Histórico, Museo Nacional de Antropología e Historia, fol. 123r; "Anales antiguos de México," Ms. 274, AH-MNAH, 2, No. 18, p. 769). The construction of the Franciscan monasteries within a varying radius around the town of Tlaxcala constitutes Phase 1 on figure 11.2, where it is shown by a solid arrow.

The friars reversed the functional relationships from the ancient cabeceras de señorío to the new establishments. In accordance with prehispanic customs, the Indian population now directed their services to these parish centers (*cabeceras de doctrina*), repairing buildings or organizing religious festivities. By the end of the sixteenth century some of the cabeceras de doctrina became subcenters of the Spanish administration (*cabeceras de partido*). In the respective villages resided representatives of the Spanish governor, who had authority in all affairs concerning both the Indian and the Spanish populations (Fondo de Microfotografía, Museo Nacional de Antropología, Serie Tlaxcala, Ro. 10, No. 425; AGN: Indios, Vol. 63, Exp. 285).

The influence of the Franciscans on the indigenous settlement pattern is difficult to measure, due to the lack of documents. They probably initiated the removal or reconstruction of nearby settlements, and it seems that the Spanish grid street plan (*traza*) was laid out in relation to the construction of monasteries. The documents suggest, however, that the traza was not adopted by the other pueblos until the late colonial period. Even some of the new cabeceras, for example, San Agustín, in Tlaxco, preserved an irregular ground plan without plazas and blocks even in the eighteenth century (AGN: México, Tierras, Vol. 624, Segunda Parte).

The indigenous settlement pattern was radically affected by the partial or total abandonment of villages after the conquest. Taking into account the pueblos which developed from barrios or were founded after the mid-sixteenth century, it seems that about 35 percent of them were deserted completely during the colonial period. According to the dates collected from different sources, this process started in 1539, peaked in the beginning of the seventeenth century, and declined up to 1768. It stemmed from the rapid decrease in population—90 percent between 1531 and 1648 (Epistolario de Nueva España, XVI, p. 9; Fondo de Microfotografía, Museo Nacional de Antropología, Serie Tlaxcala, Ro. 3, No. 125, fol. 2v). The settlements which were abandoned completely are shown as black points in figure 11.2

Faced with this situation, the Spanish crown ordered the removal of the remaining settlements to the existing cabeceras. This occurred between 1599 and 1607.[6] These displacements represent Phase 2 on figure 11.2, where they are shown by a dashed arrow. Probably the effects of the civil congregations were limited. Some pueblos preserved their location, because the authorized offical considered the ancient sites to be suitable, e.g., in the cases of San Nicolás Panotlan and San Jorge Tezoquipan (AGN: Mercedes, Vol. 59, fols. 315r, 319r; Indios, Vol. 10, Exp. 54). The inhabitants of others returned to their former localities as soon as the evacuations were finished. These resettlements constitute Phase 3 on figure 11.2, where they are shown by a light dashed arrow. Many of them were abandoned after several years. The result was a transformation of the populated space; whereas the peripheral areas were intensively affected by the abandonment of settlements, principally in the northwest, north, and northeast of Tlaxcala, in the central region only a few pueblos were deserted. With regard to the ethnic composition of the province, almost all the Otomí population disappeared, except in the region of Huamantla.[7]

Although Tlaxcala was attached to the Spanish crown by a Real Provisión ("royal order") in 1535, it could not prevent the genesis of large Spanish landed estates. Until the mid-sixteenth century landowners from the adjoining provinces infiltrated the uninhabited tierras de guerra, establishing mainly estancias; these intrusions occurred first from the north and northeast of Tlaxcala. Afterward the southwest was also affected. The Spanish infiltration constitutes Phase 1 on figure 11.3, where it is shown by a solid arrow.

Late in the sixteenth century widespread epidemics and the civil congregations favored the purchase or even the occupation of parcels within the area of the pueblos. The number of Spanish landholdings rose from twenty in 1596 to more than one hundred and twenty in 1623.[8] Apart from the estancias which invaded from the adjacent provinces, the central places of the doctrinas constituted the nuclei of expansion, because many Spaniards had settled around the monasteries. This penetration of the pueblos constitutes Phase 2 on figure 11.3, where it is shown by a dashed arrow.

The localization of large Spanish landed estates reveals that they filled up the gap left by the abandoned Indian settlements. Above all, the high percentage of deserted pueblos in the peripheral zones of northwestern, northern, and northeastern Tlaxcala promoted the formation of large, continuous areas held by the great landowners. In the south and southwest, however, the haciendas were mingled with the pueblos in some areas. Although Spanish landholdings were also founded around the town of Tlaxcala, some disappeared during the colonial period (Fondo de Microfotografía, Museo Nacional de Antropología, Serie Tlaxcala, Ro. 22, No. 22, fol. 182; Ro. 26, No. 30, fol. 588r).

The genesis of the *latifundia* led to the reorientation of socioeconomic relationships. The system of tributes and services, by which the Indians were required to support their nobility, was replaced by the system of debt peonage to the new landowners. About 9 percent of the population, which had moved to the haciendas since the sixteenth century, was affected (AGN: Padrones, Vol. 22; see also Ewald 1976; Nickel 1978). Little is known about the proportion of Indians who signed on as itinerant workers (*tlaquehuales*) because they were deprived of their lands. Within some villages (e.g., Santiago Tlacochcalco, Santa Isabel Xiloxochtlan, and San Lorenzo Cuapiaxtla), about half of the residents were employed on the haciendas (Fondo de Microfotografía, Museo Nacional de Antropología, Serie Tlaxcala, Ro. 5, No. 170, fol. 18; AGN: Indios, Vol. 67, Exp. 290). Taking into account that the majority of the large, landed estates were established in the marginal zones of Tlaxcala, we can infer spatial mobility by Indians, which was oriented principally to the periphery. The principal directions are represented by a light dashed arrow in figure 11.4.

The social and economic change of the pueblos was also produced by the immigration of foreign ethnic groups, who infiltrated the settlements along the arterial roads (*caminos reales*) and interbred with the Indian population. In 1779 Spaniards, blacks, and racially mixed people represented about 30 percent of the Tlaxcalan population (AGN: Padrones, Vol. 22, Table). The most important consequence was the spatial segregation of ethnic strata, oriented from the center to the periphery. In San Luis Huamantla the Spaniards resided principally around the plaza. The adjacent blocks were occupied by Spaniards, castizos, mestizos, and a few Indians. Toward the border of the traza the percentage of mestizos, mulattoes, and Indians increased. The nonregulated barrios outside the traza were inhabited by Indians exclusively (AGN: Padrones, Vol. 22).

This center-periphery zonation of ethnic strata has its counterpart in the occupational structure. About 58 percent of the non-Indian population of Tlaxcala was employed in crafts, 20 percent in trade and transport, and only 14 percent in agriculture (AGN: Padrones, Vol. 22). This composition suggests that the central part of the affected pueblos was dominated by nonagrarian occupations. The Indian population of the periphery, on the other hand, subsisted mainly upon agriculture. Because of the absent or reduced Indian population and the predominance of one occupation, both the towns of Tlaxcala and San Luis Apizaco can be characterized as artisan towns.

The center-periphery orientation of social and economic relationships becomes especially transparent from an analysis of the spatial mobility of the non-Indian population. Considering migrations into and within the province of Tlaxcala, the rate of mobility can be estimated at 40 percent between 1700 and 1790 (AGN: Padrones, Vol. 22). In general the town of Tlaxcala and the cabeceras de partido experienced an exodus, except for Santa María Nativitas, Santa Ana Chiautempan, and San Luís Apizaco, which attracted many migrants. An analysis of destinations within the province reveals that migrants from the town of Tlaxcala turned equally to the cabeceras de partido, the remaining pueblos, and the haciendas. Those from the cabeceras de partido preferred the haciendas and ranchos. The principal directions of non-Indian migrants are shown by a heavy dotted arrow on figure 11.4.

THE DETERMINANTS OF SPATIAL PROCESSES

The spatial processes under consideration were determined by the arrangements of interdependent factors, made up of convergent or divergent intentions of state and society. The resulting actions or attitudes influenced the development of the processes in direct, indirect, or even contrary ways. On the other hand, we should also consider the retroactive effects of a transformed environment. The corresponding elements and their connections can be presented by means of a system model (see figure 11.5).

A similar scheme is applicable to internal colonization after the Spanish conquest, directed principally to the ancient tierras de guerra. It is not clear, however, whether the related settlements were spontaneous actions undertaken by pueblos or barrios, or rather enterprises directed by persons or institutions still largely unknown. According to the few documented cases, members of the Indian nobility played an important role. Probably their principal intention was to recover or increase their former power by multiplying the number of settlements obliged to pay tribute and to serve them.[9]

Perhaps the colonization activities were stimulated in part by the reserves of cultivable land within the former borderlands. At least the level of groundwater in the plains between the Atoyac and Zahuapan rivers permitted the intensification of agriculture through the construction of raised fields.[10] On the other hand, the lack of Indian title to the land until the delimitation of the province of Tlaxcala, in 1545, facilitated the intrusion. Documents describing boundary disputes between Tlaxcala and the adjacent provinces suggest that the foundation of settlements in the borderlands was tolerated or perhaps even encouraged by the Cabildo of Tlaxcala, which was composed of members of the Indian nobility. With regard to unsettled disputes, a strong argument was simply to confront the neighbors with a fait accompli.[11]

The widespread desertion of pueblos was provoked by the rapid

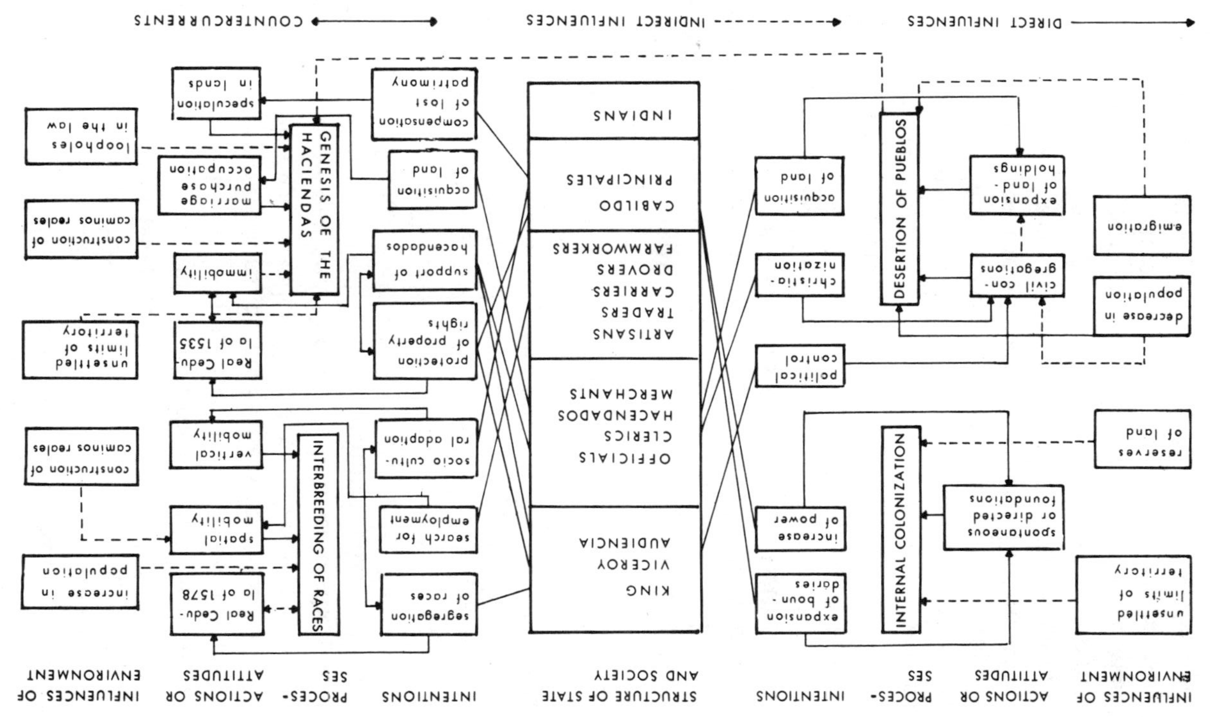

Fig. 11.5. Model of the factors determining spatial processes in the colonial period

demographic decline in the sixteenth and first half of the seventeenth centuries. The indigenous population decreased from 50,000 *hombres* in 1531 to 5,000 *tributarios* in 1648 (Epistolario de Nueva España, XVI, p. 9; Fondo de Microfotografía, Museo Nacional de Antropología, Serie Tlaxcala, Ro. 3, No. 125, fol. 2v). Among the most outstanding causes reported were diseases such as smallpox, measles, and a kind of typhoid fever (*matlazahuatl*), which had been introduced by the conquerors. Throughout the colonial period numerous epidemics plagued the Indian population, which did not possess an immunity to these infections. Severe famines developed because the cultivation of fields was abandoned in favor of labor in public works (*repartimientos*) in Mexico and Puebla, or because of the preference given to the lucrative production of cochineal (Actas de cabildo, fol. 142v; AGN: Indios, Vol. 12, Segunda Parte, Exp. 160).

The emigration of Tlaxcalans also contributed to the abandonment of pueblos. During the contact period they participated in the Spanish expeditions to other territories, where they often perished or were left behind. At the end of the sixteenth century Tlaxcalan colonists were sent by the viceroy to the Chichimec frontier, in the north of New Spain. However, colonies are reported not only from the Chichimeca, but also from Jalapa, Huejotzingo, Tulancingo, and Mexico (AGN: Vínculos, Vol. 234, fols. 14v–15v; Tierras, Vol. 914, Exp. 2, fol. 182v). Throughout the colonial period many Indians were recruited by local authorities or members of the clergy to work on haciendas or in textile factories (*obrajes*) outside of the province (AGN: Indios, Vol. 5, Exp. 574; Vol. 7, Exp. 358; Vol. 11, Exp. 473). The scarcity of lands and the periodic taxation favored these fluctuations.

The christianization of the indigenous population was handicapped by the fact that the majority lived in dispersed settlements, often remote from their cabeceras. Therefore the friars decided to remove the Indians to the monasteries. According to Motolinía (1967), the resettlers were to conserve their ancient organization, based on the tequitl system, with one hundred vecinos living in a barrio and twenty in the respective subdividions (Códice Mendieta 2: 96f). Although the clergy succeeded in resettling parts of the Indian population in other regions of New Spain, we lack similar information for Tlaxcala.

Faced with the demographic decline, the Spanish king took up the proposals of the clergy regarding civil congregations. His principal intention was to ensure the political control of the Indians. In 1598 the governor of Tlaxcala, Luís de Villanueva Zapata, was charged with the execution of the instructions, embodied in the Real Cedula of 1585 (AGN: Vol. 6, Segunda Parte, Exps. 1008f). Although it is certain that relocations took place in the beginning of the seventeenth century, the number of affected settlements remains unknown, due to the loss of the related documents. At present, only San Pablo Ocotzoquauhtla and San Bartolomé Atlixelleuian are known to have been incorporated into San Luis Huamantla.[12] The civil congregations, on the other hand, fed the ambitions of the Spanish colonists to enlarge their landholdings. Abandoned lands within the Indian communities were claimed by them as vacant (*baldíos*), which justified petitioning for a royal grant (*mercedes de tierra*). Another manner employed was to purchase or simply to occupy the parcels in question. By the second half of the seventeenth century many Indian possessed only their houseplots, despite the law which granted all lands within a limit of five hundred varas to the pueblos (*fundo legal*).[13]

The occupation of Indian land was often accomplished by the common Spanish practice of introducing cattle to the parcels which they had just acquired within the pueblos; the rapidly growing herds devastated the fields before the crops were harvested. Furthermore, the *hacendados* or their *mayordomos* recruited local residents to serve as their labor force. Confronted with this situation the Indians preferred to desert their villages (AGN: General de Parte, Vol. 5, Exp. 1151; Indios, Vol. 6, Segunda Parte, Exps. 736, 878, 902; Vol. 11, Exps. 58, 490; Vol. 12, Primera Parte, Exp. 254).

During the contact period the genesis of haciendas was effected by Spanish immigrants who became landowners by marrying into indigenous noble families. The wedding gifts made by their Indian relatives, as well as the valid rights of succession they possessed, provided the basis for estate formation. More valuable, however, were connections with the indigenous population they established on such occasions. Often the Indian wives of the immigrants, or their sisters-in-law, prepared or carried out the transactions for parcels with the pueblos (Fondo de Microfotografía, Museo Nacional de Antropología, Serie Tlaxcala, Ro. 14, No. 3, fol. 229r; Ro. 25, No. 29, fol. 1v).

The transformation of land tenure was promoted by the members of the Indian nobility. An analysis of the Tlaxcalan notarial records between 1573 and 1623 reveals that they were involved in about half of the sales, leases, or donations of land to Spaniards. Probably the majority of parcels originated from within their own dominions. The depopulation of land after the conquest deprived the nobles of their income, which was based on the tributes and services of their tenants. On the other hand, litigation involving property rights, which resulted from the intrusion of Spanish colonists, could only be financed by selling parcels from their patrimony.[14] Thus it seems natural that they would attempt to offset the loss by speculating in land transactions. Because of their social position, as well as their intimate knowledge of property holdings within the pueblos, many nobles served as ideal mediators between Indians and Spaniards.

During the early colonial period the formation of latifundia was favored by Spanish authorities, who used their position to speculate in lands. According to the notarial records, officials belonging to all levels of the Spanish colonial administration are reported to have founded estates. In opposition to the king, who ordered the protection of Indian property rights, they consistently tried to prevent or to modify the corresponding regulations (AGN: 1563, Exp. 6; Tierras, Vol. 1154, Exp. 2, fol. 3v). They were supported by the court of law in Mexico (Real Audiencia), whose members (*oidores*) were also landholders. On the occasion of lawsuits between pueblos and haciendas the court often dismissed the claim of Indian communities, or heard the allegation of the hacendados involved, which protracted the lawsuit. Thus the pueblos were forced to settle with the hacendados, since they often lacked the fees to finance the proceedings (Cartas de Indias I: 404; AGN: Vol. 10, Cuad. 2, Exp. 178). Although the Indians were acquainted with the legal procedures available to them, they failed to benefit from them because of the inertia of the Spanish colonial administration.

The transfer of Indian land was also facilitated by defects in agrarian legislation. The Real Cedula of 1572, for example, established that only parcels valued at more than 30 pesos could be sold at auction. The consequence was the division of the lands in question

(AGN: Tierras, Vol. 2699, Exp. 4; Vol. 74, Exp. 5; Mercedes, Vol. 64, fol. 135r). In the majority of the auctions documented only one bidder is reported. This suggests the existence of arrangements between Spanish colonists, hungry for land, and Indians, willing to sell.

A loophole in the law, of grave consequence, resulted from the poor financial state of the Spanish kings, due to the cost of their European wars. Therefore, all landholders were allowed to legalize defective land titles through the payment of fees (*composiciones*) beginning in 1591. In this manner the hacendados gained the possbility to sanction illegal occupations within the fundo legal. Unfortunately the property rights of the Tlaxcalan communities were incompletely protected against violations, because the Cabildo had come to an agreement with Figueroa, oidor for the whole province, by paying the sum of 1,000 pesos (Archivo Municipal de Santiago Tetla [Tlaxcala]: Documentos sueltos).

Among the environmental factors which influenced the genesis of haciendas should be mentioned the unclear affiliation of the borderlands (tierras de guerra). Thus, unsettled disputes between Tlaxcala and its neighbors facilitated the infiltration of Spanish colonists. According to the Cabildo, they used their property titles, issued to Ixtacamaxtitlan or Nopalucan, as a pretext to invade Tlaxcala (AGN: Tierras, Vol. 1154, Exp. 2, fol. 3; Mercedes, Vol. 5, fols. 112r, 182v).

It seems that the expansion of the haciendas was facilitated by the construction of arterial roads (caminos reales). The first caminos reales probably already existed before the mid-sixteenth century. These connected the city of Mexico with Veracruz, through Apam and Puebla (Trautmann 1981: 126). The location of early estates shows that the Spanish colonists tended to settle along these roads, especially in the north and northeast sections of Tlaxcala.

The interbreeding of races (*mestizaje*) played the most important part in the social and economic differentiation of the pueblos. There were also conflicts of interest between the state and the society. The Spanish king promoted racial segregation, documented in the Real Cedula of 1578 (Encinas 1945[4]: 341). The construction of lodgings (*mesones*) within the cabeceras de partido, which were reserved exclusively for Spaniards, also attempted to separate the Indian and non-Indian population. Nevertheless, the crown failed to stop the settling of Spaniards, mestizos, and mulattoes in the villages of Tlaxcala. On the other hand, the Indians tried to adopt the attitudes of the Spanish immigrants, who established skin color as an essential element in social position. Thus miscegenation with Spaniards, castizos, or mestizos was the only way to climb the social pyramid. According to the census of Revillagigedo, Indians were involved in 67 percent of all mixed marriages in the town of Tlaxcala, in between 16 percent and 35 percent in the cabeceras de partido, and in between 20 percent and 50 percent in the remaining pueblos (AGN: Padrones, Vol. 22). The higher percentage in the town of Tlaxcala was due to a higher marriage rate involving Indian nobles; they were preferred as spouses by Spaniards of lower social status, for example, by artisans, traders, carriers, drovers, and farmworkers.

Mestizaje was also promoted by the high spatial mobility of the non-Indian population searching for employment. There are remarkable differences in mobility rates with regard to ethnic affiliation and occuption. Sixty-six percent of the migrants were Spaniards, which exceeds their proportion in the non-Indian population. On the other hand, 6 percent of the castizos and 19 percent of the mestizos were migrants, percentages below their proportions in the total non-Indian population. Analysis of occupational groups reveals that 37 percent of the migrants were artisans, 32 percent traders, carriers, or drovers, and 14 percent farmworkers (AGN: Padrones, Vol. 22). The percentages within the trade and transport sectors exceed the percentages these sectors attained in the overall occupational structure.

Evidently the expansion of the non-Indian population occurred along the caminos reales. A comparison of population statistics from the late colonial period shows that nearby pueblos without Spaniards, blacks, or racially mixed people in 1779 had been infiltrated by 1791, especially in the southwest section of Tlaxcala (AGN: Padrones, Vol. 22). The influence of long-distance traffic on the occupational structure of the affected communities is apparent in Santa Trinidad, Tenexyecac, and Acatitlan, with their many mule drovers, as well as in Chachalacatlan and Santa Inés Zacatelco, with their large numbers of traders and storekeepers.

Among the environmental factors that influenced the interbreeding of races should also be mentioned the general population increase in the eighteenth century. After a long decline, the indigenous population began to rise from a reported 7,282 *tributarios* in 1763 to 62,173 *indios* in 1810 (Fondo de Microfotografía, Museo Nacional de Antropología, Serie Tlaxcala, Ro. 11, No. 440, fol. 73r; Gerhard 1972: 325). The non-Indian population grew from 800 *familias* in 1746 to 19,115 *habitantes* in 1779 (Villa-señor y Sanchez 1746[1]: 308; AGN: Padrones, Vol. 22, Table). Even considering possible errors due to the perpetuation of figures in successive accounts or the application of different census categories, the non-Indian population had increased considerably. We do not know, however, whether this growth should be attributed to higher birth rates, an elevated number of immigrants, or an increased absorption of Indians into the non-Indian population.[15]

CONCLUSION

The transformation of the cultural landscape of Tlaxcala after the conquest can be reduced to various descriptive models. The succession and directions of spatial processes have been presented using a center-periphery model. The network of determining factors, introduced by the intentions of state and the society, and modified by the influence of a transformed environment, becomes evident through the construction of a system model.

The validity of the models presented should be tested elsewhere, at different scales. At the local level it seems that the center-periphery model is applicable to large villages or towns with a mixed Indian and non-Indian population, such as the cities of Mexico and Puebla. There was a differentiation between Spaniards and racially mixed people in the center and the Indian barrios outside of the traza, which served as reservoirs of labor (Gibson 1964: 377; Liehr 1971: 39).

At the regional level there are indications that the center-periphery models can be transferred to the Valley of Mexico. Colonization in prehispanic times started from the cabeceras, which were founded in and around the lakes of the center. There was also a zonation between Nahua in the central region and the Otomí at the periphery during the contact period. The abandonment of settlements, which occurred in early colonial times, affected mainly the peripheral zones, especially in the north and northeast of the valley. The deserted regions were occupied by the large Spanish landed estates (Trautmann 1968; Gibson 1964).

At the supraregional level there are also spatial structures which can be elucidated using a center-periphery model. A similar model was developed with regard to the territories of Spanish America, based on the size of population, ecclesiastical institutions, transport system and economic activities; the result was a delimitation of four complexes with centers, intermediate zones, and peripheries around 1600 (Slicher van Barth 1979: 53–95).

It is likely that the system model presented is applicable at each level, because the majority of the critical processes considered, for example, abandonment of settlements, genesis of haciendas, and interbreeding of races, are reported not only from New Spain but also from other regions of Spanish America.[16] Furthermore, the stratified state and society were common throughout Spanish America. Modifications of the model should be expected, however, in response to the different environmental conditions found in each region.

NOTES

1. Investigations were conducted from 1969 to 1974 with the Mexico Project of the German Research Society (Deutsche Forschungsgemeinschaft), to which I am indebted for its generous support. Full results are presented in Trautmann 1981.

2. See the scheme developed by Ruppert and Schaffer 1969: 205–14.

3. Among the few villages which persisted until the present are Cuapiaxtla and Citlaltepec, founded in 1539. "Anales antiguos de México y sus contornos," Ms. 274, 2, No. 18, p. 768. México: Archivo Histórico, Museo Nacional de Antropología.

4. López de Velasco 1894: 67. The date of founding is dubious, due to falsified property titles; see AGN: México, Tierras, Vol. 1120, Exp. 2, fols. 17v–21r.

5. The most valuable statistics are found in the "Padrones de Tlaxcala del siglo XVI," Ms. 377, Archivo Histórico, Museo Nacional de Antropología.

6. Unfortunately only the orders, not the execution of the civil con-

gregations are documented; AGN: Indios, Vol. 6, Segunda Parte, Exps. 1008f.

7. Today an Otomí-speaking population still exists in San Juan Ixtenco; Anaya Monroy (1965: 65).

8. Calculated from an analysis of the notarial records in the Archivo General de Tlaxcala, Registro de Instrumentos Públicos, Vols. 1–50, copied in the Fondo de Microfotografía, Museo Nacional de Antropología, Serie Tlaxcala, Ros. 12–28.

9. In the property titles of San Luis Huamantla a Real Cedula of 1534 is cited, which is reported to confirm both the landholdings and the privileges of the Tlaxcalan nobility. It seems more likely, however, that the authorization for these settlements was deduced from the promises of the conquerors; see Ixtlilxóchitl (1965[2]: 401).

10. Contemporary raised-field agriculture has been investigated by Wilken (1969: 219–41) and Seele (1968: 153–69). With regard to the problems of dating see Trautmann (1981: 55ff.).

11. Litigations are mentioned with Zacatlan, Huexotzinco, Puebla, Tepeaca, and Texcoco; AGN: Mercedes, Vol. 1, Exp. 394; Vol. 2, Exps. 184, 513, 546; Vol. 5, fol. 129. Unfortunately the relevant documents themselves are missing.

12. Anales antiguos de México, 2, No. 18, p. 780; Archivo del Ayuntamiento de Tlaxcala: Documentos sueltos (1629). The recommendation of Mendieta to raise the cabeceras de doctrina to villas was not accepted by the crown; see Códice Mendieta 1: 138.

13. Disputes concerning the fundo legal are largely documented for the eighteenth century.

14. A good example is Francisca de la Cerda Xicotencatl, a member of the ancient dynasty of Tizatlan; Fondo de Microfotografía, Museo Nacional de Antropología, Serie Tlaxcala, Ro. 24, No. 26, fol. 105.

15. The descendants of unions between Spaniards and castizos were considered to be Spaniards.

16. On the abandonment of settlements in Peru see Schmieder (1930).

REFERENCES

Actas de cabildo del ayuntamiento de Tlaxcala (1548). Ms. 340, Archivo Histórico, Museo Nacional de Antropología e Historia. México.

AGN (Archivo General de la Nación). México.

Alvarado Tezozomoc, Hernando
1944   Crónica Mexicana. Manuel Orozco y Berra, ed. México: Ed. Leyenda.

Anaya Monroy, Fernando
1965   La toponimia indígena en la historia y la cultura de Tlaxcala.
            México: Universidad Nacional Autónoma de México.
Cartas de Indias
1970   2 vols. Guadalajara: Aviña Levy.
Códice Mendieta
1971   Documentos franciscanos, siglos XVI y XVII. 2 vols. Biblio-
            teca de Facsímiles Mexicanos 4. México: Aviña Levy.
Durán, Diego
1967   Historia de las Indias de Nueva España y islas de tierra firme.
            2 vols. Atlas. José F. Ramírez, ed. México: Ed. Nacional.
Encinas, Diego de
1945   Cedulario Indiano. 4 vols. Madrid.
Epistolario de Nueva España
1939–42   16 vols. Francisco del Paso y Troncoso, ed. Biblioteca Histórica
            Mexicana de Obras Inéditas, Segunda Serie. México: Porrúa.
Ewald, Ursula
1976   Estudios sobre la hacienda colonial en México: las propiedades
            rurales del Colegio Espíritu Santo en Puebla. Das Mexiko-
            Projekt der Deutschen Forschungsgemeinschaft IX. Wies-
            baden: Steiner.
Gerhard, Peter
1972   A Guide to the Historical Geography of New Spain. Cam-
            bridge, Eng.: Cambridge University Press.
Gibson, Charles
1964   The Aztecs Under Spanish Rule: A History of the Indians of
            the Valley of Mexico 1519–1810. Stanford: Stanford Univer-
            sity Press.
1967   Tlaxcala in the Sixteenth Century. Stanford: Stanford Univer-
            sity Press.
Ixtlilxóchitl, Fernando de Alva
1965   Obras históricas. 2 vols. Alfredo Chavero, ed. México: Ed.
            Nacional.
Liehr, Reinhard
1971   Stadtrat und städtische Oberschicht von Puebla am Ende der
            Kolonialzeit (1787–1810). Das Mexiko-Projekt der Deutschen
            Forschungsgemeinscaft III. Wiesbaden: Steiner.
López de Velasco, Juan
1894   Geografía y descripción universal de las Indias. Justo Zaragoza,
            ed. Madrid.

Maier, Jörg, Reinhard Paesler, Karl Ruppert, and Franz Schaffer
1977   Sozialgeographie. Das Geographische Seminar. Braunschweig:
            Westermann.

Motolinía, Toribio
1967   Memoriales. Luis García Pimentel, ed. México: Aviña Levy.

Muñoz Camargo, Diego
1947   Historia de Tlaxcala, México. 2nd ed. México: Publicaciones
            del Ateneo Nacional de Ciencias y Artes de México.

Nickel, Herbert
1978   Soziale Morphologie der mexikanischen Hacienda. Das Mex-
            iko-Projekt der Deutschen Forschungsgemeinschaft XIV.
            Wiesbaden: Steiner.

Ricard, Robert
1933   La "conquête spirituelle" du Mexique. Travaux et Mémoires
            de l'Institut d'Ethnologie 20. Paris: Université de Paris.

Ruppert, Karl, and Franz Schaffer
1969   Zur Konzeption der Socialgeographie. Geographische Rund-
            schau 21: 205–14.

Schmieder, Oskar
1930   Wandlungen im Siedlungsbilde Perus im 15. und 16. Jahr-
            hundert. Geographische Zeitschrift 18.

Seele, Enno
1968   Die Agrarlandschaften des Beckens von Puebla-Tlaxcala. *In*
            Berichte über begonnene und geplante Arbeiten. Franz Tichy,
            ed. pp. 153–69. Das Mexiko-Projekt der Deutschen For-
            schungsgemeinschaft I. Wiesbaden: Steiner.

Slicher van Barth, Bernard
1979   Economic Diversification in Spanish America around 1600:
            Centres, Intermediate Zones and Peripheries. Jahrbuch für
            Geschichte von Staat, Wirtschaft und Gesellschaft Latein-
            amerikas 16: 53–95.

Trautmann, Wolfgang
1968   Untersuchungen zur indianischen Siedlungs- und Territorial-
            geschichte im Becken von Mexico bis zur frühen Kolonialzeit.
            Beiträge zur mittelamerikanischen Völkerkunde VII. Hamburg.
1981   Las transformaciones en el paisaje cultural de Tlaxcala durante
            la época colonial: una contribución a la historia de México
            bajo especial consideración de aspectos geográfico-económicos
            y sociales. Das Mexiko-Projekt der Deutschen Forschungs-
            gemeinschaft XVII. Wiesbaden: Steiner.

Villa-señor y Sánchez, Joseph Antonio
1746–48   Theatro americano: Descripción general de los reynos y provincias de la Nueva España, y sus jurisdicciones. 2 vols. México.
Wilken, Gene C.
1969   Drained-Field Agriculture: An Intensive Farming-System in Tlaxcala, Mexico. Geographical Review 59: 219–41.
Wirth, Eugen
1979   Theoretische Geographie: Grundzüge einer theoretischen Kulturgeographie. Teubner Studienbücher. Stuttgart: B. G. Teubner.

12

Land Tenure and Land Inheritance in Late Sixteenth-Century Culhuacan

S. L. Cline

Our knowledge of indigenous land tenure and land inheritance patterns in colonial Mexico is being broadened and enriched by increasingly available local-level, native-language documentation. This study of land tenure and land inheritance is based on El Libro de Testamentos de Culhuacan (LTC), the largest extant, homogeneous collection of sixteenth-century Nahuatl testaments.[1] It contains the wills, written entirely in Nahuatl, of more than sixty Indian men and women from the town of Culhuacan, D.F.[2] The testaments date from the period between 1572 and 1599, the majority being from 1580 and 1581.[3] Between 1579 and 1581 major epidemics drastically reduced the population of Culhuacan and the surrounding area (Gallego 1927: 172). The Culhuacan testaments document the deaths within a short period of time of a number of people related to one another. Thus the same people appear in different roles and relationships: as testator, as recipient, and as witness. In addition the same pieces of property can be traced through several testaments.

Although a picture of Nahua landholding patterns has been constructed based on accounts of Spanish observers, Indian accounts in Spanish, and Spanish translations of native-language documents, the use of native documentation in the original language adds an important dimension to the picture. Native documents such as the Culhuacan wills were community centered. Thus the presentation of the information is not influenced by an outside audience. While many Nahuatl documents were translated into Spanish in the colonial period, important distinctions in the original Nahuatl were often lost or misconstrued. Local-level Nahuatl documentation gives a more immediate, intimate glimpse into native institutions and the lives of individual Indians than is possible using the more formal sources, such as codices, or works of ethnographic intent such as Motolinía (1971), Torquemada (1975), and others.

It is important to study Nahua patterns in specific locations; general accounts often gloss over regional or local variations. Unfortunately, for a given location, the native documentation is often scattered, or gives uneven coverage, or both. Two localized studies of Nahua land inheritance have however been done. Kellogg (1979) effectively uses lawsuits and native wills from Mexico City (1546–1606) to reconstruct patterns of land inheritance, but not land tenure. The number of extant native wills from Mexico City is small (26), and none of the testators is related to any other. Yet another localized (but preliminary) study of land inheritance is of Calimaya and Tepemaxalco, which utilizes 105 testaments made over a span of 150 years (1672–1821) (Loera y Ch. 1977). Both studies have considerable time depth, deal with specific regions, and provide the basis for comparisons of native land inheritance. The Culhuacan materials deal with a specific town and are extremely concentrated in time (1580–81).

There appear to be some problems with using wills as the source for land tenure and land inheritance patterns. It might seem that only those with large amounts of property to bequeath would make testaments, thus biasing the patterns. In the Libro de Testamentos de Culhuacan, however, several wills involve small estates, and some minuscule estates had no land whatsoever. Although the testaments do give considerable information on land tenure in Culhuacan, the coverage is not comprehensive. No complete map, cadastral, or land register exists for Culhuacan ca. 1580, which could give additional information.[4] From the wills we infer the broad outlines of the land tenure system, but by no means are all the details filled in. Testaments must be utilized to their fullest, but there are gaps in their coverage which cannot be bridged. Since the source of information for this study is almost exclusively testamentary materials, the focus is on the *orders* of testators. These orders may or may not have been carried out or later disputed. In only two cases are testaments set in a larger legal context.[5] Both indicate that divisions of estates were not necessarily immediate, amicable, or in accord with the wishes of the testators.

The testaments follow a standard form. Using formula phrases, testators identify themselves by name and *tlaxilacalli* ("ward") and affirm their religious beliefs.[6] The nonformula text of the will usually begins with the bequest of the testator's residence, followed by enumerations of fields held, and then a list of movable goods—metates, agricultural tools, clothing, and so on. After this is a list of witnesses, almost always including some of the people receiving the bequests. Standard closing formulas are followed by the notary's signature. Variations in the texts of different wills by the same notary indicate that testators' words may well have been recorded close to verbatim. Occasionally a friar notes in Spanish when property has been sold for masses.

Property owners listed each parcel of land separately. Testators ideally listed their parcels by the location, soil type, size, civil category, and previous owner. Most testators did not supply every piece of information for each parcel. For this reason, absolute comparisons of testators' estates cannot be made; however, enough information is given to make an estimate of the relative size of estates and the types of land held. Once a parcel of land was identified, the testator almost invariably indicated the disposition of the property. Usually land was either bequeathed to named heirs or ordered sold for masses.

MEASUREMENT OF LAND AND SIZE OF ESTATES

Most testators give the size of at least some of their parcels. All the terms for measurements are in Nahuatl, indicating native units. The problem of equating native units of measure to each other or to European units has been investigated by a number of scholars (Gibson 1964: 257–58; H. F. Cline 1966: 93; Castillo F. 1972; Harvey and Williams 1980). Land measurements in Culhuacan are usually given in *maitl* or *matl* (lit.: "hand/arm"), in some places equivalent to the Spanish *braza* (1.67 m; Castillo F. 1972: 211–15).[7] Occasionally the testaments indicate the measure of a *quahuitl*, "pole," or "rod" (LTC 91r, 103r). None of the testaments uses the two units of measure simultaneously; each unit is used consistently within a testament. Another measure found in the Culhuacan wills is the *cenyollotli* (lit.: "one heart"), a measure from the chest to the hand (Molina 1970: 17). The cenyollotli was some fraction of a matl (Castillo F. 1972: 215). In one Culhuacan will the length of two house plots is given in matl and cenyollotli, and the width in matl (LTC 4v). A final native measure found in the wills is the *cemmecatl* (lit.: "one cord").[8] At times no unit of measure is given for parcels, just the number of units. Quite often only one dimension is listed, perhaps indicating a square plot. Although *vara,* a Spanish unit of measure, appears in the Libro de Testamentos (LTC 76r), significantly it does not appear as a unit of measure for land, which is consistently described in terms of Nahua measures.

There are often no measurements given for *chinampas,* but only the number of chinampas in a given location.[9] However, one testator gives one dimension for two chinampas, carefully pointing out they were ten units long, not twenty (LTC 46v). Some chinampas were measured by the number of furrows (*cuemitl*) they contained, varying from as few as three to as many as twenty (LTC 10r, 13r, 24v). Other chinampas were simply described as small (LTC 38r, 42v, 63v, 81r). Some testators had chinampa land measured by size and not by the number of individual plots (LTC 10v, 91r, 103v). For example, it is possible to calculate the number of chinampas in one 380 by 20 area. Nineteen chinampas were bequeathed in that location, making each 20 by 20, if each was of uniform size and shape (LTC 10v).[10]

Fully a third of the approximately one hundred and fifty chinampa holdings were found in groups of seven. One woman had chinampas she said would have been seven if they were "complete" (LTC 64v); what she had were four large ones. Another testator had a group of just six chinampas, explaining that one had been stolen from him

(LTC 66v). Yet another testator had some chinampas counted for tribute purposes "as if they were seven" (LTC 43v). Not all testators had chinampas in clusters of seven, but the emphasis on seven is interesting. It may have been some sort of ideal number. Support for the hypothesis of seven as an ideal number for chinampas is the stylized sixteenth-century map called the Maguey Plan. The map, from an area under Azcapotzalco's control, shows each house site with seven chinampas (Calnek 1973).

There are difficulties in calculating the size of individual testators' estates, as outlined above. All testators did not use the same units of measure in listing their parcels. They often omitted listing one or even two of their parcels' dimensions. For these reasons, it is difficult to compare the holdings of the testators in absolute terms. Each parcel is listed separately in the testaments, so the total number each testator owned is known. There is enough information given to know that both men and women held both large and small estates.

LOCATIONS AND TOPONYMS

The location of a parcel is often indicated by a toponym; frequently the place-names are descriptive of soil types or terrain. The recurrence and consistency in the usage of place-names suggest that certain topographical features or areas were consistently known by a given toponym, a practice evident in contemporary Mexico.[11]

In some cases a field is designated as being next to the field of an individual already dead. A typical entry of this type is "my milpa borders on the field of Pablo Juárez, defunct" ("nomil . . . ymiltitech yn baplo [*sic*] xuarez catca"; LTC 61r). This type of entry is sometimes made in addition to the toponyms and sometimes stands alone, replacing it. The reference to a dead owner may be a reflection of swift change in owners due to epidemic conditions. Testators might know who the old owners were, but perhaps not the heirs of the deceased. Possibly not until the heirs reached maturity and reached prominence would the fields be identified with them and not the deceased owners. Many plots of land were ordered sold for masses, and the interval between someone's death and the sale of property may have left many plots without an owner. Reference to the dead owner may have been an attempt to keep some order in a system undergoing rapid change.

The careful specification of parcel locations indicates that testators were well aware of the boundaries of their land. Boundaries of fields were sometimes marked by stones (LTC 77r). The importance of boundary markers is indicated by prehispanic ordinances decreeing death for anyone who moved markers (Ixtlilxóchitl 1977[1]: 385). Occasionally someone did not know the boundaries or the precise location of a parcel. One Culhuacan man owned some land in Tlallachco, but did not know exactly where it was; when it was located, he wanted the nobles (*pipiltin*) to sell it for masses (LTC 16r). In discussing Tenochtitlan landowners who had lands elsewhere, Calnek (1975) points out that wealthy owners often had no idea where their fields were located, since they never worked them. Field boundaries facilitated bookkeeping "and bore little direct relation to the day-to-day process of cultivation" (Calnek 1975: 14). That Culhuacan owners almost always knew where their fields were located indicates there was less separation between ownership and cultivation, since most people worked their own fields. Even if they did not, the fields were not located so distantly that the testators could not oversee them.

Despite numerous recurrences of the same toponyms in different testaments and other indications of parcel locations, it is not possible to draw a map of Culhuacan and place the toponyms precisely. Some toponyms can be located generally within one of the political divisions shown on the Relación Geográfica map of Culhuacan (1580; Monterrosa Prado 1970). Others are known to be located on the Cerro de la Estrella,[12] the mountain dominating Culhuacan's landscape. Testators' separate listings of each parcel and the number of different locations of the parcels (known through the toponyms), indicate that they had scattered holdings. This is consistent with more general native landholding patterns in Central Mexico (Gibson 1964: 263–64).

LAND TERMINOLOGY: SOIL TYPES AND TERRAIN

Most parcels of land did not have a specific soil type or terrain listed with them, but enough did so that a general picture of the types then found are known. Nahuatl has a highly developed vocabulary for soils, distinguishing them by texture, organic or chemical content, color, and topographic position (Sahagún 1963{11}: 251–57; Williams 1976a, b, 1980; Williams and Ortíz-Solorio 1981). Dry land (*teuhtlalli*) and level land (*tlalmantli*) were frequently found in Culhuacan, while *axalli*, possibly sandy soil, and *tequixquitl*, salty-ashy soil, occurred occasionally.[13] Chinampas, artificial extensions of farmland into the lake (West and Armillas 1950), were the most typical kind of land owned by testators. The data give the impression of different zones of cultivation in Culhuacan; chinampas near the lake or canals, perhaps level land leading up to dry land on the Cerro de la Estrella.[14]

STANDARD CIVIL CATEGORIES OF LAND

Civil categories of land in Culhuacan ca. 1580 show evidence of the general trends in the Valley of Mexico toward elimination of some prehispanic categories of land, shifts in categories, and creation of new categories (Gibson 1964: 257ff.). According to the major sources (Ixtlilxóchitl 1977; Torquemada 1975; Zorita 1963), prehispanic categories included land attached to the office of *tlatoani*, or "major ruler" (*tlatocatlalli*); land devoted to the support of temples (*teotlalli*); private lands of the nobility (*pillalli*); lands attached to the *tecpan*, "palace or community house" (*tecpantlalli*); and lands held by the *calpulli* (*calpullalli*). The prehispanic categories are discussed first, although they do not appear to have had major importance in late sixteenth-century Culhuacan.

Tlatocatlalli, *Ruler's Office Land*

The Culhuacan wills contain only one reference to tlatocatlalli. This prehispanic category was considerably modified by the late sixteenth century. Prehispanic office land was held by the person who succeeded to the office of tlatoani. The land was not personal property and could not be sold or bequeathed (Ixtlilxóchitl 1977{1}: 90). In the colonial era many native rulers successfully argued that office land was, in fact, rulers' land, their private property (Gibson 1964: 259–61). In Culhuacan in the late sixteenth century, the only person known to hold office land did not hold the title of tlatoani, nor any other noble title.[15] The testator, Miguel Cerón, owned a 70 by 20 plot of tlatocatlalli. Significantly, he noted that he acquired the land by court judgment (*justiciatica*). Unfortunately the grounds for the award were not listed.[16] The land was probably just a fraction of the original office land.[17] In no way did this Culhuacan tlatocatlalli resemble prehispanic office lands. Cerón freely bequeathed the parcel, part going to his heirs and part being sold for masses. In spite of the change in the tenure of the tlatocatlalli, the land retained its classificatory name.

Teopanmilli, *Land to Support Religion*

In prehispanic Mexico temples were supported by specific lands called teotlalli, "sacred lands" (Gibson 1964: 257–58). In colonial Culhuacan there are references to *teopanmilli* (or *teopantlalli*), lands connected with the Christian church. The similarity of terminology suggests a similarity of meanings: "lands to support religious activity." However, there are significant differences between the prehispanic temple lands and Culhuacan teopanmilli. Although there are a scant three references to church land, they provide considerable information about its status.

Culhuacan church land was *not* residual temple land taken over by the Christian church. This is consistent with findings for other Central Mexican communities (Gibson 1964: 258). Unlike prehispanic temple lands, Culhuacan church lands did not provide generalized support for religious personnel, but yielded revenues to aid the soul of an individual donor. In the most clearcut case, one plot of land was to be rented out each year, the money to be spent on masses for the donor, a noblewoman, doña María Juárez (LTC 98r).[18] The church did not have direct control of the property. Two executors were to oversee the land and deliver the money for masses. This arrangement is similar to the Spanish institution of *capellanía*. Wealthy Spaniards would set aside incomes from property to support a priest who would say masses for the capellanía's founder. It is impossible to say whether the Culhuacan church land was created in imitation of the Spanish practice, was an independent new development, or something with local precedent. Although doña María outlined the entire procedure, she did not label the land teopanmilli. Another testator, however, located some of his fields by reference to her church land (LTC 67v). The status of that particular piece of property was evidently public knowledge.

Pillalli, *Private Lands of Nobles*

Most sources on prehispanic land tenure include the category pillalli, lands owned by nobles. The terms of tenure of pillalli contrast with prehispanic tlatocatlalli, lands attached to the office of ruler. Pillalli was owned by nobles as individuals. Some types of pillalli could be sold or bequeathed to chosen heirs.[19] In the Culhuacan testaments the term pillalli never appears. Although identifiable nobles had extremely large estates, no land was classified pillalli. It seems unlikely that *none* of the Culhuacan nobles' land derived from prehispanic pillalli. In the late sixteenth century, however, Culhuacan citizens alienated their lands with relative ease. There may have been no compelling reason to distinguish pillalli from other private holdings. Over the whole colonial period there was a shifting and elimination of native land categories. Pillalli seems to have been extinguished as a separate category in Culhuacan by 1580.

Tecpantlalli, *Land of the Tecpan*

Another prehispanic category of land is tecpantlalli, lands for support of the *tecpan,* or "palace." Those who lived on the tecpantlalli and cultivated it were called *tecpanpouhqui,* or *tecpantlaca,* "palace people." According to Torquemada (1975), the palace people worked the palace lands in individual plots. Fathers could pass those plots on to their sons, but not sell them. If a man died without heirs or moved to another place, his house and land remained in the hands of the tecpan. Palace people paid no tribute and had a higher status than commoners (Torquemada 1975[2]: 546; Ixtlilxóchitl 1977[1]: 91).

The Culhuacan testaments do not yield any direct references to tecpantlalli; but there are various parcels attached to, or in some way involved with the tecpan. Unfortunately the language in the testament in which most of these parcels are listed is particularly obscure (LTC 98rff.). Doña María Juárez, who seems to have been a resident of the tecpan, assigned parcels of land to the palace.[20] One of these parcels of land was *cihuatlalli,* "woman (wife) land," likely dowry land, but whose dowry is not clear. Some of the land she called "house chinampas of the tecpan," which a judge had assigned to the tecpan.[21] Doña María had alienated some of that land already and said that the *tlaxilacalleque* ("ward elders," or "ward people") knew about it. The rest of the land remained in her hands, because, she said, it was her property and inheritance. The relationship between tecpan land and tecpan members is not clear, and the line between institutional and private ownership of tecpan land appears blurred. The typicality of the tecpan's acquisition of land by judicial grant when many other native institutions were losing land is open to question.

Calpullalli, *Lands of the Calpulli*

The final category of land which appears in the standard sources is *calpullalli,* land under the jurisdiction of the *calpulli.*[22] According to Zorita (1963), title to the land was held by the calpulli, but the person who worked the individual plot could bequeath it to his chosen heirs. The land could not be alienated. Land which was not worked or had no one to inherit it reverted to the calpulli (Zorita 1963: 29ff.). Zorita's account is based on Las Navas's report on land tenure in the Cuauhtinchan area (Baudot 1976: 451–61). Harvey (in this volume) discusses the problems of regional diversity in land tenure; Zorita himself cautioned that there was great diversity in practice. Further, Reyes (1975, 1979) has found the term "calpullalli" in sixteenth-century Nahuatl documentation with meanings varying from "land of nobles" to "land pertaining to religious cults."

Of all the lands held by Culhuacan testators, only *two* parcels are specifically labelled calpullalli. Why more land is not called calpulli land is an interesting question. In the Culhuacan documents Gerónimo Teuhcihuatl (LTC 79r) identifies only one of his parcels as calpulli land, while the rest are simply identified by their locations. In the case of Juan Rafael Tlacochcalcatl (LTC 67v), the calpulli land was only one of his many parcels identified by civil category. Other lands of his were purchased land (*tlalcohualli*) and patrimonial land (*huehuetlalli*). Only one of his parcels lacked a civil category. The term calpullalli may have been used in his testament to distinguish that land from other types.[23]

Both testators who owned land specifically called calpulli land were residents of the ward of Coatlan. Neither parcel had a toponym indicating a location, so there is a good possibility that the land was located in Coatlan. Ward heads of Coatlan may have been more diligent in enforcing distinctions between calpulli land and other types. From these two cases of calpulli land we have information about ownership and bequest patterns. Both owners were men, but one bequeathed his calpullalli to his daughter, indicating that women could own such land. Neither man ordered the land sold for masses or otherwise alienated it, but this is not necessarily significant; neither one ordered much of anything sold for masses. In any case, we must be aware of the possibility that these two identified pieces of calpullalli are a subset of other calpulli land, not specifically called by the Nahuatl term.

Zorita (1963) reported that calpulli land reverted to the calpulli for redistribution if there was no one to inherit it. In two cases property not called calpulli land reverted to tlaxilacalleque for reassignment. One man left a small part of his large estate to the tlaxilacalleque to reassign, though he did not lack for heirs (LTC 88v). A woman (LTC 46v) left most of her property to her husband, but assigned seven chinampas to the tlaxilacalleque of Iyauhtenco for redistribution to the poor. Neither of these parcels is called calpulli land, but the ward heads took charge of them.

The question must be raised of how much control the calpulli had, even in prehispanic times, over calpulli lands. Significant variations in holdings suggest less than rigid control by the calpulli (Harvey this volume). What the calpulli was is still unclear; how it functioned in relation to land is merely part of a larger problem.

OTHER CIVIL CATEGORIES OF LAND

Unlike the categories discussed above, which appear in some form in the standard sources on land tenure, there are other terms which frequently occur in local-level Nahuatl documentation. These include *cihuatlalli,* "woman (wife) land," *tlalcohualli,* "purchased land," and *huehuetlalli* and *tlalnemactli,* "inherited land." All these terms are found in Nahuatl documentation from Culhuacan, as well as from other places. The frequency and widespread use of these terms to classify land indicate that they are fundamental civil categories at the local level. In the Libro de Testamentos de Culhuacan, purchased and inherited land appear with much greater frequency than the single mention of office land (tlatocatlalli) and the references to church land (teopanmilli). Two other land terms which occur in the Libro de Testamentos, *Mexicatlalli* and *quauhtlalli,* are difficult to classify. All of these other civil categories of land are discussed separately below.

Cihuatlalli

Cihuatlalli, "woman (wife) land," is a term which occurs with considerable frequency in local-level Nahuatl documentation. The meaning of the term is somewhat obscure, however. There is evidence from imperial-level records that cihuatlalli was dowry land. In the fifteenth century Texcoco's king, Nezahualcoyotl, gave eleven plots of land called cihuatlalli to his daughter upon her marriage.[24] At the more local level, cihuatlalli is found in a Nahuatl document from Xochimilco (1582), translated as *tierras . . . por bienes maternales,* indicating inheritance through the female line.[25] Cihuatlalli could be owned by both women and men; a man could speak of "his 'woman land'" (*icihuatlal;* Anderson, Berdan, and Lockhart 1976: 28).

In the Libro de Testmentos the only reference to cihuatlalli is to land owned by the tecpan. The parcel is listed in the will of the noblewoman doña María Juárez. She does not allege personal ownership of the land.[26] The status of the Culhuacan cihuatlalli is unclear; if it was dowry land, it was seemingly not doña María's dowry.

Quauhtlalli

Quauhtlalli presents problems of translation and, consequently, problems of classification. The first element of the compound word may derive from *quahuitl,* "tree(s)." Quauhtlalli is classed as a soil type by Sahagún (1963), fertile soil with leaf humus or rotten wood (Sahagún 1963[11]: 251). It may be that quauhtlalli simply means land with trees, or woods. If either of these definitions is correct, the term quauhtlalli describes the physical conditions of the land.

Another possibility is that quauhtlalli is a civil category of land, a type of conquered land. The derivation would be from *quauhtli,* "eagle," rather than from quahuitl, "trees(s)." Eagle knights were one of the prehispanic Aztec elite military corps. Lands awarded these warriors may well have been called quauhtlalli. Calnek (1975: 13) has found quauhtlalli classed as conquered land in Atlixocan.

The two examples of quauhtlalli found in the Culhuacan testaments do not help to clarify the meaning of the term. Two men owned quauhtlalli; one was a tlacochcalcatl and the other a tecuhtli, statuses which might have made them eligible for awards or inheritance of quauhtlalli (LTC 67v, 74r). One parcel of quauhtlalli was classified as *huehuetlalli,* "patrimonial land" (discussed below). Pablo Huitznahuatl tecuhtli willed his quauhtlalli to his two minor daughters, excluding his wife, an adult daughter, and a grandson, and a nephew. Juan Rafael Tlacochcalcatl wanted his quauhtlalli sold for masses, ignoring his wife, two daughters, and a nephew. Even if quauhtlalli was "conquered land," no pattern of preference for male recipients is evident. If quauhtlalli was merely a soil type, the choice of heirs is a less important question.[27]

Mexicatlalli

Another land term whose meaning and importance are unclear is Mexicatlalli, "land of the Mexica." In the Culhuacan wills the term appears in two different testaments, both times identifying chinampas. The terms does appear elsewhere in the Libro de Testaments. Sahagún (1963) included Mexicatlalli under the listing of provinces; he described it as good land belonging to the city of Mexico, and to the Mexican nation (Sahagún 1963[11]: 256). The term may have had a very local Culhuacan meaning, denoting land in Mexicapan, a place in or near Culhuacan. But there is another possible meaning for Mexicatlalli. Chinampas constructed in Atlixocan during Montezuma Ilhuicamina's reign were "classed simply as Mexicatlalli . . . because it was acquired through land reclamation rather than conquest" (Calnek 1975: 13).[28] Documents from Xochimilco also mention Mexicatlalli in Atlixocan. This land was cihuatlalli and not specifically identified as chinampas. The contemporary colonial translation gives for Mexicatlalli "las tierras que estan asia la parte de Mexico" ("lands that are toward the part of Mexico," i.e., facing Mexico City).[29] This gloss is somewhat dubious, but possible.

Unfortunately the Culhuacan testaments shed no light on the origin of the term "Mexicatlalli," but facts about its ownership and disposal emerge from the testaments. As previously mentioned, Culhuacan Mexicatlalli was chinampa land. Both genders could own it. In 1589 Diego Hernández (LTC 105r) listed seven chinampas of Mexicatlalli, but did not specifically bequeath them (this is relatively uncommon). Another testator, Ana Juana (LTC 50v), owned three chinampas of Mexicatlalli, which she willed to her son Juan Francisco; she said he already worked or paid tribute on it. Mexicatlalli could be bequeathed, but whether alienation was possible cannot be determined.

We can only hope that the terms "cihuatlalli," "quauhtlalli," and "Mexicatlalli" turn up in more contexts, so that we can clarify their meanings. The overall difficulty of translation and interpretation of land terms is highlighted by these examples from the Culhuacan wills.

Huehuetlalli *and* Tlalnemactli, *Inherited Land*

Two terms for inherited land are *huehuetlalli* and *tlalnemactli,* which denote separate categories of land in a document from Xochimilco, contemporary with the Culhuacan testaments.[30] Deriving from the verb *(mo)maca, nemactli* means, in a general sense, "that which is given to someone, a portion." Tlalnemactli then means "land received, a portion of land." A Spanish translation of the term gives "tierras que vienen de derecho," ("lands which come by right").[31] Pragmatically this would imply mainly inheritance and dowry, but it could also apply to judicial apportionments. Huehuetlalli, translated here as "patrimonial land," seems to have been a special category of inherited land.[32]

Patrimonial land was not any particular soil type or in any particular location; it could be chinampas, level land (tlalmantli), or quauhtlalli.[33] There is no distinct pattern of locations for patrimonial land, although several testators had holdings of it in Santiago Tetla (LTC 67v, 69r, 105v). Whether this is more than coincidence is not clear.

Both men and women owned patrimonial land, with men outnumbering women, eight to three.[34] The origin of one man's patrimonial land is interesting; the tecpan gave him huehuetlalli, which he was proceeding to alienate (LTC 61r). This contrasts with the origin of most patrimonial land, commonly stated in the Libro de Testamentos as inheritance from the testator's father or grand-father. The tecpan's involvement with patrimonial land is interesting, in light of evidence that lands of each tecpan in Cuauhtinchan, taken as a whole, were called huehuetlalli (Reyes 1978: 8–9). In general, though, huehuetlalli simply seems to be a name for inherited land.

One woman had fifteen chinampas she called "my portion of chinampas" (*nochinannemac*), which a judge gave her, possibly as a division of an estate under dispute (LTC 96r). Interestingly, this testator, María Teicuh, was one of only three women to own huehuetlalli, "patrimonial land." She was a resident of the tecpan of Cihuatecpan.

At present it is not possible to make a sharp distinction between tlalnemactli and huehuetlalli; they may in fact simply be two names for inherited land. We should be aware, however, that the two terms were used and that there may be a distinction between them.

Tlalcohualli, *Purchased Land*

Tlalcohualli was often part of Culhuacan estates. In the colonial period sales of land within the Indian community and between Indians and Spaniards were frequent. The existence of prehispanic legal rules governing land sales indicates that the transfer of property by sale was *not* a postconquest innovation (Ixtlilxóchitl 1977[2]: 385). Sahagún (1963[11]: 251) lists tlalcohualli as a land term. Very early colonial Nahuatl documents, such as the Tepoztlan census (ca. 1535), list purchased land.[35] Early colonial tlalcohualli seems to have been held by people of high status. The distinction between purchased land and other types is made in all kinds of local-level Nahuatl documentation, indicating that purchased land was a fundamental civil category.

In Culhuacan, even when purchased land was inherited and in turn bequeathed by testators, the land retained its designtion as tlalcohualli. Testators continued to note who originally owned the land and the price paid by the purchaser; this may have been an attempt to establish clear title to the property. Other property retained old identifications, as seen above with tlatocatlalli. The case of purchased land may, however, be different. If land was recognized as tlalcohualli, it could be bought and sold freely from then on, no matter how many times inherited. It would never go back to what the Spaniards called *"tierras de repartimiento,"* that is, as long as the possessor could maintain that it was tlalcohualli.

There were several sources of land for sale. About half of the testators ordered land to be sold to pay for masses. In addition, a number of Culhuacan nobles sold land, both to Indians and to Spaniards. To all appearances they did so regardless of its category. Sales were recorded in the testaments of the buyers or their heirs (LTC 60r, 82r, 94v). Occasionally testators noted that they had sold land.

Owners of purchased land were not the largest landowners; it was generally part of medium-size estates, and the parcels were not large. Male owners of purchased land outnumbered female. Only three women testators owned tlalcohualli (out of twenty-seven), and of these, one did not buy the land herself (LTC 62v, 81r, 90v). Only two of the ten males owners of purchased land (out of thirty-seven) received the land by bequest rather than buying it themselves. Both of these men received their purchased land from their fathers (LTC 60r, 66r). Only men owned more than one parcel of purchased land (LTC 60r, 67v, 82r, 103r). Two of the men who owned purchased land also owned purchased houses (LTC 94v, 106r). Men seem to have been much more involved in real estate transactions; women's participation seems to have been minimal.

The value of Culhuacan land in 1580 cannot be accurately determined from the testamentary data.[36] As often as not, the price of a plot is not given, while occasionally the price is given, but not the size or type of land. Land prices were generally low, however.

The lands that testators purchased do not appear to fall into any obvious patterns. If testators were buying land to consolidate holdings in a particular place, it is not readily apparent. There is always the general problem of knowing where the locations were in Culhuacan, but none of the plots of tlalcohualli were located in places with the same toponym as a testator's other holdings. Three different testators purchased land in a place called Calpoltitlan, implying that there was a concentration of land available for sale there. However, no one owned several parcels in that location (LTC 62v, 87r, 103r). Perhaps a testator's purchase of land in different places with different types of soil was a conscious effort to acquire land with different agricultural potentials. Some testators might have established residence through purchases of land and houses. One local merchant and moneylender seems to have acquired purchased land as part of his general business activities (LTC 66r).

LANDS ALIENATED TO SPANIARDS

It is difficult to gauge the amount of participation of Spaniards in the Culhuacan real estate market from the testamentary material. Since some Indians had thoroughly European names, it can be difficult to tell Indians from Spaniards. However, Spanish activity in the area is alluded to by the noblewoman doña María Juárez. She ordered some of her land sold, specifying that "no Spaniard is to buy it, just the citizens here" (LTC 98v). This restriction is important not only for indicating that Spaniards were engaged in acquiring Culhuacan land, but that at least one noble viewed it as a threat.

Only four identifiable Spaniards bought land from Culhuacan testators. One was Diego de Paz, one of the signers of the Relación Geográfica of Culhuacan (LTC 24r; Gallego 1927: 173). The sister and brother-in-law of the prior of the Augustinian church, fray Juan Núñez, bought a house and corral.[37] The only other Spaniard mentioned in the testaments as buying land was Pedro Ortiz, married to an Indian noblewoman (*cihuapilli*) of Coyoacan, who bought properties from different Culhuacan estates (LTC 60r, 68r, 82r).[38] He may have been systematically acquiring land.

The extent of land sales by Culhuacan Indians to Spaniards is not evident in the Libro de Testamentos. Late sixteenth-century Culhuacan land-sale records in Spanish show that Indian nobles alienated large tracts of land to a single Spaniard.[39] The parcels were in just a few locations, indicating systematic acquisition. Most of the sellers were males, but there were a number of women. With just two exceptions, the parcels were not chinampa land; Culhuacan chinampa lands tended to stay in Indian hands, supporting Gibson's general observation (1964: 409).

RENTAL OF LAND BY INDIANS

Not only did Indian testators generally own land, but some also rented land at the same time. Although Miguel Huantli (LTC 83r) owned several parcels of land (including purchased land), he sowed two others that he did not own. He left the crop, not the land, to his heirs. Another testator who owned land, including purchased land, worked a milpa for someone else for pay (LTC 60r). In two cases, people who owned purchased land rented other land. The land they bought or otherwise owned may not have been sufficient.

Children used their parents' land and had rights to the crops they planted, but not to the land. Juana Tiacapan (LTC 69r) sowed the land of her father and gave the crop to her brother. Domingo Yaotl (LTC 38r) sowed land belonging to his mother; like Juana Tiacapan, he bequeathed the crop and not the land. Since he sowed part of the land with magueys, which are slow to mature, he seems to have expected to use the land for quite a while. In these cases, testators were careful to draw the distinction between land that they owned and land they were merely using.

LAND INHERITANCE

Most testators had land to bequeath. Each parcel was bequeathed separately, even if there were just one heir receiving an entire estate. There are three general types of bequests: to the testators' relatives and associates, to the church for masses for the testators' souls, and to charity. At times testators are explicit about the reasons for a particular bequest; in general, however, bequests are given without explanation. The task, then, is to discern possible underlying bequest patterns.

In Culhuacan there were some differences in the types of land owned by men and women. Men owned more patrimonial land (huehuetlalli) and more purchased land (tlalcohualli) than women. Bequests of these two special categories of land seem to follow certain patterns.

Bequests of purchased land by both men and women were usually made to lineal descendants, children and grandchildren. Of the thirteen who owned tlalcohualli (three women and ten men), seven bequeathed part or all of it to children or grandchildren (LTC 62v, 67v, 82r, 87r, 90v, 94v, 106r). In the one case where both sons and daughters survived, the daughter shared equally with the sons (LTC 82r). Completely excluded from inheritance of purchased land were spouses, siblings, and their children. Of the six men and one woman who were owners of tlalcohualli and were survived by a spouse, not one bequeathed that land to the surviving partner (LTC 60r, 67v, 87r, 94v, 103r, 106r, 81r). But not all purchased land was bequeathed to heirs. Some testators ordered purchased land sold for masses, even though there were living heirs. When testators received purchased land as a bequest rather than buying it themselves, the land went for masses, usually for the original purchaser (LTC 60r, 66r, 81r).[40]

Patrimonial land (huehuetlalli) also was owned more frequently by men than women (eight men and three women). Evidence is fragmentary, but some patterns emerge. As with purchased land, wives are not recipients of patrimonial land. One man willed everything in his estate *except* the huehuetlalli to his wife. That land was to be sold for masses (LTC 12r). Four other men exluded their wives from bequests of patrimonial land (LTC 67v, 74r, 88r, 105r). The three women who owned huehuetlalli had no surviving spouses, but uniform exclusion of spouses from inheritance of this type of land is entirely possible. There is a slight tendency toward bequests of huehuetlalli to lineal recipients, children and grandchildren, of the same gender as the testators (LTC 93r, 74r, 105r). Women excluded siblings from bequests (LTC 63v, 69r), while men did not (LTC 66r, 88r). One man bequeathed patrimonial land to his sister, explaining that he was giving it to her because it *was* patrimonial (LTC 66r). One woman testator bequeathed patrimonial land to a femal of unknown relationship, also saying that the bequest was prompted because the land was patrimonial (LTC 63v). None of the three women ordered her huehuetlalli sold for masses, while four of the eight men did (LTC 12r, 15r, 61r, 67v). Three of the four men had no lineal heirs, while the fourth passed over two daughters, as well as his wife and sister (LTC 67v). Perhaps the land went for masses because the man had no sons to inherit.

GENERAL PATTERNS OF LAND INHERITANCE

Both male and female testators bequeathed property to their spouses in Culhuacan. This contrasts with data from Mexico City Nahuas, which indicate exclusion of husbands from the inheritance of land (Kellog 1979: 59). Culhuacan men and women usually left the bulk of their estates to their spouses if they were sole heirs; there is evidence, however, that the rights of spouses to inherit were mediated by the presence or absence of children. This is clear in the case of Andrés de San Miguel (LTC 87r), who left his house to his young son; his wife was to care for their child there, but if the child died, the house was to be sold for masses. Andrés made no further provision for his wife, for he left his land to another son. Women left property to their husbands if there were no other obligations on it. For instance, María Salomé (LTC 10r) married twice; her daughter from her first marriage received the bulk of the property that came from her father's estate. But María left property to her daughter and her second husband which had not come from her first husband's estate. Part of the grant, however, was to care for the daughter.

There is some evidence which suggests that husbands might have had automatic claims on their wives' estates. Perhaps this is why one Ana Juana (LTC 50r) was so explicit in her will to disinherit her third husband, whom she described as a great scoundrel. She requested one of the Culhuacan *alcaldes,* her son's godfather, to make sure her son, not her husband, got her property. There is no evidence that wives had similar claims on their husbands' estates. One male testator left his entire estate to his son; he apparently felt no need to explain the exclusion from the estate of his wife and his mother, who acted as witnesses to the testament (LTC 94v).

In general, testators first provided for their children and their own spouses before siblings. Women mentioned sisters more often than brothers. In one case a brother was mentioned only in order to limit his inheritance (LTC 69r). Two Culhuacan women (LTC 80v, 81r) willed land to siblings over their husbands and children; both women seemingly expected their husbands to care for the children.[41] Children of male testators never lost out because their fathers left land to brothers and sisters. If a man had no other heirs except a sibling, that person did not necessarily inherit the estate. Miguel Huantli (LTC 83r) was survived only by his sister; all his property was to be sold for masses, with the sister in charge of the sales. The Culhuacan wills have one example of an eldest brother bequeathing his entire estate to his younger siblings to the exclusion of his wife (LTC 88r). Early reports of native inheritance patterns indicate that the eldest son would inherit his father's estate and apportion his younger siblings' shares to them as they came of age (Motolinía 1971: 134–35; López de Gómara, 1943: 222–23). The sibling tie in late sixteenth-century Culhuacan does not appear to have been as strong as these earlier reports indicate.

Nieces and nephews often shared in estates, but for certain categories of property, such as patrimonial land and purchased land, siblings' children were excluded. Only two women mentioned nieces, and only one received a bequest (LTC 63v, 104v). One woman chose her nephew over her son to receive land, but she did not expect her son to live (LTC 78r).[42] Another woman bequeathed her land to her three nephews, her only blood relatives, and severely limited the inheritance of her stepdaughters (LTC 5r). Men's bequests were slightly less restrictive. If nieces and nephews were mentioned at all, they almost invariably received bequests. Nieces and nephews were not usually testators' first choice for heirs, but they did often share in estates.

Stepchildren were not popular choices for women's bequests. In one case where a woman mentioned stepchildren, she specifically limited their inheritance to property left them by their father, warning them not to claim more (LTC 5r). In another case, a stepson received nothing from his stepmother but exhortations to pay off his father's debts (LTC 49v). Thus, it would appear that the link between stepmothers and their stepchildren was extremely weak, especially when the father was dead. In contrast, the one male testator who mentioned stepchildren had a kind word for them and left the bulk of his estate to their mother, his wife. Presumably on her death the estate would have passed to them (LTC 43v).

Testators could specifically disinherit possible claimants to their estates. In the Culhuacan wills this was almost exclusively the practice of women testators, who may have felt that their estates were particularly vulnerable to claims they did not wish to honor. However, there may be a more general pattern of vulnerability of women's estates to claims. In their statements disinheriting claimants, testators were specific about their reasons for doing so. One woman disinherited her children because they had ignored her when she was sick (LTC 96r). Another woman disinherited her uncles, who had not cared for her in the traditional role of surrogate parent

Table 12.1 Male Testators' Land Bequests

Testator	Sp	mC	fC	mCC	fCC	B	Z	mSbC	fSbC	other	i.d. of "other"
12r	x										
15v										xx	stepmother, uncle
24v		x					x				
36v		x	x	x							
38r		x									
42v*	x	x?	x?								
43v	x									x;xx	godchild; stepchildren
48v*	x							x?	x?		
53r											
55r					xx				xx	x	niece's husband
56v					x			x			
60r		x								x	godchild
61r							x			x	uncle
67v	o		xx						x		
71v	x	x	x							x	godchild
73r			x				x	x			
74r	o		xxx	x				x		xxxxxxx	unknown males
75v		x	x							x	aunt
79r	x	x									
82r		xx	x								
83r							o				
84r	o	x									

87r	o	xx									
88r	o					oxx	xxxo				
91r	x								x		
94v	o	x				x				o	mother
97r		x			x						
99v		x	xx								
101r							xx	x		xx	brother-in-law; unknown male
103r	x	xx									
105r	x	x				x					
106r				x	xx						
107v			x	xx	xx					xx	son-in-law, daughter-in-law

Key to Tables

x—bequest of land

o—possible heir who receives no land

Sp—spouse

m—male

f—female

C—child

CC—grandchild

B—brother

Z—sister

SbC—sibling's child

Unknown—unknown relationship to testator

*Gender of children cannot be determined

Table 12.2. Female Testators' Land Bequests

Testator	Sp	mC	fC	mCC	fCC	B	Z	mSbC	fSbC	other	i.d. of "other"
3r		x		x							
4r								xxx		xx	SpC
10r	x		x								
41r										xx	unknown males
46v	x										
49v										o;x	SpC; unknown female
50v	o	x									
59r											
62v					xxx					xxxxx	unknown males
63v			x				o		x	x	unknown female
64v								x			
65v							x			x	grandmother
69r						o				x	brother-in-law
76v	x						x				
78r		x					oo	x			
80r	o		o			x					
81r	x	o					x				
85r										x	son-in-law
90v		x									
93r			xx		x					x	unknown female
96r*		o?	o?								
98r							xx				

100r											
104v									o		
BNP 110										xxxx	unknown males
										o	stepdaughter
T-58-4										xx	father, aunt

Key to Tables

x—bequest of land

o—possible heir who receives no land

Sp—spouse

m—male

f—female

C—child

CC—grandchild

B—brother

Z—sister

SbC—sibling's child

Unknown—unknown relationship to testator

*Gender of children cannot be determined

(LTC 65v).[43] Previously mentioned is the case of Ana Juana (LTC 50v), who disinherited her good-for-nothing third husband. Thus, actions of possible heirs sometimes had the effect of overriding traditional patterns of bequest; testators' declarations served both as explanation and justification for disinheritance.

Overall there do not appear to be major differences between the types of heirs men and women chose for land inheritance; specifically, there does not appear to have been a pattern of preference for female testators to choose female heirs, as is perceived elsewhere (Kellogg 1979: 55; Loera y Ch. 1977: 93). Indicated in tables 12.1 and 12.2 are the range of heirs chosen to inherit land; the amount each heir received varied.

SUMMARY AND CONCLUSIONS

Local-level Nahuatl documents from the colonial era are important historical sources. Native testaments have abundant material on land tenure and land inheritance. The Culhuacan collection is especially important because of the concentration of testaments for one town in a period of rapid change, 1580–81. People of relatively humble circumstances were involved in legal processes and appear in documents; the Culhuacan testators include some elites but most testators were not large property owners.

From the testaments we can infer that prehispanic land tenure was more complex than standard sources indicate. An example is the number of civil categories which consistently appear in local-level documentation but not in the standard sources. Careful specification of civil categories of land, in testaments and other Nahuatl documents, indicates the importance of such classifications. Changes in land tenure are suggested by the appearance of a new type of land to support religion, the seeming disappearnace of pillalli, and the transformation of office lands (tlatocatlalli). An important, open question is the nature of calpullalli, and more generally, the nature of the calpulli itself. While prehispanic land tenure might have restricted the alienation of land and sales to the upper stratum, it is important to note that land was alienated in significant amounts as early as the sixteenth century. Land was sold quite freely, both to humble Indians and to Spaniards, the latter by definition outside the native community. Spaniards were quite active in the Culhuacan real estate market, although this only becomes clear through Spanish land records contemporary with the Libro de Testamentos, besides one oblique reference in the Libro itself. It is vital to study native documents to understand land tenure, but also necessary to utilize Spanish records.

Patterns of land tenure and land inheritance give considerable insight into societal structure. The amounts of land each Indian owned varied considerably. Since ownership of land was an index of wealth, variations in the size of holdings indicate major variations of wealth. Some testators had no land whatsoever. The degree to which the calpulli regulated Indian lands in the colonial period (and perhaps in the prehispanic period as well) may be questioned, since estate size varied so widely. It should be stressed that variations in estate size were not determined by gender; women owned land, owned it in significant amounts, and freely bequeathed it to their chosen heirs. Women's control of land, the major economic resource, is an indication of their status in native society. However, women appear not to have been equal participants in some aspects of the landholding system. Fewer women owned patrimonial land and purchased land. Women seemingly did not participate in the real estate market to the extent that men did. The evidence that women's testaments were more subject to challenge than men's may indicate an undermining of women's rights to dispose of property freely. However, their rights to own property and to bequeath it through the legal instrument of a testament were never questioned. And females as well as males shared in estates. At times wives received property only to care for minor children; this seems to have had more to do with their status as spouse than with their gender, since husbands also received limited property rights in similar circumstances.

Patterns of land inheritance in Culhuacan appear to be at variance with those of other Nahua areas where studies of inheritance have been completed. In both Tenochtitlan-Tlateloco and Calimaya-Tepemaxalco, women seemingly preferred female recipients for their land. Culhuacan land inheritance patterns show no major differences between men's and women's bequests, except for the exclusion of stepchildren in women's bequests. The capital city is doubtless always a special case in the colonial period, with constriction of resources and major competition from Spaniards. The variation from the preliminary findings for Calimaya-Tepemaxalco may well indicate a regional variation in inheritance patterns. Further detailed studies of inheritance need to be undertaken.

The native civil category of land often defined how that property was bequeathed. For instance, spouses and siblings' children were excluded from bequests of purchased land and patrimonial land, preference being given to lineal descendants. If a suitable heir were not available, testators often ordered those categories of land sold for masses. Other categories seemingly retained some of their restrictions. This is suggested in the case of the noblewoman who held (but seemingly did not own) cihuatlalli and chinanemactli (tlalnemactli), and did not bequeath them to heirs. She did, however, bequeath land to the church for her own benefit. Presumably that was land to which she enjoyed clear personal rights.

Although there were a number of important changes in native land tenure in the sixteenth century, a number of patterns remained relatively constant. Land continued to be measured in native units. Land was described by native soil and terrain terms, and some of those terms passed into Mexican Spanish. Holdings of both men and women were scattered, and subsequent estate divisions perpetuated the scattering. Land retained prehispanic category names, even when the tenure no longer resembled its prehispanic namesake. Fields continued to be identified by the names of their deceased owners. An explicit attempt to conserve the old system was one noblewoman's restriction against selling her land to Spaniards. Local-level documentation makes possible the charting of changes in land tenure during the colonial period, but it also indicates important continuities from prehispanic times.

NOTES

1. A version of this paper was presented at the American Anthropological Association meetings, 1980. Miguel León-Portilla (1976) has published an excellent description of the corpus and two preliminary translations. An extended analysis of the Libro de Testamentos de Culhuacan is found in S. L. Cline (1981).

2. There are twenty-seven women, thirty-seven men, and one person

of unknown gender. There are posthumous declarations of an additional six people.

3. Dated wills for these years are: 1579, 2; 1580, 14; 1581, 20. Undated wills which can be dated approximately are: 1579, 4; 1580, 5; 1581, 1.

4. AGN: Tierras 58, 4 has a cadastral of one testator's land. There is nothing as comprehensive as the Codex Vergara. Códice de Sta. María Asunción, or the Oztoticpac Lands Map.

5. Bibliothèque Nationale de Paris, Manuscrit Mexicain 110 is a lawsuit between disputing heirs of an estate. AGN: Tierras 58, 4 is a divison of an estate. Both sets of Nahuatl documents were made by the Culhuacan notary Miguel Jacobo de Maldonado.

6. Tlaxilacalli alone is used, never *calpulli;* see Reyes 1975, 1979.

7. Calnek (personal comm.) believes that the two are approximately the same for the Culhuacan area.

8. Molina's dictionary (1970) gives "una suerte de tierra" as one definition. Castillo F. (1972: 222) indicates that it is a cord of determinant length. Harvey and Williams (1980: 505, n. 23) found that in Tepetlaoztoc a rope of standard measure was once kept in the town hall. Cabrera (1974: 90) gives as the definition of *mecate* (from the Nahuatl *mecatl*) "una medida agraria longitudinal de 25 varas" and a "medida agraria de superficie de 400 metros quadrados (20 × 20)."

9. At times the term *chinamitl* is used to indicate chinampas, but often just the number of chinampas are given.

10. Harvey and Williams (1980: 503) indicate there is evidence "that the basic unit of measure of land . . . was 400 square units (20 × 20)."

11. These colonial toponyms are retained in Spanish land documentation.

12. AGN: Tierras 1739, 5. My thanks to Edward Calnek for providing me with a microfilm of these documents.

13. *Tequesquite* has passed into Mexican Spanish as a loanword. See Williams and Ortiz-Solorio 1981 for other terms.

14. Culhuacan was part of the chinampa zone in the prehispanic and early colonial period, but the lake has been drained and the land there dry.

15. The title of tlatoani was still in use in Culhuacan ca. 1580.

16. *Justicia* (Spanish: "justice"), *-tica* (Nahuatl: "by means of") usually implies Spanish courts, that is, dispute, litigation, appeal, and settlement at a higher level. Possible grounds for the award might have been a connection by marriage of Cerón to a tlatoani's daughter. Cerón, however, mentions no such connection.

17. In 1552 Culhuacan Indians worked a 400 by 100 plot for the governor (González de Cosío 1952: 156).

18. The case of Miguel García's teopanmilli is ambiguous. He alleges personal ownership of the land, calling it "my church land" (noteopanmil) and put his nephew in charge of overseeing it (LTC 57r).

19. Offner (1981) has disputed Carrasco's (1978) belief that pillalli was a form of office land and not alienable.

20. Santa Ana Caltenco Tecpan was her declared residence.

21. "yn çacaapan icalchinayo tecpancalli yn quichalchinayotitia jues Juan de lus angeles" (LTC 98r).

22. Just what the calpulli was is still the subject of debate.

23. Perhaps most land was, in fact, calpullalli, but not specifically called that.

24. BNP, Manuscrit Mexicain 343, f. 3v. My thanks to Jerome A. Offner for providing me with a copy of this.

25. AGN: Vínculos 279-1-82r, 86v.

26. She does not call the land "my woman land" (*nocihuatlal*), but lists it with other parcels pertaining to the tecpan.

27. Harvey (personal comm.) points out that the question of what quauhtlalli was would have been clarified if it were identified glyphically.

28. Calnek (personal comm.) now believes that Mexicatlalli is land outside the limits of Tenochtitlan owned by Mexica. He has also pointed out to me the term Mexicatlalli is found in the Anales de Cuauhtitlan (1975: 31, 50).

29. AGN: Vínculos 279-1-82v, 86v.

30. AGN: Vínculos 279-1-114r.

31. AGN: Vínculos 279-1-115r.

32. The term literally means "old land." A Spanish translation of the Nahuatl documents renders it as "tierras antiguas." The literal translation has led to confusion of the civil category (a special class of inherited or patrimonial land) with a soil classification, "old (exhausted) land." Molina (1970) glosses *huehuetlatquitl* as "patrimonio." Kellogg (1979) glosses huehuetlalli as patrimonial land.

33. As noted elsewhere in the text, there are problems with the translation of quauhtlalli.

34. Men: 12r, 15r, 61r, 66r, 67v, 74r, 88r, 105r; women: 63v, 69r, 93r.

35. MNA-AH 550, e.g., f. 55r, owned by the head of a social division.

36. We do have data from Spanish land-sale records, AGN: Tierras 1739-5. My thanks to Edward Calnek for providing me with a microfilm of this.

37. AGN: Tierras 58-4-6r.

38. He is identified as a Spaniard in AGN: Tierras 1739-5.

39. AGN: Tierras 1739-5.

40. Tlalcohualli retained that classification even when inherited and subsequently bequeathed.

41. Both had horses and provided revenues from them for the support of their children.

42. The son did die, as a note indicates (LTC 84v).

43. The term could also refer to uncle and aunt.

REFERENCES

Anales de Cuauhtitlan (Codex Chimalpopoca)
1975   México: Universidad Nacional.
Anderson, A. J. O., Frances Berdan, and James Lockhart
1976   Beyond the Codices. Berkeley: University of California Press.
Baudot, Georges
1976   Utopie et Histoire au Mexique. Paris: Privat.
Cabrera, Luis
1974   Diccionario de Aztequismos. México: Ediciones Oases.
Calnek, Edward E.
1973   The Localization of the 16th Century Map called the Maguey
             Plan. American Antiquity 38: 190–95.
1975   The Organization of Urban Food Supply Systems: The Case
             of Tenochtitlan. Spanish translation *in* Las Ciudades de Amér-
             ica Latina y sus Areas de Influencia a través de la Historia.
             Jorge Hardoy and Richard P. Schaedel, eds. Buenos Aires:
             Sociedad Interamericana de Planificación.
Carrasco, Pedro
1978   La Economía del México Prehispánico. *In* Economía política
             e ideológica en el México prehispánico. Pedro Carrasco and
             Johanna Broda, eds. México: CIS-INAH, Edit. Nueva Imagen.
Castillo F., Victor M.
1972   Unidades Nahuas de Medida. Estudios de Cultura Náhuatl
             10: 195–223.
Cline, Howard F.
1966   The Oztoticpac Lands Map of Texcoco, 1540. Quarterly Jour-
             nal of the Library of Congress 23(2): 77–116.
Cline, S. L.
1981   Culhuacan, 1579–1599: An Investigation Through Mexican
             Indian Testaments. Ph.D. dissertation, University of Califor-
             nia, Los Angeles.

Gallego, Gonzalo
1927   Relación geográfica de Culhuacan. Revista Mexicana de Estudios Históricos 1(6): 171–73.
Gibson, Charles
1964   Aztecs Under Spanish Rule. Stanford: Stanford University Press.
González de Cosío, Francisco
1952   El libro de las tasaciones de pueblos de la Nueva España, siglo xvi. México: Archivo General de la Nación.
Harvey, H. R., and Barbara J. Williams
1980   Aztec Arithmetic: Positional Notation and Area Calculation. Science 210: 499–505.
Ixtlilxóchitl, Fernando de Alva
1977   Obras Históricas. México: Universidad Nacional.
Kellogg, Susan
1979   Social Organization in Early Colonial Tenochtitlan-Tlatelolco. Ph.D. dissertation, University of Rochester.
León-Portilla, Miguel
1976   El libro de testamentos indígenas de Culhuacan. Estudios de Cultura Náhuatl 12: 11–31.
Loera y Ch., Margarita
1977   Calimaya y Tepemaxalco. Cuadernos de Trabajo del Depto. de Investigaciones Históricas. México: Instituto Nacional de Antropología e Historia.
López de Gómara, Francisco
1943   Historia de la conquista de México. 2 vols. México: Robredo.
Molina, Alonso de
1970   Vocabulario en lengua Castellana y Mexicana y Mexicana y Castellana. México: Porrúa.
Monterrosa Prado, Marianao
1970   El plano de Culhuacan. INAH Boletín, 39.
Motolinía, Toribio de Benavente
1971   Memoriales o libro de cosas de la Nueva España. México: Universidad Nacional.
Offner, Jerome A.
1981   On the Inapplicability of "Oriental Despotism" and the "Asiatic Mode of Production" to the Aztecs of Texcoco. American Antiquity 46: 43–61.
Reyes, Luis
1975   El término *calpulli* en documentos del centro de México. Paper presented at El Seminario de Verano sobre Organización Social del México Antigua, CIS-INAH, México.

1977   Cuauhtinchan del siglo XII al XVI. Wiesbaden: Franz Steiner Verlag.

1978   Documentos sobre tierras y señoríos en Cuauhtinchan México: Instituto Nacional de Antropología e Historia.

1979   El término *calpulli* en documentos del siglo XVI. Paper presented at the 43rd International Congress of Americanists, Vancouver, B.C.

Sahagún, Bernardino de

1963   General History of the Things of New Spain. Charles Dibble and Arthur Anderson, trans. Vol. 11. Santa Fe: School of American Research and University of Utah Press.

Torquemada, Juan de

1975   Monarquía Indiana. México: Porrúa.

West, Robert C., and Pedro Armillas

1950   Las chinampas de México. Cuadernos Americanos 40: 165–82.

Williams, Barbara J.

1976a   Aztec Soil Science. Boletín, Instituto de Geografía 6: 115–20.

1976b   Aztec Soil Classification and Land Tenure. Paper presented at the 42nd International Congress of Americanists. Paris.

1980   Pictorial Representations of Soils from the Valley of Mexico: Evidence from the Codex Vergara. Geoscience and Man 21: 51–62.

Williams, Barbara J., and Carlos A. Ortíz-Solorio

1981   Middle American Folk Soil Taxonomy. Annals of the Association of American Geographers 71: 335–58.

Zorita, Alonso de

1963   Life and Labor in Ancient Mexico: The Brief and Summary Relation of the Lords of New Spain. Benjamin Keen, trans. and intro. New Brunswick: Rutgers University Press.

Archival Sources

AGN   Archivo General de la Nación, México. Citation by ramo, volume, and expediente.

BNP   Bibliothèque Nationale, Paris.

LTC   Libro de Testamentos de Culhuacan, private collection of Ignacio Pérez Alonso.

MNA-AH   Museo Nacional de Antropología, Archivo Histórico, México.

Note on Contributors

Woodrow Borah is Professor Emeritus, Department of History, University of California, Berkeley. He is a specialist in the historical demography of Latin America and has written extensively on that topic.

Pedro Carrasco is Professor of Anthropology at the State University of New York at Stony Brook. A specialist on Mesoamerican ethnohistory, he has written various books and articles.

S. L. Cline is an Assistant Professor of History, Harvard University, and specializes in Mesoamerican ethnohistory and colonial Mexican history.

Ursula Dyckerhoff is at the Institute für Völkenkunde, University of Munich, and has conducted extensive research with the Mexico Project.

H. R. Harvey is Professor of Anthropology at the University of Wisconsin, Madison.

Frederic Hicks is Professor of Anthropology at the University of Louisville. He has written a number of studies on Texcocan ethnohistory.

Jerome A. Offner is the author of the forthcoming *Law and Politics of Aztec Texcoco* as well as several articles.

Hanns J. Prem is Professor of Anthropology, University of Munich.

Teresa Rojas Rabiela is a researcher affiliated with the Centro de Investigaciones y Estudios Superiores de Antropología Social. Her speciality is pre-Hispanic agriculture, and she is the author of a book on hydraulic agriculture.

Wolfgang Trautmann is with the Universität Essen, Geography Seminar. His extensive archival work in Tlaxcala has resulted in a book and various articles.

Barbara J. Williams is Professor of Geography, University of Wisconsin, Rock County. Her specialities are ethnopedology and historical geography of Mexico, and she has written numerous articles in these fields.